Day by Day

Refining Writing Workshop Through 180 Days of Reflective Practice

Ruth Ayres and Stacey Shubitz

Foreword by Carl Anderson

Stenhouse
PUBLISHERS
www.stenhouse.com

Stenhouse Publishers
www.stenhouse.com

Credits
Pages 7, 51, 93, 141, 187, and 231: Wordle images courtesy of http://www.wordle.net. Images of Wordles are licensed by Creative Commons. Wordle is an online tool that creates "word clouds" from words used in a piece of text. The more frequently a word is used in the original text, the larger it appears in the word cloud. In this book, the authors have created Wordles for each chapter opener.

Page 101: Excerpt from "My Writer's Notebook" by Brod Bagert used by permission.

Pages 293 and 295: The Small Moment Story Writing and Quick Publish Assessment forms were created by Stacey Shubitz with Artemis Kakorus and Christina Rodriguez in May 2007.

Library of Congress Cataloging-in-Publication Data
Ayres, Ruth, 1977-
Day by day : refining writing workshop through 180 days of reflective practice / Ruth Ayres and Stacey Shubitz.
p. cm.
ISBN 978-1-57110-809-8 (alk. paper)
1. Creative writing. 2. Workshops. 3. English language--Rhetoric--Study and teaching. 4. Writing centers. I. Shubitz, Stacey, 1977- II. Title.
PE1404.A97 2010
808'.042071--dc21
2010020492

Cover design, interior design, and typesetting by Designboy Creative Group

Manufactured in the United States of America

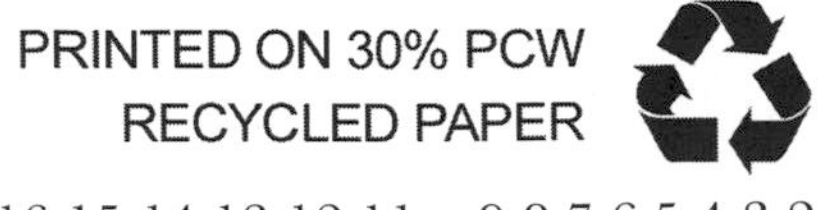

16 15 14 13 12 11   9 8 7 6 5 4 3 2

For Bo, Jami, Jordan, and Kyler,
who taught me to believe not only in the power of writing workshop
but also in myself as a teacher.
Thank you.

—*RAA*

In memory of Carol Snook,
my first-grade teacher, who encouraged me to write.

—*SAS*

Contents

List of Cycles and Discussions

Chapter 1: Routines

Chapter 2: Mini-Lessons

Chapter 3: Choice

Chapter 4: Mentors

Chapter 5: Conferring

Chapter 6: Assessment

Foreword

By Carl Anderson

Recently my family traveled to Bali. When we arrived, we met Simpen, a guide who would help us explore southeastern Bali. During our time with him, Simpen led us on adventures as varied as visiting the village of Tenganan—where my wife, Robin, purchased beautiful Balinese textiles—to trekking through the nearby rice fields. Simpen even brought us to his home, where his wife, Vani, showed my children how to make offerings to the gods out of palm leaves. Simpen's generosity with his time, his knowledge of Balinese culture and history, and his enthusiasm for his home helped us feel comfortable immediately. He helped us fall in love with Bali.

As I read each page of *Day by Day: Refining Writing Workshop Through 180 Days of Reflective Practice*, I couldn't help but think that the authors, Ruth Ayres and Stacey Shubitz, are just like Simpen. What wonderful guides they are for teachers who want to deepen their knowledge of teaching writing and become more thoughtful, reflective educators.

The authors' extensive knowledge of teaching writing comes from years spent instructing students and coaching teachers. Ruth taught seventh graders in northern Indiana; Stacey taught elementary school students in New York City and Rhode Island. Ruth is now a writing coach in Indiana; Stacey is a literacy consultant in Pennsylvania. They are uncommonly generous educators. For several years, they have been sharing their thoughts and insights about teaching writing via their popular blog, Two Writing Teachers (http://twowritingteachers.wordpress.com). Although both lead busy lives, they still manage to post regular entries about an incredible range of topics related to teaching writing, and have helped teachers far and wide become part of an online community devoted to this important topic.

Day by Day is the natural next step for these two talented and inspiring writing teachers. In the book, they focus on six topics central to teaching in a writing workshop: routines, mini-lessons, choice, mentors, conferring, and assessment. For each of these topics, Ruth and Stacey offer three courses of study, or "cycles," in which they provide a wealth of practical information about ten key aspects of the topic. Throughout each cycle, they include "Challenges" for teachers to try out in their own teaching, and ask questions in "Reflective Practice" sections to help teachers think about the results and refine their practice.

This is a book that asks readers to take an active stance toward their learning, a stance that will reward them with new knowledge, new teaching points, and new techniques that become part of their teaching repertoire.

The journey toward becoming an excellent writing teacher is a challenging one. It helps to have guides along the way—colleagues, mentor teachers, coaches. By reading *Day by Day*, teachers can invite Ruth and Stacey, two wonderful guides, into their lives. I have no doubt that teachers will be enriched by what they learn from this experience. Not only will this outstanding professional book help them think and learn about many important aspects of teaching writing, I believe it also will provide new energy to teachers who want to fall in love with teaching writing all over again.

Acknowledgments

> The elements of our characters are constructed from the fragments
> of people we meet throughout our lives.
> ***—Matt Oliver***

We're delighted Zsofia McMullin reached out to us about Stenhouse's Online Reviewers Club in 2008. One thing led to another, and we were introduced to Bill Varner, our editor. We appreciated his low-pressure style, which allowed us to chart our own course and provided us with the direction we needed. A tremendous amount of thanks to Chris Downey, who took our manuscript from a Word document to book form, patiently answering all of our questions along the way. In addition, we are grateful to all of the folks at Stenhouse Publishers for believing in this project.

Thank you to all of the Two Writing Teachers blog readers. You've made us realize our voices matter.

Ruth:

After writing an entire book, you would think the acknowledgments would come easily. Not so for me. How can I possibly acknowledge everyone who has helped me become who I am at this moment in time? What if I leave someone out? What if I put a name in the wrong order?

"What if you just write it?" my husband finally said to me. So once again I find myself balancing my laptop on my knees, just writing.

I wrote this book because my parents, Pam and Kevin Myers, taught me I could do *anything* as long as I set my mind to it. They have always been my biggest advocates and continue to offer unyielding love and support.

I wrote this book because my *little* brother, Jeff Myers, and I learned at a young age that if you are going to dream big then anything is possible with hard work, imagination, and a little humor.

I wrote this book because educators at Wawasee Community School Corporation have pushed me to continue refining my practice. As a rookie, I joined a team of seventh-grade teachers who showed me firsthand how to put students' needs at the forefront of instruction. Tammy Hess and Lori Dixon first introduced me to writing workshop. For many years, we worked together to discover the pure meaning of writing workshop instruction.

I wrote this book because my first principal, Russ Mikel, taught me to back up every single choice I made as a teacher with research. He made me into a reader of professional books. I will be changed forever by his belief in me.

I wrote this book because my curriculum director, Joy Goshert, expects my best and then some. She has taught me to consider all sides of a situation and to proceed with grace and tact.

I wrote this book because of the teachers who invite me into their classrooms. It has been an adventure blending their knowledge of specific grade levels and my knowledge of writing workshop to discover a result better than any of us could have come to on our own. Except, of course, when things flop. I thank you even more for your grace on those days.

I wrote this book because of the students who have graced my classrooms.

I wrote this book because of the generous professional development of the All Write!!! Consortium. Mindy Hoffar and the All Write!!! Consortium coaches have opened many doors to me, and I am eternally grateful. Mary Helen Gensch has listened to my thinking grow, supported me over the years, and shared tips on how to stay sane while running a household of five.

I wrote this book because of the encouragement of Carl Anderson and Penny Kittle. They both were right—writing a book is the best way to deepen my understanding of writing workshop.

I wrote this book because Deb Gaby, reading coach extraordinaire, allows me to talk candidly about literacy with her. I'm thankful for her fidelity.

I wrote this book because Barb Bean opened her classroom year after year to me. I'm thankful for hours of reflection together and her belief in public schools, friendship, and prayers.

I wrote this book because I have friends who encourage me that my voice matters. I couldn't have been a writer (and everything else) without the support and prayers of a few close friends: Heidi and Kurt Stout, Tricia and Scott Stan, Rebecca Nguyen, Nancy Ducey, and Eldonna Warren.

I wrote this book because Stacey Shubitz commented on my first blog and flung open the door to collaboration like I've never known. I appreciate Stacey's loyalty and commitment. I'm most thankful, however, for her constant friendship. I'm looking forward to the next leg of our journey.

I wrote this book because my children believe their mom is a writer. Throughout the process, I worried I was spending too much time on the computer and not enough time in the backyard. However, they all want to grow up to be writers, so this must have been a positive experience for them. Hannah, Stephanie, and Sam fuel me with their constant creative insights, giggles, and hugs.

I wrote this book because my husband, Andy, shouldered my share of the household chores, kept my teacup full, and when that wasn't strong enough, transitioned me to coffee. He stayed up late while I finished drafts, lured me out of bed with a cup of coffee too early on Saturday mornings, and constantly encouraged me. All of this and he never once complained. Thank you for being my biggest fan.

And, I wrote this book because, "I can do all things through Christ who strengthens me," Philippians 4:13.

Stacey:

My parents bought me a pair of Asolo hiking boots in 1989 when they sent me off to summer camp. They hoped a pair of sturdy boots would encourage me to climb mountains. The boots were used only once in the summer of 1989, because I went on a day hike and found it tedious. The next summer my parents sent me to summer camp again, with the same barely worn hiking boots. This time, I used them for two daylong hikes leading up to an overnight climb. In July 1990, I climbed to the top of Mt. Washington, the highest peak in northeastern United States. I reached the summit, with just a few scrapes, taking time to enjoy the view and some unexpected waterfalls along the way. However, the trek back down Mt. Washington was tough. Going down the rocky side of the mountain felt nearly impossible to me. With positive affirmations and assistance from the counselors and other girls who climbed with me, I was able to descend the mountain and proudly wear a T-shirt that said, "This body climbed Mt. Washington."

Writing this book was a lot like climbing Mt. Washington. Parts of the writing process felt straightforward, while others were problematic. As I received help making it through the rocky patches of Mt. Washington, I have received a lot of support on my writing journey as well.

I've come to rely on my parents, Marcia and Gerald Shubitz, for their wisdom. They have guided me through the twists and turns of life. Thanks to their guidance and support, I've been able to achieve nearly everything I've wanted to accomplish. I am grateful to them for their unconditional love.

George P. Gonzalez and Dimitres Pantelidis believed in me, as an educator, even when I doubted myself. I am thankful to have had the support of both of these men as I began my career at P.S. 171 in Manhattan.

Pat Werner, my first literacy coach, spent countless hours helping me understand what workshop teaching was about. I doubt I would have wanted to become a literacy specialist if it hadn't been for Pat, who understood the balance coaches must strike between being a mentor and being a friend.

I am grateful to my former students at P.S. 171 and at The Learning Community for teaching me how to teach writers.

Linda Schaefer, my mother-in-law, is a literacy coach in Connecticut. She has always been willing to "talk shop" with me at any time and has helped me grow as a teacher of reading and writing throughout the years.

The ideas in this book stand on the shoulders of the incredible people I learned from while I was a graduate student in the Literacy Specialist Program at Teachers College. I'm extremely grateful to my professors, Lucy Calkins, Marjorie Siegel, and Stephanie Jones, as well as my instructors, Grace Enriquez, Kristin Rainville, and Kathy Brody, who continually inspired me and pushed me to think about the teaching of reading and writing in new ways.

I have been fortunate to attend the Teachers College Reading and Writing Project's Summer Institutes every summer since 2005. Special thanks to my past Writing Institute instructors, Carl Anderson, Tiffany Davis-Nealy, Mary Ehrenworth, Cory Gillette, James Howe, Lester L. Laminack, Maggie Moon, Jen Serravallo, and Emily Smith, for helping me gain a deeper understanding of the intricacies of writing workshop.

I have had a number of colleagues who helped me grow as an educator and got me laughing when I needed it most. Thank you to Leana Abulencia-Shapli, Cathy Derouin, Lila Jorge, Caroline Marandino, Halli Moskowitz, Christina Rodriguez, Neris Roldan-Figueroa, Wendy Sanderson, Kate Smith, Sarah Tukman, Abi Wilson, and Christine Wiltshire.

Emily Kretchmer is the kind of friend everyone should be lucky enough to have. She has been present and helpful through *all* of the stages of this book, which even included a day filled with chocolate and fun for Ruth and me around Boston. I'm fortunate to call her my friend.

I'm blessed I had the opportunity to write this book with my friend and co-blogger, Ruth Ayres. Ruth not only has an incredible understanding of writing workshop, but she also has a fantastic way with children. I have learned so much from her since we've met and look forward to many more years of professional growth and friendship with her.

Finally, from the day I told my husband, Marc Schaefer, that Ruth and I were submitting a book proposal to Stenhouse, he has been enthusiastic. Marc has always known I wanted to write, as well as teach, and has supported my desire to make that dream a reality. I could not ask for more.

Introduction

A journey of a thousand miles begins with a single step.
—Confucius

Teaching writing in a workshop setting is rewarding work. To see growth over time, to celebrate as young writers take ownership of their work, and to have all the components of writing workshop, mini-lessons, conferring, and sharing work together is exhilarating. At the same time, teaching writing in a workshop setting is hard work. To plan mini-lessons, to understand the diverse needs of a classroom of writers, and to lift the level of each writer, while at the same time nourishing and building confidence, with only having a short amount of time—often sixty minutes or less each day—is a tall order.

This book is for anyone who believes in the power of writing workshop and wants to continue to refine his or her practice. We realize the teaching of writing is complex, and it is not just nice to know you are not alone on this journey, it is a necessity. If you have ever wished for daily doses of encouragement, tips, challenges, advice, and understanding during the school year, this book is for you. It is for the writing teacher who wants to reflect on her practice but would like a personal guide. It is for the administrator who wants to offer coaching to his staff, but does not have enough funds.

Too often, isolated islands of teachers attempt best practice, yet lack support from a teacher across the hall or even in the building. In addition, because of cuts in education budgets across the United States, literacy coaches are often nonexistent or overextended and are not available to work as closely with teachers as they would like. Therefore, we want to be the comforting colleagues at the end of the rough day and the people who rejoice with you when things go well. Through this book, we hope to renew, refresh, and reinvigorate the way you teach. We want to walk beside you on this journey, as you become a reflective practitioner, so you continue to have the energy to provide the best writing instruction to your students day by day. They deserve it.

Some teachers study texts together outside of school hours or during preparation periods. If you do not already have a community of other teachers to commiserate with about the teaching of writing, use this book to create one. While it is possible to become better teachers of writing in isolation, reflecting on our own, it is ideal to have a small group to trek alongside. As Parker J. Palmer attests in *The Courage to Teach: Exploring the Inner Landscape of a Teacher's Life* (1998):

> *If I want to teach well, it is essential that I explore my inner terrain. But I can get lost in there, practicing self-delusion and running in self-serving circles. So I need the guidance*

> *that a community of collegial discourse provides—to say nothing of the support such a community can offer to sustain me in the trials of teaching and the cumulative and collective wisdom about this craft that can be found in every faculty worth its salt. (142)*

Perhaps finding a small group or even a single colleague to collaborate with seems daunting. In that case, we encourage you to head online to find others to support you. The blogosphere is filled with educators who want to share, connect, and inspire one another. A quick search on Google will reveal many blogs devoted to literacy education. If you need a starting place, we invite you to start on our blog, Two Writing Teachers. We are living proof that collaboration across cyberspace is possible and significant.

This book is divided into six chapters: assessment, choice, conferring, mentors, mini-lessons, and routines, which are the pillars of writing workshop. Woven into each chapter are several reflections about celebration, since we feel it's important to make time to celebrate small triumphs as well as full-class accomplishments.

You will notice each chapter is broken into three cycles, ten-day sections, which allow you to explore a topic with more specificity. For instance, the chapter on routines is divided into three cycles. The first cycle walks you through structures you can implement during the beginning of the school year. The second cycle focuses on routines you can develop around writer's notebooks. The third cycle helps you develop routines for publishing celebrations. Say you pick this book up in December, once your workshop is well under way. You might skip the first cycle on routines and choose to begin with another cycle that will be more pertinent based on where you are in the school year.

There are several ways you can use this book to improve your practice:

- **A Cycle at a Time:** Each cycle contains ten discussions about a particular aspect of the teaching of writing. We encourage you to read through one discussion per day so you can try out the challenges contained at the end of each one. By the end of a ten-day period, we expect you will have enhanced one area of the teaching of writing. At that time, you can proceed to another cycle in any other chapter of the book.
- **A Chapter at a Time:** Each chapter contains three cycles, which includes thirty days of intensive professional development in one particular area. We intentionally structured each chapter's cycles in an order that feels like a natural progression to us. While you may explore the cycles in any order you wish, we do not think you can go wrong by doing them in the order in which they are written. By intentionally focusing on a particular area, teachers can create a richer and more challenging environment for their students.
- **All Year Long:** You can also use this book as a day-by-day guide as you teach writing workshop over the course of a year. If you are going to use this entire book throughout the school year, then consider perusing the

chapter introductions first so you can chart your own course of professional development with this book.

If this book sounds a bit like the Choose Your Own Adventure books of the 1980s, then you're on to something! Every teacher is different. Everyone has different needs. It's up to you to plot your own course to improve your teaching practice so you can help your students become more proficient writers.

Throughout this book, we have gathered questions to help you develop the habit of reflective practice. Just as you would prepare for any other journey, it is important to prepare for this one as well. Find a space to house your written reflections. This can be a notebook, a document on your computer, or a blog. Then find time to write. Ten minutes a day is sufficient to respond to the reflective practice questions. Taking the time to respond, in writing, will help you become more intentional about your teaching decisions. Finally, seek out other teachers of writing, in person or online, who are also working to refine their writing workshop instruction. Share your insights, struggles, and triumphs with them.

Are you ready to chart new territory? Let's take a step forward together and begin.

Track Your Journey

After reading the chapter introductions, make a plan for how you will use this book. The following charts offer a brief description of each cycle, as well as space for you to make a reading plan and record the date when you complete a cycle.

Chapter 1: Routines

Plan to Read	Finished Reading	Cycle Description
		Cycle 1: *Revving Up* Some basic routines to help your writing workshop run like a well-oiled machine.
		Cycle 2: *Writer's Notebooks* Routines to make writer's notebooks more effective.
		Cycle 3: *Publishing Celebrations* A variety of ideas to make celebrations meaningful.

Chapter 2: Mini-Lessons

Plan to Read	Finished Reading	Cycle Description
		Cycle 1: *Meaningful Mini-Lessons* Ways to make mini-lessons more effective.
		Cycle 2: *Teaching Conventions in Mini-Lessons* Ideas to consider when making choices about teaching conventions in writing workshop.
		Cycle 3: *Making Our Teaching Stick* Considerations to make our lessons indelible.

Chapter 3: Choice

Plan to Read	Finished Reading	Cycle Description
		Cycle 1: *Physical Choices* Ways to provide students with choice over the materials in writing workshop.
		Cycle 2: *Moving Toward Independence* Helping students take ownership in their writing decisions.
		Cycle 3: *Living the Life of a Writer* How to encourage students to live as writers outside of the classroom.

Chapter 4: Mentors

Plan to Read	Finished Reading	Cycle Description
		Cycle 1: *Students as Mentors* Tapping into the power of using students' writings as mentor texts.
		Cycle 2: *Teachers as Mentors* Using your own writing as a means for instruction and understanding.
		Cycle 3: *Published Authors as Mentors* Considering how to pick and use quality mentor texts to teach students a variety of craft moves.

Chapter 5: Conferring

Plan to Read	Finished Reading	Cycle Description
		Cycle 1: *Conferring Basics* A series of discussions to help you think about the building blocks of conferring in a new way.
		Cycle 2: *Peer Conferring* Creating a classroom climate conducive to peer conferences.
		Cycle 3: *Lifting the Level of Our Conferences* How to hone your language, help you reflect with colleagues, and beef up your record-keeping systems.

Chapter 6: Assessment

Plan to Read	Finished Reading	Cycle Description
		Cycle 1: *Formative Assessment* Considerations about forming opinions about students' strengths and needs.
		Cycle 2: *Summative Assessment* Discussions about grading and balancing different perspectives at the end of a unit.
		Cycle 3: *Standardized Tests* Practical ideas to align preparation for a writing prompt as close to an authentic workshop experience as possible.

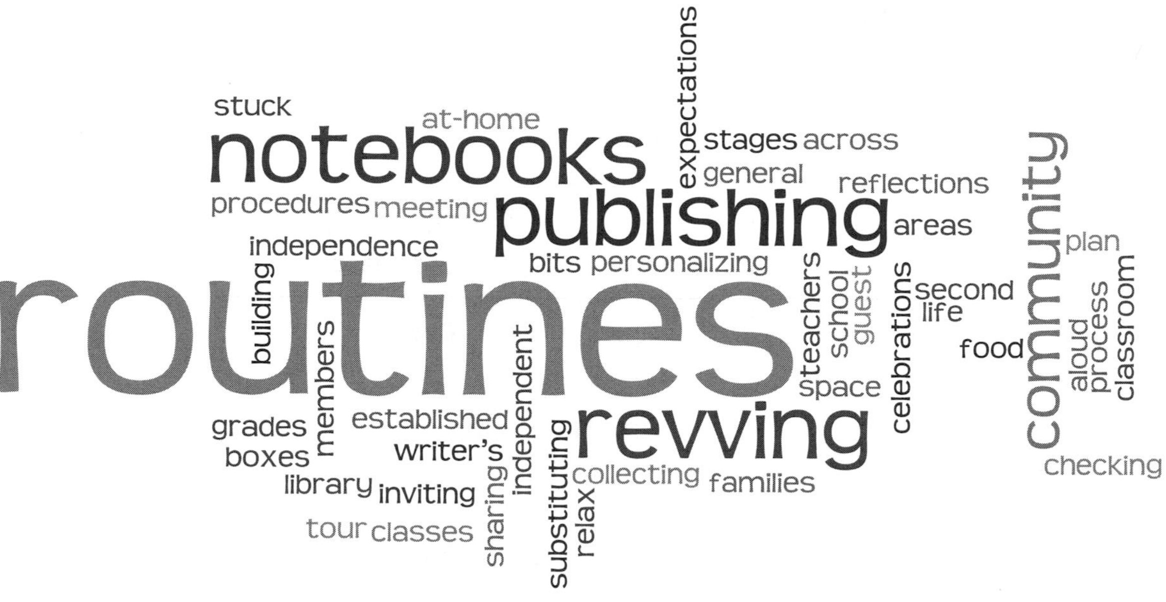

Chapter 1: Routines

We've all heard, repeatedly, that "children thrive on routines." We're sure that, as an educator, you've seen the truth behind this statement many times. Regardless of the population you teach, we're sure you'll agree that nearly all children do better when clear structures are in place. Consistency and fairness are key to ensuring procedures are carried out in the classroom.

Through the years, we've created routines and structures for our writing workshops. Those routines and structures, which are carefully thought out and explicitly taught to students, help transitions happen quickly so we can maximize our time spent teaching mini-lessons, conferring, and engaging in sharing.

Here's what you can expect to uncover in the pages to come:

- **Cycle 1: Revving Up**
  If you're ready to start a new school year, this is the section for you! However, this cycle is also applicable when you're returning from a school vacation and looking to add new structures into your workshop to get your students back in the writing groove.
- **Cycle 2: Writer's Notebooks**
  You know writer's notebooks matter, but if you're looking to use them in a more meaningful way, then consider carving out some time to hone the way you and your students use writer's notebooks.

- **Cycle 3: Publishing Celebrations**
  There's no need to hire a party planner to make your next publishing celebration one your students and invited guests will remember. By considering a variety of ways to celebrate students' writing, you can host a meaningful celebration each time.

Whether you want to tweak existing routines or develop new ones, it makes sense to reflect on the procedures and structures for writing workshop. Join us as we do some in-depth thinking about the well-oiled machine that helps our writing workshops run with the precision of a Swiss watch.

Cycle 1: Revving Up

Establishing General Procedures

A few strong instincts and a few plain rules suffice us.
—Ralph Waldo Emerson

Classroom management is the key to establishing a functioning classroom where students are safe and productive. My first principal, Dimitres Pantelidis, gave me a copy of *The First Days of School* by Harry K. and Rosemary T. Wong three months before I started as a fifth-grade teacher. I read it from cover to cover, highlighting sections that piqued my interest and dog-earing pages containing passages I wanted to incorporate into my teaching practice, such as the "Give Me Five" procedure for garnering students' attention (2009, 185). Thanks to *The First Days of School*, Mr. Pantelidis, and a host of other colleagues at P.S. 171, I survived my first year of teaching.

I began to tweak some of my classroom routines and created routines for each subject area I taught before starting my second year of teaching. I even created a classroom handbook, which I spent the first week of school reviewing with my students. At first, I felt as though I was implementing too many structures for my students to remember from subject to subject; however, I quickly found my second year was running much more smoothly than my first. Was it the kids, or was it the routines I created? Perhaps it was a little of both.

There are several procedures I implemented that helped writing workshop run more smoothly:

- **Assign notebook-checking days:** All students were required to turn in their writer's notebook to me weekly. Their checking day was assigned at the beginning of the year. Parents were informed of students' notebook-checking days, and reminder notices were placed near students' coat hooks and on their desks so they'd remember to turn their notebooks in on a given day.
- **Help students to come prepared:** I kept a list of items students needed to bring to each subject's mini-lesson on the wall of my classroom. If they needed additional items, I would verbally tell students what they should bring *in addition* to listing those items on the classroom whiteboard. As the year went on, I would only list the additional items needed for the mini-lesson on the whiteboard so students would know where to look for help if they were unsure of what to bring to the rug, thereby making them less dependent on me.
- **Lead mid-workshop interruptions from a consistent spot:** There are always students who become engrossed in their writing and do not look up when you interrupt their writing time with a phrase like, "Writers, may I have your eyes?" Therefore, showing your students the spot you will stand *every time* you do a mid-workshop interruption will help them anticipate where to find you when they hear your voice amid the silence in the room. Lucy Calkins taught me that you must wait for every single writer's eyes to be on you before you begin your mid-workshop teaching. While that can feel like an eternity when you first teach this to your students, it will happen faster as time goes on.
- **Provide a place for students to turn in work:** I labeled stackable trays by subject area and used those trays as places where students turned in their work. I expected all writing work, such as drafts, to be turned in to the "writing workshop" tray. I always placed a stapler next to the stackable trays so students could attach multiple pages together. Keeping a couple of writing implements next to the trays are advisable so forgetful students can place their names on their work before turning it in.
- **Use a rain stick to call students to the meeting area:** As suggested by Emily Smith, a Teachers College Reading and Writing Project staff developer, I purchased a thirty-inch rain stick and used it as a signal to regulate movement to and from the meeting area. This is a calming way to signal students that a transition needs to take place. I shook the rain stick five full times to give students time to get from their desks to their rug spots.

These are a few of the many procedures I taught my students during the first weeks of school. I consider these among the most important procedures for creating a productive writing workshop. When clear procedures are implemented and rehearsed, students see the value in following them so that learning time is maximized.

Challenge: Brainstorm a list of all of the procedures you want to teach your students this year. Then, set aside time to teach these procedures and to rehearse them with your students.

Reflective Practice:

- What were the most challenging procedures to teach your students for writing workshop? Why do you think they were challenging to teach and/or for your students to internalize?
- Are there any procedures you taught that need to be differentiated to fit the needs of particular students in your class? How will you make exceptions to the rules without looking like you're playing favorites?

Creating a List of Classroom Expectations

A master can tell what he expects of you.
A teacher, though, awakens your own expectations.
—Patricia Neal

Our students have a strong understanding of the norms of school. They have experienced being part of a classroom community and have ideas about what works well and what doesn't. So why not empower students to set their own expectations for writing workshop?

When I first asked myself this question, I generated a fairly pessimistic list of reasons why students shouldn't create their own rules. However, one of my core beliefs is to empower and trust students to find meaning. I decided students should develop the heart of classroom routines.

Before starting my first year of teaching, two of my mentors urged me to invite students to generate their own list of expectations. They helped me sort out my nonnegotiable expectations for writing workshop:

1. Become a stronger writer.
2. Be respectful.
3. Come ready to learn.

Then I asked students to talk with a partner about what these expectations would look like in our classroom. Each partnership teamed with another partnership and shared some of their ideas. Small groups compiled a list of expectations they all agreed on. Next, we came together in our meeting area to share our ideas.

I was astounded by the results. Sure, there were typical responses, such as "Don't make fun of other people" and "Treat other people how you want to be treated." However, there were also expectations such as "Write important stories" and "Voice your thoughts and opinions."

I've witnessed students from second grade through high school generate their own lists of expectations for writing workshop. I've found it is most powerful to generate this list of expectations after students have lived as writers for a few weeks.

I also talk with my students about what happens if someone chooses not to follow the expectations. I'm always impressed by this discussion. It affirms that students know and appreciate the norms of school. By creating a student-generated list of expectations, students feel ownership over writing workshop.

Challenge: Develop a list of expectations for writing workshop *with* your students. Even if you've already created workshop rules, take some time to elicit student input about the expectations for writing workshop. Post these expectations in a prominent place in the classroom.

Reflective Practice:

- What are your nonnegotiable expectations for writing workshop?
- How can you boil these expectations down to something general for students in order to start a discussion?
- How did creating a list of expectations differ from creating a list of classroom rules with your students?

Choice in Writing Process

A writer is not so much someone who has something to say
as he is someone who has found a process that will bring about new things
he would not have thought of if he had not started to say them.
—William Stafford

The way I revise is probably different from the way you revise. This is also true for the young writers in our classrooms. Revision may look different for each of them. As teachers, it is important to give many strategies for a given part of the process. We should not only allow different strategies to meet the needs of our students but also provide opportunities for students to pace themselves according to their individual needs. Some writers take longer to draft; others spend little time planning. In writing workshop, it is crucial to push ourselves to provide an atmosphere where the nuances of each writer's process can be fostered.

This is easier said than done.

To accommodate the many needs of the writers in our classrooms and to empower them to find a meaningful writing process, we must establish specific procedures. To compile this list, I remembered one of the most reluctant writers ever to stand before me. Jordan didn't want to do anything that didn't involve a soccer ball. Yet, over the course of the year, because I consistently followed through on a handful of procedures, Jordan was empowered to find a personalized writing process. By May, Jordan wrote for sustained amounts of time and had the needed skills to face any writing challenge successfully. These procedures empower students to discover their own preferences when it comes to the writing process.

- **Set deadlines (and mini-deadlines):** One commonality among writers is that they have deadlines. It is the truth of a writer's existence. To help students think through their work as writers, we can help them set mini-deadlines for the different parts of the process. We can ask students to plan when they will complete a draft or embark on editing. This process can be as simple as asking students at the beginning of writing time to determine what they will accomplish for the day or asking older students to map out their own mini-deadlines on a calendar.
- **Listen to reason:** Sometimes it's easy to assume students are skipping a particular step of the writing process, such as revision. However, if we listen when we confer, students will share a crude revision process. Too often, we conclude that students are skipping major parts of the writing process, when what they really need is to learn to refine their current process.
- **Insist on boundaries:** In an environment where everyone is working at their own pace, it is easy to become distracted. As teachers, we must set clear boundaries for work time. When may students leave their work area? Where should they work? What kinds of conversations are helpful? These are all questions to consider when establishing procedures to help students work independently.
- **Respond with grace:** Our students are not experts when it comes to writing. In fact, they are quite the opposite. Most of what they do as writers is an approximation. They are *learning* how to be writers. Therefore, they are bound to make silly choices from time to time when it comes to personalizing their writing process. There will be some days when the freedom in writing workshop chokes them, days when there are so many possibilities it is difficult to make a choice and stay on task. At times like these, it is imperative to respond with grace and understanding. We redirect and set them back on the path.

If the procedures we develop do not empower students to find their unique writing process, then they are insignificant. We know when our procedures empower because even the most reluctant writers will awaken.

Challenge: Consider the procedures you have in place to encourage students to work within their personalized writing process. Make changes to increase the opportunity for students to work according to their individual needs.

Reflective Practice:

- How do your current procedures help or hinder students in developing a personalized writing process?
- Considering the previous bulleted list, which procedure would be most helpful to establish in your writing workshop?

Getting Stuck and Working Through It

Good judgment comes from experience,
and experience—well, that comes from poor judgment.
—Anonymous

There were many times when I was working on this book that I got stuck. Every now and then staring at the blank computer screen would yield some new writing. Sometimes a quick diversion (i.e., checking my e-mail or looking at my Facebook "Live News Feed") would help me get back on track. Other times, I had to walk away from my desk for a stretch break. Finally, there were occasions when I'd ask Ruth, "Am I on track with what I'm writing right now?" Regardless of how badly I got stuck, I had a variety of ways to work through the tough spots independently.

We want our students to become independent so they can work through rough patches in their writing when they get stuck. This means we must give students the space they need to work through the hard parts even when it looks like they're not working at all. Spending five minutes looking out the window might be all a boy needs to get back on track. If he's looking out the window instead of writing *every day*, then perhaps he *is* daydreaming. As teachers, it's our job to know the difference so we don't shut down kids' abilities to *think* as they write.

I recently read Roy Peter Clark's *Writing Tools: 50 Essential Strategies for Every Writer*. When it comes to getting stuck, Clark offers this:

> *If you want to write, here's a secret: the writer's struggle is overrated, a con game, a cognitive distortion, a self-fulfilling prophecy, the best excuse for not writing. "Why should I get writer's block?" asked the mischievous Roger Simon. "My father never got truck driver's block." (2006, 3)*

Our classrooms should become "No Writer's Block Zones" so our students never throw up their hands and claim, "I have writer's block!" as a way to excuse themselves from writing. Instead, it is incumbent upon us, as teacher-writers, to have open dialogues with our students about what *we* do, as writers, when we get stuck and need to get back on track.

Challenge: Have students do a little writing about what they do when they get stuck during the writing process. Ask them what helps them get back on track. Then, using their reflections about how they've overcome challenging writing situations in the past, lead a class discussion wherein students discuss ways to overcome "getting stuck."

Reflective Practice:

- How did the open forum you created help your students exchange ideas about independence in the writing workshop?
- What did you learn about your students' resilience with writing as a result of the discussion you lead?
- How did speaking openly about the writing process, regarding the ways you get back on track, go *with* your students?

Communal Supplies

Either you deal with what is the reality,
or you can be sure that the reality is going to deal with you.
—Alex Haley

I used to feel like the Pied Piper when I gave my students a tour around the classroom during the first week of school. They'd line up, single file, for an orderly tour of the classroom. I would show them around the room so they'd know where everything they might need was located. The tour included the math center's manipulatives, the classroom library, and the classroom writing center. In fact, by my fourth year of teaching, I affixed a handwritten banner to the top of the writing center that read, "This is *your* Writing Center. Enjoy it & take care of it." During the Pied Piper tour, I made sure I stressed this point so my students would know that they'd be responsible for straightening it up at the end of each school day and for restocking it with supplies when they ran low.

In addition, my classroom always contained supply caddies at the center of each table or cluster of desks, which housed writing implements, colored pencils, felt-tipped markers, crayons, and handheld pencil sharpeners. I always saw communal supplies as a necessity in my classroom so students would never have to waste time asking, "May I borrow your pencil?" or "Can I use the blue crayon?" I held a guided discovery (Denton and Kriete 2000, 15–18) of the supply caddies on the first day of school to teach students how to responsibly access, use, and put away all of the materials in the supply caddies.

Some kids who came to my classroom never had the experience of accessing their own materials. If you find that's the case with some of your students, then I highly suggest implementing procedures for taking, using, and returning communal supplies. When an expectation is set for how students should care for materials, they use them for academic purposes all year long.

Challenge: Plan a classroom walk-through for your students that will support their independence with regard to knowing where materials are and how to access them.

Reflective Practice:

- What did your students learn about the way to access materials for writing workshop during the classroom tour?
- How will you restock supplies when they run low? Will you have a student notify you or will you enlist your students' assistance to replenish supplies?
- What's your plan if you notice your students aren't properly caring for communal supplies?

Meeting Areas Are for Everyone

Coming together is a beginning. Keeping together is progress.
Working together is success.
—Henry Ford

When I first learned about writing workshop, I jumped in with both feet and accepted the method in its entirety. One of the most difficult switches I made was asking the teenagers in my seventh-grade classroom to join me in a meeting area. It was an unconventional approach, at best, and near insanity, at worst. Developing a meeting area was one of the biggest paradigm shifts I had to undergo as a middle school teacher who believed in writing workshop. At the time, I didn't realize just how much the success of writing workshop would hinge on the establishment of a meeting area.

Several years later, I became a writing coach and began working in elementary classrooms. I encountered many upper-elementary teachers who didn't have a meeting area, nor did they want to create one. I didn't push them to have one, which was a big mistake! In all of the classrooms where there wasn't a meeting area, writing workshop flopped.

My second year as a writing coach, I developed a short list of nonnegotiables when I worked with teachers. "Establish a meeting area" was first on the list. Success in writing workshop hinges on developing a community of writers. When we come together in a meeting area, it is like a coach calling his or her team into a huddle. We're here for some important instruction, and then we're going to "break" and head off to work hard.

When establishing a meeting area, consider these items:

- **Space:** It is necessary to have enough room for the entire class to sit comfortably together. In some classrooms, space is a limited commodity. In this situation, we move desks out of the way to create space for a meeting area. Even young students can learn to move desks and chairs in a matter of seconds when writing workshop is about to begin.
- **Seating:** Many teachers choose to assign seating in the meeting area, by having students sit in rows. This often helps the mini-lesson begin quickly. Often with older students, I prefer to have them sit in a circle (or an oval). Sometimes as students get older, they are uncomfortable sitting on the floor. Consider ways students might sit on furniture such as chairs or benches in the meeting area.
- **Supplies:** A well-stocked meeting area will make life easy during mini-lessons. Some of the items I consider necessities include chart paper and markers, an overhead projector or document camera, tape or glue sticks (for mini-charts), and pencils for student use.

Today, I consider a meeting area an essential element of writing workshop. Even when I work in high school classrooms, I ask students to meet with me together. It is one of the best ways to establish the routine and expectation of participating in a community of writers.

Challenge: Consider the effectiveness of your meeting area. Make changes to help you become more efficient during mini-lessons. If you have never developed a meeting area, make plans about how to include this essential part of writing workshop.

Reflective Practice:

- What do you like best about your meeting area?
- What would you like to see improved about your meeting area? How do you think the changes you're planning to make will enhance student learning?

Plan Boxes

A goal without a plan is just a wish.
—Antoine de Saint-Exupery

Isn't it nice when students know exactly what to do at the end of a mini-lesson? It's even better when they can work independently for the entire period without seeking assistance from us or their peers. Having students who always know what to do and how to sustain themselves for stretches of time was something I wished for when I started teaching. However, my wish didn't come true right away because most of my students needed help self-managing their learning.

In September 2006, after learning about plan boxes from my professor Lucy Calkins, I began to implement them daily in my writing workshop. *What a difference these little boxes made!* After integrating plan boxes into writing workshop I cannot imagine how my students, or I, ever got along without them.

Plan boxes are tools that help students self-manage their independent writing time. I asked my students to create a plan that would help them determine what they would do during independent writing time. However, students need to receive explicit instruction about how to create a plan box (Figure 1.1), because planning ahead is not intuitive for many children. In addition, it is helpful to share other students' well-written plan boxes (Appendix A) so children can begin to get an idea about the ways in which their classmates are spending their independent writing time.

I have worked with and consulted with many teachers who have grown frustrated with the use of plan boxes after a couple of weeks. While having students plan for the way they'll use their time can start off slowly, and may feel arduous to check, I assure you that consistent use of plan boxes will help your students manage their time better, thereby becoming less dependent on you. Students who have trouble developing plan boxes can rehearse what they might do during the workshop by verbally telling you their plans. Once they get the hang of explaining how they'll use their time, you can transition them into writing their plan down.

You can transition students from the mini-lesson to independent writing by checking their plan boxes. I insisted on having my students wait quietly while I checked their peers' plans so I could converse with my students and ask clarifying questions when necessary. If a student's plan didn't make sense, I had them rework their plan and return to my chair once they revised their plan. If a student's plan reflected that they needed help, I had them write in their notebook until I was able to pull them in for a conference or a strategy lesson. Finally, if a student's

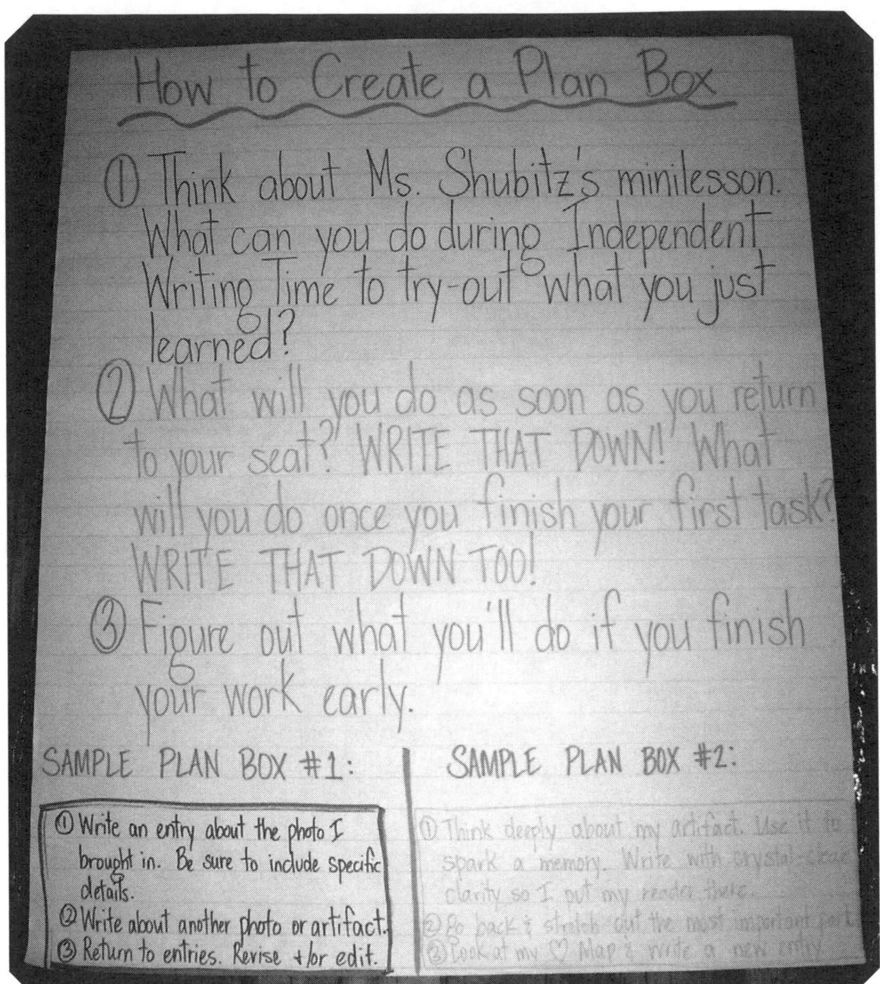

Figure 1.1
This chart was created in early September. It remained on the wall until mid-October and served as a reminder to students about the steps they needed to think about when they created a plan box at the end of each mini-lesson.

plan was on target, I put a smiley face on their plan box and said, "Off you go!" Checking plan boxes daily, before students left the meeting area, reinforced the necessity to manage one's time efficiently.

Challenge: Set aside time to instruct your students about the importance of reaching their writing goals through careful planning. Guide them through the plan-making process by first having them think about how they'll use their independent writing time. Next, have them tell their writing partner what they'll do first, second, and third (if they finish early). Finally, have your students write down their plan in their notebook (either in the next blank space or in a separate "plan box" section of their notebook) and show it to you before they leave the meeting area. Your students' plans will not always be elaborate—some will be a simple list, while others may be a few sentences in length. As long as the child writes a plan that seems like it will sustain them for the entire independent writing time, approve it.

Reflective Practice:

- Did any of your students take more than three minutes to craft a plan for their independent writing time? How will you support them in planning more quickly going forward?
- Were any of your students not adhering to their plans? How did you get them back on track? How will you get them to stay on track with their plan during the next writing workshop *without* a reminder from you?

Be Honest!

Honesty: The best of all lost arts.
—Mark Twain

Honesty makes us or breaks us. It is such a basic understanding, yet it often takes years to grasp. Just like other people, writers value honesty. It is important to be honorable when claiming words and ideas as our own. Since this is a basic principle for writers, we ought to teach this in writing workshop.

The one thing that makes my blood boil is dishonesty. Losing my temper isn't an option in the classroom, however, so I ask children who have claimed someone else's work as their own, "What were you hoping to get by copying this work?" Their responses reveal a variety of motives behind plagiarizing, as well as provide insight in how to address academic dishonesty.

- ***"I asked for help and the person helping me wrote some of the words to show me how to make my writing better."*** In this case, the person helping could be a support person within the school, a family member, or a friend. Often when people work with reluctant writers, their help turns into doing, and the work is no longer the student's. It is important to have a conversation with the student to ensure her understanding of using her own words on writing projects. It is also imperative to have a conversation with the person "helping" so this form of plagiarism does not happen again.
- ***"I was researching for my feature article and found these facts. I included the Web site in my Works Cited list. I changed a few of the words.***

See, I took out two words here, and I changed this **and** ***to a period and capitalized this sentence."*** This student knows writers research to find facts, and he also knows not to copy word for word when using research. His motives are not self-centered; however, he clearly hasn't mastered the art of paraphrasing. In this case, I would teach the student how to paraphrase the information and would give him the opportunity to check over the rest of his work to ensure there aren't any other incidents of plagiarism. Then, I would assess and score the writing from a fresh standpoint. If there are still places of plagiarism, I would talk with the student again. If it is evident the student knowingly turned in plagiarized work a second time, I would follow the consequences of academic dishonesty as defined in the school handbook.

- ***"I was trying to elaborate on my reasons, so I researched on the Internet. I thought those were good ideas, so I added them into my persuasive letter."*** Unlike the previous student, this writer has more of a self-serving motive behind her plagiarism. In this incident, the student chose to use someone else's ideas instead of working toward her own meaning. It is important to explain that using someone else's ideas is just as dishonest as using someone else's words. When we get ideas from someone, we should give credit. This student should have an opportunity to cite her source and develop her own ideas. She should resubmit her work for full credit. If she turns in plagiarized work a second time, the school's consequences of academic dishonesty should be followed.
- ***"I was in a hurry, and this was the easiest way to get my story finished."*** This is a true case of academic dishonesty. The student realized he didn't have his work complete and chose to take someone else's words to submit as his own. This could include swiping work from the Internet or having someone write it for him. In this instance, it is essential to follow through with the firm consequences of academic dishonesty in your school.

With older students, we should explicitly teach academic honesty early in the school year. As writers become more experienced, there becomes less "wiggle room" regarding plagiarism. Still, like all other aspects of writing workshop, it is important to ask questions and listen to answers to get to the root of the problem. Often an important teaching point will ensue out of a conversation about plagiarism. Although it is difficult, paying the consequences of academic dishonesty is a lesson that will stick with students long after they leave our classrooms. The world needs more honest people; we have the opportunity to help instill this value in our students.

Challenge: Determine your response to students who claim other people's words or ideas as their own. Decide whether you will respond to individuals like I would, or whether there will be a blanket policy for everyone. Also consider some key lessons with regard to plagiarism.

Reflective Practice:

- What is your (or your school's) policy for plagiarism? How will you communicate the policy for academic dishonesty with your students?
- What kinds of questions will you ask students who have plagiarized to learn their motivation behind the plagiarism?

Routines and Procedures for Guest Teachers

There cannot be a crisis next week. My schedule is already full.
—Henry Kissinger

I loved attending professional development (PD) sessions when I was a classroom teacher. I always returned invigorated and full of new ideas. However, there was usually some kind of fallout between my students and their guest teacher whenever I took off to attend a PD. Inevitably, I'd have to pick up the pieces and put my class back together again after many a day off. It took a while for me to figure out why they'd crumble when I left in the early years. Over time, I realized it was because the guest teachers weren't familiar with the routines and procedures of my classroom. As soon as students sense that a guest teacher doesn't know classroom protocol, they take the liberty to malign that person in lieu of "doing the right thing."

If you work in a school with in-house substitute teachers, then I highly suggest inviting them to observe your writing workshop before your absence. If their schedule permits them to spend some time in your classroom, then have them come in and see how workshop flows, from the mini-lesson to the share time, so it can run similarly when you're away. If the guest teacher cannot schedule time to be in your class before your absence, then write thorough plans for writing workshop, which should include:

- Materials students must bring to the meeting area
- The teaching point
- Mini-lesson (I used to script out everything, including the demonstration, as if I were the guest teacher delivering the mini-lesson. This eliminated the need for the guest teacher to do prep work and allowed the students to receive the exact instruction I would have taught them that day.)
- Routine for transitioning students from the meeting area to independent writing
- Conferring plans (Leave a list of possible teaching points to help the guest teacher. Give the guest teacher access to your conferring notes so he or she can record the students he or she meets with when you're out.)

- Provide expectations for independent work time, with notations about procedures for leaving the classroom or having a peer conference
- Write up a mid-workshop teaching point and explain where it should be delivered
- Explain how students will return to the meeting area to share

Advance planning not only helps guest teachers feel more comfortable but also helps to keep your students' daily routine intact. Furthermore, planning for a writing workshop you won't be teaching allows *real teaching* to go on during your absence so your students are productive while you're away, thereby making your return much sweeter.

Challenge: Write down the procedures you have in place for writing workshop. Be sure to write them so an outsider who has never stepped into your room before can follow this guide and lead your class in the event of your absence.

Reflective Practice:

- Now that you have created a comprehensive guide to the routines of your writing workshop, how will you make your guide user-friendly and succinct so guest teachers, who don't have a lot of time to prepare, can carry out these routines?
- Will you share the guide you created with your students so they're aware of it? Will you ask them for input or will you rely on yourself to capture everything a guest teacher should know about the way workshop runs in your class?

Routines for Sharing

We have a routine we go through and without question there is a comfort level there.
—Tony Clark

"I want to share today!"

"Is it my turn to share?"

"Pick me! Me! Me!"

Sometimes share time can demonstrate the survival of the persistent. Students who are most vocal have the opportunity to share, and everyone else becomes a captive audience. By establishing procedures for share time, we are able to tap its power so all students' voices are heard.

- **Track who has shared:** Develop a system to ensure every voice has an opportunity to share. Marking in my conference notes when students share is a convenient way to track those who have shared. Another option is to create a visual to hang in the share area. By putting students' names on cards, along with a clothespin next to each name, a simple system is established. When a student shares, the clothespin is moved to the other side of the chart, next to the name of the student who shared. This visual is especially useful in primary classrooms where everyone wants to share every day.
- **Set a precedent:** The purpose of an end-of-workshop share is to discuss our learning as writers. This is a critical part of membership in a community of writers. When we ask one another "How did this help you be a better writer?" or "What are you learning about being a writer?" we lift our share sessions to a higher level. By always including this component in our share sessions, it becomes the precedent for students to follow.
- **Location, location, location:** Establish places for different kinds of share sessions. Where will students meet for a whole-group share? How will they sit for a whip-style share? When talking as partners, where will they sit? Location is an important routine to develop so share sessions will be successful.
- **Signal the end:** Develop a catchphrase for the end of sharing time. One option is to provide a notice of the share session coming to the end. For example, you may say, "This is the last writer to share" or "Two minutes until we must end our conversations." Some other possible phrases to close the share session include "Writers, you should be proud of your work today" or "Tomorrow we will pick up where we left off."

By envisioning the share session and thinking through some of the necessary procedures so the share goes smoothly, we will have productive and effective shares.

Challenge: Consider some of the routines associated with share sessions. Choose one to focus on during upcoming writing workshops.

Reflective Practice:

- What works well during share time?
- What would you like to change about share time?
- What procedures would help your share time run more smoothly?

Cycle 2: Writer's Notebooks

Personalize Writer's Notebooks

I think we have stories because they help us understand who we are.
—***Jodi Picoult***

I keep in mind, when launching writing workshop, that until students know I genuinely care about them as people, they will have little desire in learning how to become stronger writers. A writer's notebook becomes an indispensible tool for me to learn about the idiosyncrasies of the students sitting in my classroom. To build relationships, I ask students to personalize their writer's notebooks.

Since I expect students to write the things that matter most to them, I share my own notebooks with them. I show them the cover, a collage of the things that really matter in my life. I spend time talking through a few of the photos and words that grace my notebooks.

Some of my notebooks have a large collection of words and images; others are simple. All have one commonality—they reveal important parts of my life. I challenge students to design a cover that reveals pieces of their lives.

After I share my notebooks with students, we create a chart titled "Ways to Collect Bits of Life." Then we list possible ephemera to collect. The list ranges from candy wrappers to photographs to clothing tags. As we capture the possible ways to collect bits of life, ideas swirl around the classroom. Students leave school with a mission to find meaningful bits of life to decorate their writer's notebooks.

Some teachers give students quart-sized plastic bags in which to gather ephemera. This helps to ensure the items students gather to decorate with will be flat and fit on their writer's notebooks. The plastic bag also serves as a concrete reminder for students to complete their homework when they arrive home. Another option is to slip a small note inside the bag so parents can help gather ephemera with their children (Appendix A). It is important to give students a few days to gather important bits of their lives.

On a specific day in writing workshop, students spend time decorating their writer's notebooks. They use the ephemera they brought from home and also use donated scrapbooking supplies, stickers, and images they cut from old magazines. As students decorate their notebooks, they naturally begin sharing stories from their lives. We get to know one another through the decorating process.

Personalizing notebooks provides an opportunity for a hodgepodge of students to get to know one another and be transformed into a community of writers.

Challenge: Personalize your own writer's notebook and share it with your students. Give them an opportunity to personalize their writer's notebooks too. (As a way to garner more supplies, ask parents for old or gently used scrapbooking supplies, as well as magazines for students to cut up.)

Reflective Practice:

- What did personalizing your writer's notebook reveal about your life? What did your students' notebooks reveal?
- How can you encourage your students to tell stories about their lives as they decorate their writer's notebooks?
- What is different about the community of writers in your classroom after personalizing writer's notebooks?

Writer's Notebook Expectations

What one has to do usually can be done.
—Eleanor Roosevelt

Each year, when I handed out new writer's notebooks to my students, I included a list of guidelines for my students' writer's notebooks. The guidelines were essentially a list of expectations I had for my students' notebooks. Some were meant to nudge students toward doing their best work, others were meant to instill order and control, while other guidelines were to provide students with support when the writing process felt challenging.

My goal in creating a list of expectations was to foster positive writing behaviors without impeding students' creativity. Some of the expectations I had for my fourth and fifth graders' notebooks work were

- **Write your entries in separate paragraphs:** Entries that are one long paragraph are difficult to follow, so I encouraged my students to start new paragraphs whenever their idea changed, a new person began speaking, or the setting changed.
- **Vary topics:** It's easy for young writers to write bed-to-bed stories daily. It's important to nudge students toward varying their topics by being careful observers of the world and by giving them strategies to generate different kinds of entries so their writing is diversified.
- **Write on the front and back of each page:** During my last three years in the classroom, my students received writer's notebooks that were either provided

by the school or through donations from patrons of DonorsChoose.org. In an effort to make sure students were using their notebooks efficiently, I asked them to start a new page only when it was sufficiently full with writing. If two words of an entry continued on to a new page, I asked my students to draw a line and start their next entry below that one, so that I could also teach them how to live the life of a *green* writer.

- **Write legibly, but not in your neatest handwriting:** I included this expectation because many of my students' families would judge their writing based on their penmanship. While neat handwriting is important, I didn't want my students to be slowed down to please their families. My "rule" was this: If I can read your handwriting, then it's perfect for your notebook.
- **Use conventions:** While the notebook is the writer's place to experiment, it should also serve as a tool to improve their writing. I asked my students to use conventions as they wrote so that their writing carried meaning, because writing devoid of conventions is hard to understand.

We want our students' notebooks to show evidence of their learning. If we set a few clear expectations, then we will see the tracks of our teaching when we look across their notebooks at the end of the school year.

Challenge: Create a list of expectations that you will have for your students' writer's notebooks.

Reflective Practice:

- Are all of the things you wrote expectations rather than rules?
- How will you teach your students what you expect of them when they write in their notebooks?

Collecting Bits of Life

Life becomes precious and more special to us when we look for the little everyday miracles and get excited about the privileges of simply being human.

—Tim Hansel

There is so much power in the ordinary, routine, and daily living we do. Yet so often this living just passes through us like the air we breathe. Suddenly, the week is over. Suddenly, it's the weekend. Suddenly, the New Year is upon us. And if we haven't documented the everyday living, then suddenly, things have changed and we don't know what happened or how. Yet, it's not so sudden. Day by day all those little things add up to big meaning.

Collecting bits of life makes the living of it much richer. By teaching students ways to collect bits of life, we help them to find meaningful writing topics. Here are some ways to encourage students to collect bits of their lives.

- **Collect ephemera:** By collecting the "stuff" we would normally throw away, we are able to see patterns emerge. How often do we drive through to pick up dinner? What does the note left on the counter reveal about life right now? Why is a page from a tear-off calendar important?
- **Make a list:** Lists are an easy way to document life. Lists using a repeating line, such as "Today I . . ." or "I wish . . ." are a quick way to capture life. Lists detailing the contents of a backpack, desk, or under the bed are another way to record bits of life.
- **Draw a map:** Place is often a rich source of meaningful ideas. When we collect maps of important places in our notebooks, memories often flood us. Encouraging students to be specific in their maps empowers them to find important memories. As students zoom in on a place—instead of the entire backyard, just the secret hideout; instead of their house, just their bedroom—they will be rewarded with a copious amount of writing ideas.
- **Jot a quick write:** Donald H. Graves and Penny Kittle (2005) crack open the power of quick writes in *Inside Writing: How to Teach the Details of Craft*. They share two powerful rules for quick-writing. First, write the entire time, and second, write about something that matters. Providing students time to quickly record memories and thoughts gives them the opportunity to find topics they are interested in writing more about.
- **Use thinking stems:** In *Comprehension Connections,* Tanny McGregor (2007) shares thinking stems, which are phrases to encourage students to reflect on an idea. Phrases such as "This makes me realize . . . ," "I used to think, but now I believe . . . ," and "This is important because . . . " prod students into reflection. As they reflect on the bits of their lives, they are able to pinpoint those ideas that are most meaningful.

By collecting bits of life and then pushing ourselves to reflect on them, we are able to live powerful lives. This is why I believe in writer's notebooks for our young writers. It gives them a spot to sift through all the little moments that make up their lives and find the common themes. It's not just the physical book that makes an impact. It is helping students develop a habit and routine of collecting bits of their lives and then pushing them to find big meaning in the little bits of life.

Challenge: Spend two weeks daily collecting bits of your life in your writer's notebook. Notice ways you document the ordinary moments of your life. Spend time reflecting on this process so you can teach students to do this same work.

Reflective Practice:

- What were some common kinds of entries you collected in your writer's notebook? (Add these ideas to the ones in this reflection to empower your students when collecting bits of life.)
- How did focusing on the small, ordinary moments of life influence you as a writer?

Dropping Everything to Write

The great art of writing is the art of making people real to themselves with words.
—Logan Pearsall Smith

During my fifth year in the classroom, I began to draw inspiration from Don Graves and Penny Kittle's *My Quick Writes* notebook, which accompanies *Inside Writing: How to Teach the Details of Craft* (2005). Although they were originally designed for use with high school students, I began adapting some of the writing stems for my fourth graders during times when we had just a few moments to write because of an assembly or field trip disturbing the usual flow of our school day. I also began collecting "Stories in Hand" sparks from Jessica Sprague (2008), for my kids to use in a quick-write-like session, which I called "rapid writes." I projected a bunch of sparks or quick write stems onto the projector screen and encouraged students to choose one. I chose one to write too, and then everyone went off and wrote rapidly about the topic they chose for ten minutes. At the end of ten minutes, everyone shared their writing with their writing partner or with the whole class.

Getting students in the habit of writing about themselves for a short period during the school day gets them excited about the written word. Often students weren't finished writing when time was over, so they'd finish their writing at home later that evening. Since students had freedom of topic choice during rapid write sessions, just as they do in writing workshop, they were heavily invested in their writing. Often pieces that were written during rapid write sessions turned out to be seeds for published pieces of writing.

Providing students with a semistructured, but short, time for writing *outside* of the writing workshop instills a greater love of writing. Students come to see that their words matter and that writing matters since it's valued at multiple points during the school day.

Challenge: Carve out fifteen minutes of the school day, at least once a week, when you provide your students with time to *just write*. Consider a list of topics students can write about so they spend most of the short time allocated to writing rather than thinking about what they could write.

Reflective Practice:

- Did you write alongside your students? How did this uninterrupted time for writing help you as a writer?
- What were your students' reactions to this unstructured time for writing?
- How will you go about infusing this type of writing time into your daily or weekly schedule while still fitting in everything else you're supposed to teach?

Using Writer's Notebooks Throughout the Writing Process

I enjoy the process of writing. The torment comes in getting my bottom on the chair and in front of the typewriter."
—Caryl Rivers

Collecting bits of life and envisioning writing projects is one of the main purposes of a writer's notebook. It is a superb tool for collecting, envisioning, and planning writing. However, writer's notebooks can be a powerhouse for other parts of the writing process too. As we shift our mind-set of the writer's notebook as a tool to use before writing to a tool to be used throughout writing, we will realize we can use writer's notebooks to help us:

- **Draft:** Writer's notebooks can help us experience freedom as writers when we use it to take risks with craft. One primary way my students and I use our writer's notebooks during drafting is working with mentor sentences. We try to emulate the mentor sentences with a few of our own lines that could become part of the current drafts we are writing. (We don't use the writer's notebooks to write entire drafts. This would make our notebooks fill up too quickly!)
- **Revise:** A large part of revision is being willing to play with language. Writer's notebooks provide a safe place to take these risks. We can write a new lead or ending, crack open a sentence to create a more powerful image, or play with mood by reworking a few lines of the setting. The writer's notebook also provides space for revision, something draft paper sometimes lacks. It is important to teach students how to indicate on a draft that a revision is located in the notebook so it isn't forgotten when it comes time to publish.
- **Edit:** Besides using the notebook to jot down a few possible spellings for a difficult word, we can also use it to experiment with different conventions for a sophisticated sentence. Do you want a dash or parenthesis? A semicolon or a period? By exploring different possibilities for punctuation within the covers of our writer's notebooks, they become a tool to support the editing phase of the writing process.

- **Publish:** We can teach our students ways to use their notebooks for publishing. They can sketch ideas in the notebook. For example, designing a scrapbook page or drawing a character for a short fiction story they plan to illustrate helps lead into the publishing phase. Another option is to make a list of potential places to submit writing.

Writer's notebooks have great potential as tools to be used throughout the writing process. As we push ourselves to use our own writer's notebooks during different phases, the possibilities will become evident and endless for ways our students can use them too.

Challenge: Use your writer's notebook throughout your next writing project. Look for ways that you can use it beyond collecting, nurturing, and planning. Then document the ways your notebook has become a tool to support you in the different phases of the writing process. Use these notes to help plan upcoming mini-lessons to empower students to use their notebooks throughout the writing process as well.

Reflective Practice:

- During what part of the writing process was it most natural for you to use your writer's notebook? During what part was it most difficult for you to turn to your writer's notebook for support?
- How did using writer's notebooks throughout the writing process support your students throughout the unit of study?

Caring for Notebooks

Success is the sum of details.
—Harvey S. Firestone

Sometimes success lies in the details. This is true when it comes to writer's notebooks. An essential detail with notebooks is teaching students to care for them. Although it doesn't take as much responsibility as caring for a pet, a measure of responsibility is required for caring for notebooks. Here are some of the key responsibilities to ensure notebooks are successful.

- **Date and title:** Although there are more elaborate organizational systems for notebooks, almost everyone can work within this one. The date is necessary to know when an entry is written; the title is important to know what an entry is about. Encourage students to draw a line between entries so they can be located more easily.

- **Don't tear out pages:** This poses a problem in bound notebooks because it breaks the binding and causes many pages to fall out. In all notebooks, if pages are torn out, then there won't be enough pages to collect entries. All attempts at writing, even the not-so-good ones, ought to be honored. Hence, encouraging students to leave their "bad" writing in their notebooks so they can examine it at a later date empowers them to engage in reflection.
- **Close your notebook:** If bound notebooks are left open, then spines will crack and pages will be lost. In spiral-bound notebooks, pages can easily be torn out if the notebook isn't closed.

We take care of the things that matter most to us—as writers this includes our writer's notebooks. By taking the time to discuss ways to care for our notebooks, we place value on this important tool.

Challenge: Consider how you will instill a sense of responsibility in your students to care for their writer's notebooks. Think through possible ways to respond to students who lack responsibility for their writer's notebooks.

Reflective Practice:

- What will be the biggest battle you will fight when it comes to caring for writer's notebooks?
- How will you instill a sense of responsibility in your students to care for their writer's notebooks?

Checking Writer's Notebooks

Simplicity is the keynote of all true elegance.
—Coco Chanel

When I started teaching, I often yearned for things to be simpler. I remember many days on which I wolfed down my sandwich in less than five minutes so I could check as many writer's notebooks as possible. After realizing this wasn't healthy for my digestive system, I created a structure for checking writer's notebooks at lunchtime that helped me create a manageable routine.

At the beginning of each school year, I informed my students I would be checking their writer's notebook once a week on a designated day. I often reminded students of their checking day in the same way that I reminded them to turn in particular homework assignments at the beginning of the school year. Designating a special place for them to turn in their notebooks for checking proved useful. Returning students' notebooks after lunch, complete with the assessment rubric and my comments on sticky notes, provided them with both direction and personalized feedback, which helped them improve their writing. Finally, I reminded students to turn in their writer's notebook when they returned from an absence.

Many teachers grapple with grading writer's notebooks because they're so personal. Aimee Buckner, author of *Notebook Know-How: Strategies for the Writer's Notebook*, regularly reviews and grades students' notebooks since she views notebooks as "a learning process" (2005, 111). As a result, she advocates grading notebooks with a rubric that will help students become better writers. She states:

> *The rubric helps parents know what is expected of students. It helps students know and understand how this translates into progress. It helps me focus my assessment of the notebook on qualities that I know will lead to better writing. (2005, 111–112)*

Checking and grading students' notebooks can feel daunting because it usually means giving up your lunch period since we don't want students to be at home without their notebooks at night. However, once this lunchtime routine is manageable, it becomes an enjoyable part of your daily routine as a teacher of writing, because it allows you to get to know your students more intimately while helping them become stronger writers.

Challenge: Make a plan for checking your students' writer's notebooks. You might want to create a schedule that allows you to check the same number of notebooks every day of the week. Consider days that you do or do not have preps, because that extra time can be used to check notebooks.

Reflective Practice:

- Does your plan for checking writer's notebooks feel manageable?
- Now that you've streamlined your checking process, how do you feel?

Starting a New Notebook

Use your notebook to breathe in the world around you.
—Ralph Fletcher

When Christian was in my fourth-grade class, he "finished" five or six notebooks that year. In reality, he never finished a single notebook. One day he confided in me about the reason he never wrote "till the last page." Here's a close approximation of our conversation:

I walked into the hallway and saw Christian standing at his backpack shaking his head. "What's wrong?" I asked.

"Ms. Shubitz, I never finish my writer's notebooks. I always leave a few pages blank at the end of an old one when I start a new one. I don't know why I do that."

I smiled. I knew why. "I do the same thing, Christian," I replied.

His eyes widened. "You do!?"

"Mmm-hmm," I said. "You and me: we're alike in that way. I can never use a notebook till the very end. Too scary. What if you run out of pages when you are ready to write an amazing story or see something that you've got to write down. Then what?"

"I know exactly what you mean!" he said. "I once had to write on the back cover of a notebook."

Christian was living like a writer. He wrote voraciously and therefore needed to make smart decisions about when it was time for *him* to begin a new notebook.

Christian went through many notebooks in one year, whereas other students might complete two. Regardless of the number of new notebooks a student needs, each notebook should begin its life with some fanfare. First, encourage students to personalize their new notebook by gluing photographs to the cover, inserting favorite poems, or by taping in magazine clippings of their favorite bands or movie stars. Second, make sure to insert the same items, such as inspirational quotes or poems such as "My Writer's Notebook" by Brod Bagert, into each student's notebook in the fall. Third, if your students divide their notebooks, remind them to take a few moments to section their new notebooks in a similar fashion. Finally, if you're in the midst of a unit of study when a student begins a new notebook, encourage him or her to keep the existing notebook close at hand so it can be referenced when necessary. Whether it's a student's first notebook or sixth notebook of the school year, young writers always should be encouraged to make each notebook their own.

Challenge: Create extra copies of lists, poems, quotations, guidelines, or other items that you insert into your students' writer's notebooks. Put these items into a folder so they're ready to go when any student begins a new notebook during the school year.

Reflective Practice:

- Do you want to vary the items you insert into your students' new notebooks from what you put in their notebooks in the fall?
- Will you hold on to students' notebooks once they finish each one (and give them back at the end of the school year) or will you allow students to keep each completed notebook? What do you think the benefits and detriments would be of each system?

At-Home Writing Spaces

Writing is the only thing that, when I do it, I don't feel I should be doing something else.
—Gloria Steinem

During my college years in Washington, D.C., I used to go to the National Gallery of Art before every history exam (my minor was history) to study in an atmosphere that was devoid of distractions. I bragged to my friends about how wonderful it was to have a space to go to, even if it was a Metro ride away, which enabled me to focus on studying for an exam. My time at the National Gallery was a treasure! Because of this experience, I encourage students to find writing spots at home. Most students do not have a gorgeous place such as the National Gallery of Art to inspire them as writers and readers, so they need to create such a place. When children have a special place they want to go to for writing, it will inspire them to get into a daily writing routine.

Young writers need writing spaces too. Whereas many children often do their homework around the kitchen table with their siblings, the work of a writer is often done without the distractions of others. Having a special place to write usually helps a writer grappling with the best way to get words down on the page. Some young writers may choose to write on a lap desk in the corner of the living room, while others may choose to lay out their notebook or draft on their bed. Some writers may choose to work in silence, while other writers might have an MP3 player punctuating the sound of their pen.

Some of my former students have created study carrels for themselves to help them focus. One fourth grader once placed photos of his family and quotes he loved on the inside of his cardboard study carrel so he could be inspired to write more when he came to that part of his homework. Please realize, I'm not suggesting that we encourage our students to create boxes or study carrels for themselves (albeit a cool idea). Rather, I want us to encourage our students to seek out writing spaces at home that will inspire them to do their best writing. And, if they cannot seem to find a space at home that helps them get into a regular writing routine, then it is incumbent upon us to work with our students' families to help them create these special spaces.

Challenge: Work with one of your most reluctant at-home writers to create an at-home writing routine. This could be as simple as talking about designating a particular spot at home for writing, or it might mean making a home visit to help create a writing spot.

Reflective Practice:

- How did the student's at-home writing change as a result of creating a writing space?
- What have you learned by helping this student that you can use to help other students make writing a priority at home?

Sharing Notebooks Across Grade Levels

Our best thoughts come from others.
—Ralph Waldo Emerson

Small groups are scattered throughout a classroom, each group huddled around a single writer's notebook. What makes these groups unique is that they consist of second, third, and fourth graders—and the second graders are doing most of the talking!

Christi Overman's second graders had studied writer's notebooks for nearly a month. They used Marissa Moss's Amelia's Notebook series and *Max's Logbook* (2003) as mentor texts and learned to collect important parts of their lives—emotions, dreams, memories, thoughts, observations, and ephemera. Their notebooks were filled with rich writing possibilities. Meanwhile, Barb Bean's and Lori Jones's multiage classrooms were ready to embark on launching writer's notebooks. (At the time, our state testing was in the fall, so the first unit of study in writing workshops of upper grades was a writing prompt genre study.) As a way to introduce notebooks, they invited Christi's students to share their notebooks.

This provided an authentic audience for the second graders as they shared not only their writer's notebooks but also their thinking and their process of collecting entries in their notebooks. They thumbed through their notebooks, narrating the reasons they created various entries and how they helped them as writers.

"I'm working on a comic strip and these are my main characters," Nick said to the older boys.

"This is a map of my dog. See the mud, her slobber, and bits of grass and leaves from the woods? I'm thinking my first story is going to be about my dog," Katrina told her group.

"I love office supplies," Marley said as she showed the page she filled with different office supplies. "I'm not sure how I'm going to use this in a story, but getting to use office supplies sure makes me want to write!" Her grin is enough to convince anyone that office supplies should make us all want to write.

At the end of the share session, the multiagers left with brains filled with ideas for collecting in their own writer's notebooks. "When do we get to start?" they asked repeatedly. The second graders returned to their classrooms with pride. They walked a little taller and smiled a little broader after sharing their notebooks. The self-confidence they gained served them well as they began to draft in writing workshop the following day.

Today, our state testing has been moved to the spring. Therefore, all grade levels launch notebooks at about the same time. However, this doesn't stop us from sharing across grade levels. It is a great way for students to get new ideas for the kinds of entries they might collect in their writer's notebooks, as well as a prime way to rehearse stories before drafting. By sharing notebooks, writers are able to see patterns and common themes emerge that they may miss when looking through their notebooks alone. Most important, though, the pride transforms writers of all ages when other students affirm them.

Challenge: Make plans with another classroom to share writer's notebooks. Help students prepare by giving them time to practice talking about their work as a writer when using writer's notebooks. Encourage them to talk beyond the ideas on the page and to tell more of the story or the thinking behind the entry.

Reflective Practice:

- What are some issues that could arise during the share session? How will you be proactive to prevent any problems?
- How did sharing across grade levels help your students?

Cycle 3: Publishing Celebrations

Reflect and Relish Growth as Writers

Winners take time to relish their work, knowing that
scaling the mountain is what makes the view from the top so exhilarating.

—Denis Waitley

Celebrations are a time to rejoice in the finished product. That's not the only thing we should celebrate, though. Celebrations are also a good time for us to reflect and relish our growth as writers.

As students are finishing their published work, it is a good time to ask them to complete a writing analysis, which is a reflection about their writing process. If students are engaged in writing workshop, then they aren't too young, nor are they too old, to delve into a bit of reflective practice. I've watched the power of this kind of reflection in five-year-olds and fifteen-year-olds. Each time, I am fascinated.

I've learned that students often know more about writing well than they are able to execute in a piece of writing. I've learned that students often attempt sophisticated writing moves, and these moves often flop in the piece of writing. Before I started having students engage in reflective practice, I was often disappointed with their work. Now, as I read their reflections and take into consideration their attempts at sophisticated writing, I am able to view their writing with new eyes. This perspective allows me to see the attempts to write well and gives me a more accurate understanding of the writer.

Some questions that are most powerful on these pre-celebration reflections are as follows:

- How did you use your plan to write well?
- What will you change about the way you plan on your next piece?
- What did you do to write your best first draft?
- How did you decide what to revise?
- How will you refine your revision process next time?
- What helped you most while checking your writing for Standard English?
- What did you do best as a writer on this piece?
- What do you like best about your published piece?

For younger students or those less experienced with reflective practice, I often design a reflection that guides students through the process of reflective practice. To begin, empower students to consider basic practices of being a writer. Here are some examples:

- I used my writer's notebook to make a plan.
- I wrote my best first draft.
- I revised my writing for clarity.
- I checked for spelling, capitalization, and punctuation.

A simple scale is another way to ease students into reflective practice. The following scale empowers even the least experienced writer to engage in reflection.

- I did an exceptional job.
- I could have put forth more effort.
- I didn't understand.
- I didn't do this.

When we push students to consider their growth as writers, we give them a gift that outlasts the cookies and punch at the celebration. It is by looking back and making plans to move forward that we grow as writers.

Challenge: Create a pre-celebration reflection for your students. (Appendix E has samples of writing analyses that could be modified for pre-celebration reflections.) Consider questions that will give you insight into the kinds of decisions students are making as writers.

Reflective Practice:

- How will you use the reflections to help you assess your students as writers?
- How will you encourage your students to take the time necessary to reflect on their personal writing process?

Guests from the School Community

Celebrations are the juice of life.
—John D. Hofbrauer, Jr.

All writers need an audience. A sure-fire way to get a captive audience to listen and respond to student writing at ten thirty in the morning or two o'clock in the afternoon is to invite another class to attend your students' publishing celebration.

At the beginning of each school year, I'd often invite students I had taught during the previous year. By having former students as guests, I received assistance teaching my new students how to move through a publishing celebration, because previous students knew my expectations. If it's not possible to invite a group of your former students, then consider inviting another class from your grade level to join in the festivities.

Regardless of which class was invited, I tried to speak with the other teacher before setting a definite time for the party, so we could find a mutually convenient time. Once the teacher accepted, a couple of my students delivered a printed invitation to the other teacher, or placed it in the teacher's mailbox, so it could be shared with the class. Excitement was generated when the invitation process began.

As the months of the school year went on, I asked my students for input about which classes they'd like to invite to our publishing celebrations. Often classes with siblings or cousins were suggested. As long as the content of the published pieces was age appropriate (i.e., inviting kindergarteners to a fourth-grade memoir celebration never seemed like a good fit), I usually followed through with the invitation requests.

Finally, regardless of the class I chose to invite, my students and I always delivered invitations to all of the school administrators, support staff, specialists, and service providers (Appendix A). While my students knew it would be hard for all of them to attend, we regularly were treated to a handful of extra visitors who sat alongside students and listened to their published pieces of writing before offering feedback. There was something exceedingly special about watching my students interact with the principal, the school receptionist, the speech pathologist, or the lunch coordinator inside our classroom. Traditional dynamics were changed since a celebration of published writing allows people to see one another in a new light.

Challenge: Initiate a conversation with your students about your class's upcoming publishing celebration. Find out who they're interested in inviting *and* why. If their rationale sounds good, then enlist their help to extend the invitation.

Reflective Practice:

- Which grade levels did your students wish to invite to the publishing celebration and why? How did you feel about your students' choices of invitees?
- How did your students react when you told them you'd be inviting adult members of your school's community?

Inviting Families

A family, although not a necessity, is the ultimate luxury.
—Eric Pio

Nothing brought a smile to the faces of my fourth and fifth graders like the entrance of a family member to a classroom publishing party. Regardless of their relationship at home, I noticed my students were thrilled to have a sibling, parent, cousin, aunt, uncle, or grandparent attend a classroom publishing celebration.

It's challenging for adults to take time off from work, especially when they're working more than one job, to attend school-sponsored activities in the middle of the school day. However, by varying the times of celebrations, it is usually possible for all parents to show up to one publishing celebration at least once during a given school year. For instance, one month I'd try to schedule a breakfast celebration; the next month, I'd try to schedule the celebration at lunchtime, and the following month I'd try to schedule a celebration at the end of the school day. Another option is to consider hosting a celebration outside of school hours.

When I taught, I found that extending invitations to all parents in advance of the publishing party is useful. I used to disseminate printed invitations in my students' backpack mail and via e-mail. If your students' parents are tech savvy, you might use an electronic invitation service, such as Evite or MyPunchbowl, which will ask them to RSVP online so you can get a better projection of who to expect. Regardless of the method of inviting, I sent invitations home in the languages spoken by my students' families. Family members who speak Spanish feel included when they can read the piece of paper that's coming home to them.

Although we don't need family members to make publishing celebrations more festive, they certainly add a new dimension to any classroom celebration. While a child might struggle with writing at home, I've noticed that having a family member present to celebrate the final product can help a child's family understand how much he or she has accomplished in the classroom. Furthermore, families celebrate their children, one-on-one, in a special way when they honor them by attending this type of in-class celebration.

Challenge: Keep track of family members who attend publishing parties. Consider sending a quick thank-you note to any family member who attends a publishing celebration. After three celebrations, phone home to any student whose family member has not attended. It could be that your invitations aren't making their way home and therefore a personal invitation might make the difference when trying to get all parents into the classroom. However, this would also provide an opportunity to find a time that is convenient for a family member.

Reflective Practice:

- How will you communicate your expectations for the celebration to family members (e.g., inviting them to read and respond to more students than just their child)?
- How will you help students whose family members can never make it to school for a publishing celebration so they don't feel left out?

Preparing to Read Aloud

The thing about performance, even if it's only an illusion,
is that it is a celebration of the fact that we do contain within ourselves infinite possibilities.
—Sydney Smith

The first time I hosted a celebration and invited students to read aloud, I was left feeling a little let down. I was a middle school teacher, with three classes. All day long, I listened to student after student bungle reading aloud their writing. After hearing more than seventy poorly read pieces, I vowed that the next time would be different.

As the next celebration neared, I decided to hold what I called a "Silent Celebration" instead. In this gallery-inspired celebration, students displayed their writing and a comment sheet on their desk and then walked around the room reading and commenting on other people's work. Student feedback on this celebration was mostly positive, but some still wanted to read their work aloud.

As the final celebration of the year neared, I caved to their requests and agreed to host a celebration in which students would have the chance to read aloud. To keep my promise to myself, we used several writing workshops leading up to the celebration to prepare. To kick off this line of thinking, we brainstormed how speakers keep things lively for the listener. Here is the list that evolved:

- Speak clearly and loudly enough for everyone in the room to hear.
- Use inflection.
- Pause for emotion.
- Make eye contact with the audience.
- Change your face to go with the story. If it is happy, look happy.

I then took these snippets and made a small "cheat sheet" of notes for each student to use as they practiced reading their writing aloud. As we passed the sheets around the mini-lesson area, many students looked perplexed. "What do you mean, practice?" someone asked.

I sat for a moment and collected my thoughts. *They didn't practice reading aloud?* I shared with them the importance of practicing reading aloud to make it interesting for the reader. We talked about performing our writing and the importance of practicing. Students used the remainder of writing workshop to practice reading aloud. I encouraged students to practice at home in front of a mirror or with their family members.

The day before the celebration, we had a dry run in small groups. Students practiced in a more formal way by standing in front of a small group and reading their writing. The small group then offered feedback based on the list we brainstormed earlier in the week.

On the day of the celebration, I encouraged students to take a minute to silently read their writing to imagine what it would sound like in front of the class. I enlarged the list of good qualities in a speaker and taped it to the podium. As students finished reading their writing, I asked them to choose one quality to keep in mind when they were reading aloud.

Explicitly teaching the nuances of reading aloud well was worth the time we invested. The celebration was enjoyable and the writing was honored as student after student stood before us and read aloud in engaging ways. However, the benefits didn't stop at the end of the celebration. Students continued to put into action reading aloud well in future share sessions and celebrations.

Challenge: Develop a list with your students of qualities speakers must use to keep listeners engaged. Take a few minutes to make mini-versions of this list so students can internalize these ideas by practicing with them.

Reflective Practice:

- What do your students do best when reading aloud? What is the one thing they should develop as a group?
- What piece of your writing will you use to model an effective read-aloud for your class?

Responding During the Celebration

What is the shortest word in the English language that contains the letters: abcdef?
Answer: feedback. Don't forget that feedback is one
of the essential elements of good communication.
—Unknown

I've always thought of publishing celebrations as part work and part fun. When I was a classroom teacher, I always planned to have my students share their writing work first and then allotted adequate time for them to socialize and eat some sweet treats before getting on with the rest of the school day. Regardless of the type of format students will use when sharing their writing, it's important to keep the focus of the celebration on students' writing, even if a student's birthday happens to fall on the same day as the celebration. After all, *the writing* is what's being celebrated.

When you extend an invitation to another class, it's prudent to inform the other teacher of what you expect out of her students. When inviting students from younger grades, you can have them deliver feedback to your students orally, with pictures, or in one sentence. However, for students in upper elementary grades, I always requested that their teacher show them how to give targeted feedback since it is often demoralizing for students who have worked diligently throughout an entire unit of study get to the end of a piece and have the peer say, "It was good."

It has been my experience that we must teach others how we want them to respond to writing. Therefore, I always share a copy of the feedback form my students are going to ask invited guests to fill out. If I can't speak with the teacher directly, then I leave a short note, asking him or her to review the feedback form with his or her students so they know what it looks like (Appendix A). Further, I request that they teach their students how to do one of three things:

- Inform the writer of something specific he or she did well.
- Tell the writer about a personal connection you had to their writing.
- Let the writer know how their writing has inspired you to do something differently as a writer.

I have found that students as young as first grade can come into an upper elementary school classroom and provide targeted feedback to older students *if* their teacher takes the time to teach them how to do this. Having specific comments fuels young writers and makes them even more proud of the accomplishment they're celebrating.

Challenge: Collaborate with your students to create a feedback form to use at your next publishing celebration, keeping in mind what they hope to gain from the feedback form they create.

Reflective Practice:

- Is the feedback form developmentally appropriate for the respondents (if you're inviting students from other classes)?
- How will the feedback form help your students grow as writers?

Thinking Up a Theme

I love any and all celebrations where you celebrate creativity.
—Brad Paisley

Themes are a fun way to add a little spice to your celebrations. However, that's not the only reason to consider a theme. They also provide another teaching opportunity. By connecting an appropriate theme to a celebration, we are able to provide students with experiences that build background knowledge. Consider the following ideas for enriching writing workshop celebrations.

- **Poetry jam:** It was common in the 1960s for groups of people to bring their snappin' fingers and gather 'round for a poetry jam. Dressing as beatniks, playing some Beatles hits, and sippin' on smoothies are ways to teach more about the era.

- **Campfire stories:** What better way to celebrate the conclusion of a narrative study than to gather around a campfire and share stories? This celebration provides an opportunity to teach oral storytelling skills and gives students the chance to consider ways the audience can become active participants in the storytelling. By using a repeating line or sound effects, the audience is able to become a part of the storytelling. The campfire doesn't have to be real—I've been known to build one out of rulers and paper in the middle of my classroom—but if it is, there is the possibility to teach fire safety (and how to make s'mores!).
- **Red carpet event:** At the end of one trimester, Tifani Beer and I joined our classes to celebrate with black-tie style. With formal invitations, attire, and decorations, our students came to an awards celebration that rivaled the Emmys. We gave awards to every student, in such categories as Best Use of a Metaphor, Outstanding Lead Writer, and Most Likely Writer to Make You Cry. Students brought their best work of the year to place in a gallery celebration. Many wore formal attire (like their teachers), and we concluded with a breakfast. We had rich opportunities to teach civility and formal manners in a fun atmosphere.
- **"I've been published!"** Although this is not a theme for a celebration, it is a great theme for a bulletin board. Especially appropriate in the midst of a persuasive unit, students can add clippings of their published letters to the editor or responses they receive from persuasive letters that were sent. This gives students an opportunity to share with others the power of their words.

With these ideas as a starting point, the possibilities for a theme celebration are endless. Consider ways to extend your teaching about culture or civility during a celebration. Enthusiasm for writing increases as students are drawn into the magic of a themed celebration.

Challenge: Make a list of possible theme celebrations in your classroom. Consider ways to teach culture or civility in a way that connects to the unit of study. After choosing a theme, take a few minutes to make a list of details that could tie your celebration together in a more meaningful way.

Reflective Practice:

- How will the celebration enrich your students' learning?
- How will you encourage your students to be active participants in the celebration? When will you inform parents and provide time for students to prepare?

Party Planning

Sharing food with another human being is an intimate act
that should not be indulged in lightly.
—M. F. K. Fisher

What's a party without food? Frankly, I don't know because I'm a believer in pairing celebrations with something delicious to eat. It's my belief that the inclusion of food at a publishing party makes it more festive, so I always set aside some time to plan a publishing celebration menu with my students.

A few days before the celebration, spend about five minutes figuring out what students will bring. Create a sign-up list so you can balance the number of bags of chips students bring with the napkins and plates you'll also need. A sign-up list is useful because it will allow you to remind students of the specific item they signed up to bring the day before the party.

Don't think you have to forego food just because you work in a school with a healthy food mission. If you are hosting a breakfast party, you can serve whole-wheat bagels, low-fat cream cheese, and juice. For a midday party, consider serving fruit, vegetables, cheese, crackers, nuts, and sparkling water.

Two final points to remember when serving food at a publishing celebration: First, make sure you know what your students can eat. If the school's nurse isn't sure, then send home an allergy questionnaire to avoid surprises (Appendix A). Second, wait until all students have shared their writing with several people before serving food. I learned, the hard way, that sharing comes to a halt once food is served. Plus, allotting time for eating and schmoozing at the end of the celebration allows students time to work on those ever-important socialization skills.

Challenge: Plan a menu for your upcoming publishing celebration with your students. Although it's easy to have students sign up to bring junk food, consider talking with them about healthy choices and then create a menu of healthier options together. Take time to preselect students who will help with distributing food and drinks at the celebration and talk about an efficient cleanup system.

Reflective Practice:

- Did you have too much or too little food for the people present at the celebration? How will you change your planning list next time to make sure students bring in enough food?
- Was there ample time for everyone, including you, to sit back, relax, eat, and celebrate the hard work accomplished?

Fill the Community with Student Writing

Words, once they are printed, have a life of their own.
—Carol Burnett

When I visited the Manhattan New School, we went to a local pizza joint for lunch. As I looked at the whimsical art on the walls, I realized it was student writing. More students' writing popped out at me as I looked around the restaurant. I couldn't help but smile and was instantly drawn into the stories.

This writing was an unexpected lunch treat. Leaving the restaurant, walking down the street with buildings towering over me, I realized the genuine gift writing is to people. We don't even have to know our audience, and we can bless them, simply by putting our words out in public. Thoughts tumbled in my mind about ways to make my students' writing accessible to community members. The following are two of the publishing projects my students developed when I returned and shared with them my experience at the pizza place.

- **Main office magazine:** We used the term *magazine* loosely, but basically this was a compilation of writings and images around a specific topic, such as winter or patriotism. A due date was established; students submitted their pieces to an editor (me) and then finalized their work. We used page protectors bound with a plastic slide and left the magazine on an end table where people could browse as they waited.
- **Class anthologies for doctors' offices:** As my students and I brainstormed places people wait and read, doctor's offices topped our lists. We began to create class anthologies at the end of most units of study. We made multiple copies of each anthology and when someone went to the doctor, they took a copy of the anthology with them. Since students took responsibility for distributing the anthologies, we discussed the polite way to ask permission to leave an anthology in a waiting room.

In both the main office magazine and the anthology, I included a letter to the public, explaining writing workshop and our daily work as writers. I also addressed the need to accept student errors in writing. Since I was working with teenagers, I did a thorough final edit; however, errors still found their way into our publications. I wanted our readers to understand that our purpose in publishing was not for perfection, which often leads to only one outcome—a decrease in motivation for writing. Instead, our purpose for publishing was to share our writing because it is good for the soul. I wished the reader the same blessing I had in the Manhattan pizza place, as they looked beyond the errors and into the beauty of the words.

As a writing coach, I've watched other classes infuse the community with their writing. They have

- **Placed poetry on grocery bags:** We asked a local grocery store for a stack of paper bags. Students then wrote their poems and drew a picture on each bag. The bags were returned to the store, used to bag groceries, and brightened days.
- **Designed placemats:** One class used their writing to decorate placemats. After laminating them, they donated the placemats to a local nursing home.
- **Created note cards:** Students created several note cards with the same design and an original poem, leaving the inside blank for a personal message. They then placed them in a basket. Anyone who contributed to the note card basket could swap their designs with others. By adding envelopes and ribbon near the note card basket, it was easy for students to create a bundle of note cards to give as a gift. Of course, they could also use the note card and send it through the mail.

Flooding the community with student writing doesn't have to take a lot of time or energy. By making a plan and empowering students, we will soon find the whimsy of student writing in communities across the country.

Challenge: Brainstorm with your students ways to fill your community with student writing. Have them consider places people wait and the way writing could be posted in these places.

Reflective Practice:

- What happened to students' energy levels as you discussed putting their writing in the community?
- What kinds of procedures will you have in place to ensure a final edit of students' work?
- How will you educate the public about the work of young writers, as well as the acceptance of writing errors in student work?

Community-Based Celebrations

"A community needs a soul if it is to become a true home for human beings. You, the people, must get it this soul.
—Pope John Paul II

It's convenient to host a publishing celebration in your classroom during the school day. However, hosting every publishing party in your classroom isn't the *only* way you can celebrate with your students. Moving beyond the classroom walls to the school library or to another common room in your school has distinct possibilities. These venues are especially useful when more than one class at a time is celebrating and sharing published work.

However, sometimes we have to get out of school when we want to throw a celebration. First, in an age when some states are banning students from bringing food from home into the classroom, it's often necessary to hold a celebration outside of school if you want to have food at the party. Second, because many adults work during the school day, it's nice to bring a celebration or two into the community in the early evening or on a weekend, so more people can be part of the festivities. Finally, having a celebration outside of school showcases the importance of the students' writing work and gives them a greater audience.

Popular places for out-of-school publishing celebrations are public libraries or local bookstores, which are often accustomed to hosting open mikes or author celebrations. Other options are community rooms at firehouses, grocery stores, or local businesses, which often can be used for an hour at a time free of charge to a school group. Since free space is a precious commodity, you will need a group of volunteers to help you set up before and clean up after the publishing celebration so you're invited back. While you can enlist the help of your students' parents, consider asking a couple of your friends or family members to help with this endeavor. This way, you have even more members of the community present at your class's celebration.

Stepping out into the community is one way to reach beyond the walls of your classroom to your students and their families. Everyone's a little different outside of the confines of school. While stepping out of your comfort zone might feel uncomfortable at first, it will position your students and their families to feel more at ease and will, in turn, help you develop a stronger relationship with them when you come together to celebrate, regardless of your venue.

Challenge: Plan to head into the community to celebrate your students' writing. Locate and confirm a venue at least a month in advance. Notify your students and their families about the location and date as soon as you secure it so they can plan to attend. Make sure to put a start and end time on the invitation and request that families stay for the duration of the celebration rather than drop off and pick up their child.

Reflective Practice:

- How will your preparations for an out-of-school publishing party differ from an in-school celebration?
- Plan for the flow of the publishing celebration just as you would if it were in your classroom. Will you allow time for students to mingle with one another or will you get right down to business? Think about the sharing format (e.g., open mike, partner share) you will use.

Here's to Writing Workshop!

The more you praise and celebrate life, the more in life there is to celebrate.
—Oprah Winfrey

In *Independent Writing*, Colleen Cruz (2004) suggests toasting the first published pieces in writing workshop. Tony Miller and his third-grade class invited me to join them in celebrating their first published work of the school year.

We started in the traditional way, coming together in the meeting area for the mini-lesson. "Writers," I began, "often come together to celebrate their writing." Their smiles beamed at me. "Something they also do is spend time reflecting on their growth. So we will do the same thing." They nodded in agreement. "Then, we'll make our writing public by hanging the published writing on the bulletin board in the hallway." Recognition of the new bulletin board was evident on their faces. "Finally, like all great celebrations, we'll end with a toast." Some students knew exactly what this meant, since they'd attended weddings or other celebrations with toasting. Others were clueless, so we spent a few minutes defining a toast.

Students left the meeting area and went off to work on their reflections. A comfortable silence settled over the classroom. As they finished their reflections, they hung their work on the bulletin board. After each piece was placed on the bulletin board, the student would stand back and admire it.

When everyone was back in the classroom, we passed out glasses of apple juice. Tony revealed a "Congratulations Writers" banner on the SmartBoard. His students oohed and awed. He raised his glass. They grew silent. He proceeded to toast his students in honor of becoming writers together. He acknowledged his own growth as a writer and teacher of writers, as well as his pride in their hard work. As he finished, he bumped his glass even higher in the air, invited us to toast with him and announced, "To writing workshop!"

"To writing workshop!" A chorus of voices joined him. Then Tony opened the floor to anyone who wanted to stand and toast. A litany of voices followed.

"I'm proud of myself, but I'm even more proud that we all did this together!"

"I'm glad we have writing workshop."

"I'm proud of all of us for publishing."

"Our writing looks nice out on the board; we all did a good job."

Student after student stood and voiced their joy of writing and their pride in being a writer. The simple invitation to toast writing workshop unleashed powerful words and filled everyone in the room with encouragement to continue writing. This made for a very good day in writing workshop.

Challenge: Write out a potential toast for your next writing celebration. Follow Tony's lead and include both the way you have been influenced by writing workshop and the things you've noticed about your students. Make a plan for a toast in an upcoming writing workshop.

Reflective Practice:

- How have your students impressed you in writing workshop?
- How has writing workshop influenced you as a teacher? As a writer?

Chapter 2: Mini-Lessons

Mini-lessons deepen instruction bit by bit over time. Through short and explicit lessons, students learn the essential elements of writing well. We consider curriculum standards, our own writing lives, and the needs of our students when determining mini-lesson topics. By weaving together these needs, we find an effective balance in our instruction.

Because mini-lessons are given a limited amount of time in writing workshop, we must make the most of each moment. Therefore, this chapter includes a look at creating meaningful mini-lessons, teasing out the teaching of conventions, and helping mini-lessons stick with our students. If lifting the level of your mini-lessons is one of your interests, consider the following:

- **Cycle 1: Meaningful Mini-Lessons**
  Meaning is the heart of writing well, as well as at the heart of effective mini-lessons. This cycle focuses on ways to make mini-lessons more meaningful.
- **Cycle 2: Teaching Conventions in Mini-Lessons**
  Many of us seek to weave grammar instruction into the content of writing workshop. This cycle provides ten ideas to consider when making choices about grammar instruction within writing workshops.

- **Cycle 3: Making Our Teaching Stick**
  The true indicator of learning is whether students remember the lessons over time. If your goal is to make your teaching indelible, this cycle is for you.

As our instruction builds over time, our students will grow in their understanding of how to write well. Enjoy teaching in explicit ways, as well as watching your students put the teaching points into practice.

Cycle 1: Meaningful Mini-Lessons

Keeping It Authentic

You can teach a student a lesson for a day; but if you can teach him to learn by creating curiosity, he will continue the learning process as long as he lives.
—Clay P. Bedford

Lately, I've been struggling with the vast amount of activities, skill builders, mini-lessons, and so on touting their effectiveness for student writers in the guise of writing workshop. At every turn, there is a new gimmick promising to grab students' attention in the name of writing workshop.

Yet if we choose the teaching point of the mini-lesson wisely, then we won't need a gimmick to get students interested. They will already be interested because the lesson meets their needs as writers. The writing work they are engaged in is enough to fuel their interest in the mini-lesson.

In *The Writing Workshop: Working Through the Hard Parts (and They're All Hard Parts)* (2001), Katie Wood Ray and Lester Laminack write:

> *If we have set the workshop up well, and students are interested in what they are working on as writers, then they have real reasons to be interested in what we are saying in our focus lessons. This is actually one of my main teaching goals. I want students to be interested in my lessons because they have their own reasons (as writers) to be interested in them, and although I stab around at the extent to which I'm successful at that with different students, I still maintain that as a goal. (146)*

This is my goal as well: to gain student interest in a mini-lesson because it is worthy of their attention. I don't want to manipulate students into "buying" a lesson because I'm a good salesperson. I want them to believe in a lesson because it helps them become a better writer—not just a better writer for one day on one piece of writing, but a better writer forever.

I've been struck by the fine line between a gimmick and an authentic experience for our students. It all boils down to the teacher's focus. Authenticity is achieved when we focus on the needs of the writers in our classrooms as opposed to producing perfect pieces of writing. When this becomes our goal, workshop innately matters to the writers in our classrooms, and we don't need to coerce them into paying attention to the mini-lesson.

Challenge: Take a close look at the motives behind your mini-lessons. Are you offering lessons that matter? Determine your students' attitudes toward the mini-lesson by noting their body language, engagement, and feedback. Spend time reflecting on ways to make upcoming mini-lessons more authentic.

Reflective Practice:

- How do your students act during the mini-lesson?
- What are some ways your mini-lessons can become more authentic?

Lessons They Can't Help but Remember

Tell me and I'll forget. Show me, and I may not remember. Involve me, and I'll understand.
—Native American Saying

It was a dreary Friday afternoon in early February 2009. Because of a scheduling change, writing workshop was moved between lunchtime and our weekly craft project. A student was having an issue with her peers, which created a disruption. She was dismissed from the classroom until she could regain her composure. Because of the disruption, I was feeling frazzled as my students arrived at the rug for the mini-lesson, notebooks in-hand, waiting to hear what I had to say.

I looked at my lesson, which was printed out and placed inside sheet protectors beside my classroom's document camera. I looked at the teaching point that said, "Writers often search their writing for lines such as these looking for ways to highlight them, because highlighting a particularly strong line can also highlight a particularly strong idea. One way to make a powerful line stand out is by repeating it here and there across a piece of writing" (Calkins and Chiarella 2006, 181). My mini-lesson was supposed to be an outgrowth of a mid-workshop teaching point on refrains contained in Calkins and Chiarella's *Memoir: The Art of Writing Well*. I was set to use an example of the refrain Sandra Cisneros repeats in her story

"Eleven," as well as refrains several of my former students wove into their published memoirs. However, as I glanced over my prepared lesson, I wasn't feeling it. I looked outside at the gray, rainy sky and still wasn't inspired. I looked at my students, whose eyes were fixed on me, waiting for me to begin teaching, and I couldn't go on with the lesson I had planned.

I excused myself from the meeting area for a moment and walked to the other side of the classroom trying to psych myself up to teach this important lesson. I took a few deep breaths, reassured myself that I could to it, turned, and walked back to my class, who were chatting quietly with one another. Once I arrived back at the meeting area it occurred to me that I could deviate from my plan and teach the mini-lesson in a different way.

I turned off the document camera and faced my students. My lesson began something like this:

> *Writers, many of you listen to music on the radio and hear songs by famous singers. In fact, we listen to a lot of songs when we do our activities at morning meeting. There's something that most songs have in common with one another, regardless of the singer. Nearly every song contains a chorus or a refrain, which is a part of the song that repeats over and over.*
>
> *Let's take Beyoncé's song "Single Ladies," which most of you have heard. Now, I don't know if Beyoncé wrote her song or had a songwriter do it, but either way, she wanted to get her point across in the song and repeated the big idea of the song over and over. "If you like it, then you should've put a ring on it. If you like it, then you should've put a ring on it." (Some students started to sing along with me until I made a conductor's "cut" sign.) This phrase is repeated many times in "Single Ladies." I think she did this because it's like the woman telling the man who she used to date that if he loved her so much, then he should've given her an engagement ring and asked her to marry him. But he didn't. And now, there's a song about her new life. See, Beyoncé is smart. She repeated the most important line multiple times. This was done to emphasize her point.*
>
> *Writers do this too.*

And then, I went into my literary examples.

At the end of the mini-lesson, it was evident from their plan boxes that three-fourths of my students were going to try weaving an important line of their writing throughout their memoir. In fact, to keep the inspiration for refrains going, I played popular music softly during independent writing time that day. By share time, I discovered many of my students had a better understanding of refrains, because their drafts now contained beautiful refrains, which reflected the main idea of their piece, repeated artfully throughout their writing.

The following Monday I overheard a group of my students talking in the hallway before school started. They were wondering whether I'd sing Beyoncé for them again during writing workshop. Rather than poking my head out into the hallway and saying, "That was a one-time only performance," I said nothing. Instead, I relished that they'd probably never forget the day when their fourth-grade teacher taught them how to weave a powerful line throughout their writing by using "Single Ladies" as a mentor text. The refrain lesson was dynamic and engaging. Therefore, the teaching stuck. The objective was met. They will always remember.

Challenge: Shake things up in an effort to get your students more engaged in your mini-lesson. While you're still going to be the one speaking through the connecting and teaching parts of your lesson, think about ways you can creatively involve your students while you teach so that the lesson sticks.

Reflective Practice:

- What did you do out of the ordinary today?
- What was your students' response when they had a greater involvement or sense of engagement in today's mini-lesson?
- What makes you think your students will remember today's lesson more than others you've taught in the past?

Strings of Mini-Lessons

If one does not know to which port one is sailing, no wind is favorable.
—Seneca

During the summer of 2005, I did something that felt a little scary. While I'd like to say it was like climbing up Annapurna or bungee jumping, it wasn't exactly a physically risky terrain I conquered on my own. Rather, the summer of 2005 marked the first time I crafted my first unit of study on my own at the Teachers College Reading and Writing Project Summer Reading Institute. One of the first things my instructor, Grace Enriquez, taught was to plan the "bends in the road" for our unit. Essentially, the bends in the road are the skills you're planning to teach students during a unit of study.

Once you figure out the bends in the road of your unit, you can then craft the teaching points, or the strategies, to teach your students how to master these skills. Grace taught me that to connect a teaching point to my bends in the road (or the strategies to the skills I want to teach), it helps to link them by adding the word *by* between the teaching point and the bend.

For instance, let's say you're teaching a realistic fiction unit of study. One of the bends in the road for this unit of study might be "Writers create characters that seem like real people." You'd need to write a string of mini-lessons to teach your students how to do this. As you are writing your mini-lesson teaching points, you'd want to make sure they connect to the bend in the road. For example, your first mini-lesson might be, "Writers craft dialogue that moves their story forward." To make sure it matches the bend in the road, you'd put the teaching point together with the bend in the road to see whether the sentence made sense. When put together, it would read, "Writers create characters that seem like real people by crafting dialogue that moves their story forward." If the sentence makes sense, then the teaching point matches the bend in the road and will therefore help you to teach your students a strategy for mastering a given skill.

As you might look at a map before you travel to an unfamiliar place, think through the bends in the road when you craft a unit of study. It helps to know exactly which three to five skills we want our students to attain during a unit of study so that we can plan mini-lessons accordingly.

Challenge: Look at your next unit of study in writing workshop. Record the skills you want your students to be able to walk away with once the unit is over. Those are your bends in the road. Then flesh out your teaching points, making sure they match up to the bend in the road they fall within, connecting them with the word *by*. If the sentence doesn't flow or make sense when you link it with the word *by*, then it's time to recraft the teaching point(s).

Reflective Practice:

- How is planning with bends in the road in mind similar to or different from the way you've planned units of study in the past?
- What happened when you linked the teaching points with the bend in the road using the word *by*? Did you have to recraft any of the teaching points so they'd fit into the bend?

Responding to Needs

Find a need and fill it.
—Henry J. Kaiser

The thought of teaching in response to student needs can be overwhelming. Exactly what should I teach? And how will I know? Sometimes we make it too hard. We are simply looking for the needs of a classroom of writers and then teaching in response to these needs. How do we identify these needs for our mini-lessons?

One way is to pay attention to the teaching points in our conferences. When we confer with students who have a strong understanding of the teaching point from the day's lessons, our conferences will push the student to have a deeper understanding. This is often a viable option for a future whole-group mini-lesson. By contrast, if we find ourselves reteaching in our conferences, chances are there are other students who are confused as well. If this is the case, an upcoming mini-lesson may need to focus on the same teaching point to clarify it for the whole group.

Observing the students in our classroom work as writers is another sure-fire way for teaching points to become apparent. Do students appear stuck and not able to carry on? Are students off task? Are students using classroom resources? When I observe students working well as writers, I note their behavior, which can become another teaching point. By noticing the behaviors of students and then asking, *How could I help my students write more effectively?* mini-lesson ideas become abundant.

Finally, another possibility for a mini-lesson is to have students help teach the mini-lesson the following day. The way students are able to learn from their peers is always remarkable. Anytime we can facilitate this opportunity, the richer our writing workshops become.

Our mini-lessons are our best shot at instructing the majority of our students. Realistically, we are not going to meet the needs of every single writer. Some will already know and understand the teaching point, and others will not be ready for it. By using these techniques, we can meet the needs of the bulk of our students. This is one reason we keep our lessons short—so we don't waste other students' time.

Challenge: Create a space in your conferring notes to keep a list of potential mini-lessons. (You could write in the margin, on the back of your conferring notes, or on a sticky note.) Be on a constant lookout for possibilities and jot them down.

Reflective Practice:

- Taking a look at your list of possible mini-lessons, which are the most important to teach?
- Why are these the most important?
- How could you go about teaching these lessons in the most effective way?

Effective *and* Short

I never teach my pupils; I only attempt to provide the conditions in which they can learn.
—Albert Einstein

My mom is an expert quilter, and several years ago, I asked her to teach me. Her excitement when I first asked for her help put my nerves at ease. She loves to quilt, and she believed I could become a quilter too. We went to quilt stores together. We walked around the store, ideas filling our heads as we browsed through the fabrics. She offered advice as I pulled bolts of fabric off the racks. "This pattern is too big . . . look at the red running through this fabric; it could work," she said. As she ran her finger across the quilt pattern, she showed me how to figure the amount of fabric to buy.

Mom's instruction didn't stop there. At each stage of the process, she was beside me. Teaching me, watching me, and coming back after I completed some of the work. In the end there was a quilt I could never have made without her, yet I felt as though it were my own. Since then, I've made many more quilts, each time working more independently.

I learned to quilt by quilting. I held the rotary cutter and sliced the fabric. I sewed the stitches. I ripped them out when they didn't work. I pieced the blocks.

I remember this when I sit down in the meeting area to teach a mini-lesson. It is best to learn by doing, receiving short bits of instruction along the way. Here are a few ways to keep mini-lessons short so students have more time to write:

- **Stay focused:** We must determine a single teaching point and stick to it.
- **Watch the clock:** If I've been talking for ten minutes, I start wrapping it up.
- **Use part of the text:** A sure way to make a mini-lesson too long is by reading an entire text. By reading a text outside of the mini-lesson and then teaching from a portion of it during the lesson, the lesson is succinct and the time is short.
- **Practice:** I talk out my lessons ahead of time, often in the car on the way to school. I watch my car clock to make sure the lesson is short. If it is too long, I consider what to eliminate.
- **Don't ask for input:** The mini-lesson is teacher directed, so most of the talking is done by the teacher.
- **Think in series:** We don't have to teach everything at one time! Tomorrow will provide another opportunity to teach more deeply about a concept.

We learn to write by writing. To learn, we must spend time doing the thing we want to master. Babies learn to walk by walking; teenagers learn to drive by driving; writers learn to write by writing; teachers learn to teach well by teaching.

Challenge: Consider the list of ways to keep a mini-lesson concise, and think about what tends to be a cause for lengthy mini-lessons in your workshop. Then spend a few days intentionally keeping your lessons short and effective.

Reflective Practice:

- What is the average length of your mini-lessons during a week?
- As you increased your awareness of the length of your mini-lessons, what did you notice about your instruction?

Strong Connections

Good teaching is one-fourth preparation and three-fourths theater.
—Gail Godwin

I recall learning about the architecture of a mini-lesson from Lucy Calkins, who was my professor for three semesters at Teachers College, during the first summer institute I took with her in 2005. She contended that teachers had to "sell" the lesson during the "connection" portion of a mini-lesson; the connection needed to inspire and uplift the students. I wasn't sure how to inspire, uplift, and sell something to my students while simultaneously educating them.

After listening to Calkins speak of how to make the connections of lessons more meaningful so they would hook the kids, I realized that mini-lessons were composed of excellent teaching points that were missing *ruach*, the Hebrew word for "spirit." If I was going to connect with my students in a meaningful way, then I realized I'd have to infuse more ruach into my classroom. If I were going to inspire my students to listen to what I had to say, intently, for ten to fifteen minutes, then I needed to jazz up my mini-lesson with some ruach! But how does a teacher instill a greater sense of ruach into a short time span? That's what I had to figure out.

To learn how to infuse a greater sense of ruach into my mini-lesson connections, I looked to the most vibrant place I knew at the time: Congregation B'nai Jeshurun, or BJ, my former synagogue, which is located on Manhattan's Upper West Side. Every Friday night, BJ holds two Kabbalat Shabbat Services, since there are more than 600 people who attend each one. People from all walks of life gather together at both services to chant the prayers, which start the Sabbath. However, the chanting of the prayers is unusual because there is musical accompaniment and full congregation participation and engagement throughout the seventy-five-minute service. People leave BJ's Friday night services feeling reenergized and revitalized. Surely, there was something I could learn about teaching from the ways the clergy and musicians inspired the congregation each Friday night.

The clergy was always prepared for Friday night services. However, it wasn't just their preparation that inspired me—it was their willingness to be open with the congregation when they spoke and when they prayed, which in turn caused congregants to become more emotionally involved in the service. On occasion, the clergy would stop the service if and when they felt as though the members of the congregation were emotionally detached from what was happening. This made me reflect on what I was doing as a teacher. I realized, by watching the rabbis at BJ, I'd have to make myself vulnerable if I wanted my students to become emotionally invested in what I was teaching.

I connected what Calkins said about hooking my students with the ways the clergy from BJ revitalize their congregants every Friday night. I realized that no matter how prepared I was, I had to act as if I wanted to sell my lesson to my students. No amount of preparation would help me deliver my message if I didn't become emotionally invested in every lesson I taught. Therefore, I started to spend the greatest amount of time on the connections of my mini-lessons, because I realized that if I was prepared to inspire my students as authentically as possible at the start of the lesson, the rest would follow.

Challenge: Work toward crafting stronger connections this week. Do this by thinking about what inspires and invigorates you so that you can think about ways to tap into that same power when you stand up before your students.

Reflective Practice:

- Look back on the mini-lesson connections you delivered this past week. Were they inspiring and invigorating for your students or were they boring?
- Rate them and think about how you could've strengthened them, or consider what made them great.
- How did your students respond to your stronger connections? Were they more engaged while you taught? Did they produce better work?

Active Involvements: Learning by Doing

We learn by example and by direct experience
because there are real limits to the adequacy of verbal instruction.
—Malcolm Gladwell

The first two parts of the mini-lesson are spent activating our students' prior knowledge and teaching a new strategy for them to try as writers. By the time we finish our demonstration, we get to see whether they "got it," because we actively involve our students in the mini-lesson. It's at this point of our lesson that we find out the strength of our teaching after presenting the strategy just moments before. While there may be a couple of students who might not grasp every concept you teach, you want all of your students to be able to accomplish successfully the task you give them in the active involvement part of your mini-lesson.

An important lesson I learned from Lucy Calkins about teaching mini-lessons was that what we ask our students to do during the active involvement should match what we demonstrated during the "teaching" part of the mini-lesson. Essentially, if your demonstration was clearly executed, then your students should be able to complete the active involvement without your help. This is crucial because you want your students to use the strategy you taught them independently that day and every day thereafter if they're doing that type of writing.

As you know, an active involvement should last approximately two minutes. Sometimes your students will work independently, and sometimes they'll work with their writing partner. Sometimes you'll debrief what you noticed, and sometimes they'll share what they wrote. Regardless of the combination, walking around the meeting area during this time is imperative so that you can determine who understands and who doesn't. If you notice a couple of students misunderstanding what to do, you can jump right in and coach them until they're back on track. If you find students raising their hands to ask, "What were we supposed to do again?" or you notice confusion, then it's time to stop the active involvement and reteach the strategy in another way so that your students can apply the strategy.

Even the best-planned mini-lesson can go awry. There were times I planned a demonstration and an active involvement that I thought every student would understand. However, during the actual mini-lesson, sometimes my students didn't understand. Early on in my career, I'd often chastise myself for this. As time passed, I figured out why the active involvement went astray. That helped me prevent a similar problem from occurring in the future. Most of the time, after reflecting, I discovered the teaching in the first half of the mini-lesson didn't adequately prepare my students to be successful with the active involvement task. Therefore, as time went on, I asked myself, "Does the active involvement match the teaching I did earlier?" every time I wrote a lesson. If the answer wasn't always "yes," then I went back and tweaked the lesson until it did.

Lucy Calkins's keynote address at the 2009 Teachers College Reading and Writing Project Summer Institute for the Teaching of Writing was about teaching the inner writer. She talked about writing strategies. She asserted that "a strategy is only a tool if it's meant to accomplish a purpose." Hence, our students should be able to see the purpose of what we teach when they're actively involved in the mini-lesson. If they're trying out and experiencing the strategies we've taught them, then strategies are acquired and placed into their writer's toolbox for years to come.

Challenge: Think about your most recent successful mini-lesson. What did you do as a teacher when you demonstrated the strategy that clicked with your students when they arrived at the active involvement? Brainstorm ways that worked and think about ways you can replicate that kind of teaching.

Reflective Practice:

- How can you engage all of your students in the active involvements you're planning for the upcoming week?
- Do you need to do anything differently to plan improved active involvements? If so, what? If not, how will you continue doing amazing work?

Concrete Images for Support

There is plenty of courage among us for the abstract but not for the concrete.
—Helen Keller

I do Pilates three times a week. My first Pilates instructor, Amie Cunha, started training me a little over a year after I had neurosurgery. I was weak when I came to her and needed as much help as I could get. Because I lacked core strength, Amie gave me verbal cues to help me maintain proper form as I exercised. For the abdominal series, I placed a small ball between my knees. The ball wasn't actually part of any of the abdominal exercises. Yet Amie insisted I squeeze my knees into the ball to keep my lower body as still as possible. About a year after I started Pilates, I rarely needed the ball for abdominal exercises because I had been trained to keep my lower body still during abdominal work.

Our students also need concrete images for support. When my former colleague, Kate Smith, and I were trying to get our fourth graders to write about their emotions, Kate suggested giving the students colored candies to represent different emotions. It's pretty hard to ask kids to think of times they felt six different strong emotions. However, by having them use different colored Skittles to represent each emotion, it became fun for students to start listing when they felt angry like the red Skittle or calm like the orange Skittle. While I asked my students to use Skittles to represent strong emotions on a September morning, I reminded them, in the link of the mini-lesson, that any time they were searching for something to write about, they could think of a strong emotion and then write detailed stories that reflected that strong emotion.

When Ruth teaches primary-grade writers to revise their stories to include more dialogue, she hands out "call-out bubbles," which she cuts up and places in baskets around the classroom. Then, as students try to insert the real words their characters say, they write the words inside of the call-out bubbles and tape them onto their draft. As these children grow into more experienced writers, the need for these bubbles will diminish. However, while they're learning dialogue writing, these bubbles serve as a concrete tool to help students with the revision process.

As dedicated workshop teachers, we do what it takes to get the teaching point across to our students in mini-lessons. Even if you find yourself doing something gimmicky, it's probably not a gimmick, but rather a concrete tool that's helping the writers in your classroom gain greater independence.

Challenge: Make a list of all of the concrete tools you use to support your students as writers. Ask one or more of your colleagues to do the same. Discuss the tools you use and ascertain whether you can implement any of your colleague's tools into your teaching practice.

Reflective Practice:

- What is useful about using concrete tools to help your students in writing workshop?
- How do you decide when to introduce a new concrete tool to help the writers you teach?

Endless Possibilities for Teaching from Text

Stop thinking in terms of limitations and start thinking in terms of possibility.

—Terry Josephson

One key to a meaningful mini-lesson is to show *and* tell (Ray and Laminack 2001). One way to show is to use a text. Simply placing an overhead projector on the floor in the meeting area and a text on a transparency allows us to show students writing moves. In more tech-savvy classrooms, text can be shared using a document camera or an interactive whiteboard. By shining text on the wall of our meeting areas, we give students a clear understanding of what we are teaching.

When I first started teaching writing workshop, I had a misconception about using text in mini-lessons. I thought the only text I could use was from children's books. Today, I've learned the vast possibilities of text to teach mini-lessons.

- **Picture books:** Because many of these texts are short, they enable us to teach a concise mini-lesson.
- **Excerpts from novels:** We can teach important mini-lessons by using a page or two from a novel.
- **Published writing:** We can find texts to teach mini-lessons not only from trade books but also from magazines, newspapers, and anthologies.
- **Blog posts:** Blogs have made publishing possible for amateur writers. There are many examples of strong writing that can become possibilities for mini-lessons.
- **Student writing:** I often have the most success when teaching with students' writing. As I confer with students, I keep my eye out for students who are working well. When I see evidence of this in their drafts, I make a copy to use in the future.

- **Teacher writing:** When I'm teaching the process of writing, I tend to gravitate toward using a text I've written in the mini-lesson. This allows me to show students my thinking work. Of all the possible texts to use in mini-lessons, this is the only option that allows students behind the scenes.

It takes more than talking to teach writers in a mini-lesson. When we couple the explanation with a concrete example, our teaching becomes more meaningful.

Challenge: Consider the list of potential texts to use in a mini-lesson. Make a plan to use a type of text you've not used often in your mini-lessons. As you stretch yourself to try something new, remember that this is what we ask students to do each day in our mini-lessons.

Reflective Practice:

- Which type of text are you most comfortable using in your mini-lessons? Why?
- How did it feel when you stretched yourself to try something new (or something you don't normally do) in your mini-lesson?
- How does this connect to the way your students feel as they attempt new ideas in writing workshop?

Bookend the Mini-Lesson

What would life be if we had no courage to attempt anything?
—Vincent van Gogh

Part of becoming a stronger writer is tackling new concepts. Since I'm aware of this necessity, I often insist on students attempting the mini-lesson skill in their writing work for the day. This attempt may be in their writer's notebooks or in their drafts. If they do not like the result, they do not have to keep it. They simply have to try.

When I would like everyone to try a concept, I will often use a bookend share to close writing workshop. Carl Anderson has said the purpose of this kind of share is to bookend the mini-lesson. We want to encourage our students to take risks as writers and stretch themselves to try new things. This type of share provides a great avenue for formative assessment. We are able to determine whether students understand and apply the teaching from the mini-lesson.

Another advantage to this type of share is the potential to collect student-generated mentor texts. As students share in response to the mini-lesson, we can easily gather texts to teach future mini-lessons on the same topic. Another way to gather crucial information for upcoming mini-lessons is to be aware of the misconceptions and approximations students share in response to the mini-lesson. This share may be executed in many ways.

- **Author's chair:** A few students read aloud their writing inspired by the mini-lesson.
- **Highlight share:** Students share their process of applying the mini-lesson to their writing.
- **Partner share:** In pairs, students share their writing as well as their processes.
- **Response group share:** Students gather in small groups to reflect on their work as writers and challenge one another to become even stronger.
- **Whip share:** Each student chooses a sample of his or her writing to share with the class. As students sit in a circle, someone reads a line aloud and then the share progresses from student to student around the circle.

It would be a disservice to end every writing workshop in this manner. However, from time to time, it is important to encourage young writers to try new concepts. By celebrating their attempts, we give them the courage to take more risks in the future.

Challenge: Consider a key concept you would like your students to attempt as writers. Make a plan to teach this in a mini-lesson and then use a bookend share to wrap up writing workshop.

Reflective Practice:

- How do you encourage your students to take risks as writers?
- What information about your students did you glean from the bookend share?

Cycle 2: Teaching Conventions in Mini-Lessons

The Power of Conventions

Children need models rather than critics.

—Joseph Joubert

A difficult part of writing workshop for me to get my head around was how to weave conventions into my instruction. I've been on the extremes: from grammar using a traditional drill and practice grammar book to almost zero grammar instruction in writing workshop. The good and bad news is there was no difference in the abilities of the two groups of students when it came to writing in Standard

English at the end of the year. I realized my grammar instruction, traditional drill and practice or no instruction, was a wash. Students weren't changing in their ability to use Standard English.

Then I listened to Janet Angelillo share her ideas about the power of punctuation. Instead of focusing on using conventions in the right way, she helps students see the possibilities of conventions. I began teaching conventions in mini-lessons by posing questions such as, What happens to your voice when you read an exclamation point? What does an ellipsis make you feel as a reader?

As I shifted my attitude from using conventions correctly to using conventions for meaning, my students' understanding of conventions surfaced. This was exciting! For the first time, my grammar instruction was making a difference.

In Angelillo's book *A Fresh Approach to Teaching Punctuation: Helping Young Writers Use Conventions with Precision and Purpose* (2002), she discusses devoting entire units to punctuation studies. With my success in a few mini-lessons, I decided to follow Angelillo's advice and plan a punctuation unit. This unit improved students' punctuation as well as their awareness. As my students noticed and named different conventions and then determined their purpose, the level of their writing improved.

When our single focus is using conventions in the right way, few of our students will grow in their understanding of Standard English. By contrast, when we model the power of conventions and show possibility, our students latch on to new understandings and grow as writers.

Challenge: Consider a possible mini-lesson that would show the possibility of a specific convention. To push yourself into a true inquiry-based lesson, choose a punctuation mark to tap into its power. Consider a guiding question for your mini-lesson like I did.

Reflective Practice:

- How is your attitude changing regarding teaching grammar?
- What is the attitude of your class regarding using conventions? What kinds of changes are you noticing?

Stage Directions for Writing

I am not an actor or theatre person at all, but everybody around me is—and punctuation is kind of like stage directions. I think if the punctuation and the layout are right, they give you a clue on how to read it.

—Natalie Babbitt

Every Thursday during the two years I taught fourth grade, my students were put into small groups and given one of the class's weekly vocabulary words to act out. Each group was given several minutes to plan and rehearse their skit. As I walked around the classroom and listened in to what the students were doing, I noticed each group planning where they'd move, where they'd gesture, and where they'd finish each skit. Whether or not they knew it, the students were creating stage directions so their scenes would move fluidly and thereby help the audience understand the vocabulary word their actions were trying to portray.

I turned to Dan Feigelson's *Practical Punctuation: Lessons on Rule Making and Rule Breaking in Elementary Writing* when I prepared to teach a unit on conventions. Feigelson's book proved to be an invaluable resource. I especially appreciated the appendix of in-depth interviews Feigelson conducted with a variety of writers about punctuation. From his interview with Natalie Babbit (2008, 202–205), I was able to liken the use of punctuation in writing to stage directions in theater when I was trying to help my students deepen their understanding of all those little dots on the page. This example was powerful for my students because they always saw the need for creating "stage directions" for their Thursday morning skits.

Before I shared the Babbit quote with my students, they used punctuation whenever they felt like it. They knew they were supposed to put a mark at the end of a sentence but never really thought about *why*. Once they understood that readers need "stage directions" for their eyes and brains as they read texts, they used punctuation purposefully, because they finally understood the necessity of all those dots, lines, and squiggles. I used a few mini-lessons to model the way I used punctuation as stage directions for my reader. As a result, the meaning of my students' writing was enhanced when they began using a variety of punctuation marks intentionally.

Challenge: Get your students to become more intentional about their use of punctuation during a mini-lesson. Find a creative way to model how punctuation helps readers understand what to do—where to pause, stop, speed up, or express emotion. Be sure to collect the writing your students do after this particular mini-lesson so you can document how their use of punctuation was enhanced because of your teaching.

Reflective Practice:

- What's different about the way your students are now using punctuation marks?
- Are there any punctuation marks your students are misusing? How will you instruct them to use those marks properly so their "stage directions" are clear to their readers?

A Sign of Growth

Grammar is a piano I play by ear. All I know about grammar is its power.
—Joan Didion

This is a fact: errors in student writing are a sign of growth. Constance Weaver teaches this in *Teaching Grammar in Context* (1996). When we accept this notion, our mini-lessons can approach grammar instruction from a positive standpoint. No longer do we focus on correcting our writing, but we focus on what students are ready to learn based on their errors.

For example, second-grade writers are notorious for stringing their thoughts together with the word *and*. Sometimes there can be more than one *and* per line of writing and only one period—at the end of the page! We may be tempted to say, "Use more ending punctuation. You can't have an entire page of writing and only one ending punctuation mark. Go back and add the ending punctuation."

However, we could recognize the overuse of the word *and* as a sign of growth. These young writers are ready to write compound sentences. They are using a conjunction to join two thoughts, but they don't know how to control this type of sentence. At this point, we can approach our mini-lesson with, "I've noticed you are using many *and*s in your writing. When writers use conjunctions to join two thoughts together it is called a compound sentence. Let me teach you how compound sentences are punctuated so they don't become run-on sentences."

When we learn to identify the types of errors our students make, our mini-lessons become more powerful. As more experienced writers begin to use subordinate clauses in their writing, they show up as sentence fragments. A student may write: *I ignored my mom's warning. Even though I would get in trouble later.*

If we tell students, "Stop writing sentence fragments," they often are unable to find and correct these errors. By contrast, we can say, "You are the kinds of writers who are becoming more sophisticated by using subordinate clauses. I'm going to teach you how to punctuate subordinate clauses so they are not standing alone as sentence fragments." Now students are able to develop multiple understandings: how to identify a sentence fragment, how to identify a subordinate clause, and how to punctuate this type of sentence properly. The instruction can continue with mini-lessons on varying sentence types to make writing stronger.

Ali Edwards writes in *Life Artist: Scrapbooking Life's Journey*, "It is OK to let go of that high-school English teacher who lives in your head. The one who's always correcting your sentence structure, making sure you have a proper noun and verb in every sentence, reprimanding you when you don't follow the 'rules'" (2007, 118). When I first read this, it stopped me in my tracks. *Hey*, I thought, *she's talking about me!* As writing teachers, our job is to help students write well. Edwards, who helps people across the globe learn to write their stories, is giving the advice to let go of the high school English teacher in your mind. I want to be the kind of teacher whose voice students hear when they get ready to write. I want my voice to be one of encouragement and help. To do this, I must always allow errors to point me toward writers' signs of growth.

Challenge: Look through your students' writing and identify common errors in your class. Identify the root of the problem. What are your students attempting as writers and what do they need to know to make their writing more conventional? If you are unsure, find the grammar expert in your building and ask for help. There are also many online resources to help identify grammar issues.

Reflective Practice:

- What are some common errors in your classroom of writers?
- How will you approach your mini-lesson to help students learn to write more conventionally?

Writing Under the Influence of Mentor Sentences

It is requisite for the relaxation of the mind that we make use,
from time to time, of playful deeds and jokes.
—St. Thomas Aquinas

When I first started teaching, the Daily Oral Language (DOL) program was a part of the curriculum. In this program, students are shown incorrect sentences and expected to make them correct. It didn't take long to realize there was little transfer between the DOL sentence corrections and student writing. Students could perfect the incorrect sentences, but their writing was still filled with conventional errors.

As I considered the power of mentor texts in teaching other aspects of writing, I wondered about using mentor sentences to teach conventions. Armed with piles of research countering the use of isolated programs such as DOL to help students learn grammar, as well as research that showed the power of modeling strong writing for students, I went to my principal and asked whether I could replace the DOL sentences with mentor sentences. He gave his blessing, and the following day I put a model sentence on the board.

It was like pumping fresh air into our classroom as I turned off the deficit mentality of grammar instruction. Our approach to grammar was not only more positive but also more meaningful. As students analyzed mentor sentences and considered how the writer was communicating effectively, they would then pull out their writer's notebooks to practice writing their own sentences. Often these practice sentences would show up in subsequent drafts.

Our mentor sentences came from many different places. At first, I pulled them from picture books, often depending on some of my favorite writers, such as Jane Yolen, Patricia MacLachlan, and Angela Johnson. Then I pulled them from favorite young adult writers—Jacqueline Woodson, Kate DiCamillo, and Sharon Creech. Often a book talk could then be linked to our mentor sentences. Soon students noticed mentor sentences in their own reading. As they showed these to me, we added them to our lineup. Eventually, each student was required to bring a mentor sentence for the class to analyze. As we shifted into different genre studies in writing workshop, our mentor sentences shifted as well. We would find sentences from Rick Reilly and Leonard Pitts when we studied editorials or from Eloise Greenfield and Georgia Heard when we studied poetry.

Often we would linger with a mentor sentence over the course of several days. When a mentor sentence was especially rich in conventions or language, we revisited it. This desire to revisit a sentence was another major difference in our attitudes compared with DOL.

As students shared the sentences they constructed based on the mentor sentences, they used the language of grammar to share their work. I was impressed with the sophisticated ways they were able to speak about their work. This was another significant difference as I shifted my approach to mentor sentences.

However, perhaps my favorite part of shifting our attention to mentor sentences was the playfulness it created in our writing. As we used our notebooks to write our own sentences, influenced by mentor sentences, we took risks and played with language. There was little pressure to conform to a single right way and plenty of opportunity to take risks with language. I found myself stretching and growing as a writer in this safe environment where I had the luxury of not having to write perfectly. I wasn't the only one; my students were stretching and growing as writers too.

Challenge: Spend some time with mentor sentences in your class. Find five to ten minutes in your day to spend with mentor sentences. In our busy classrooms, the secret is to consider what activity you will replace with mentor sentences. Consider what you are already doing in your classroom regarding grammar instruction that mentor sentences could teach. Another option is to study a mentor sentence in your mini-lesson.

Reflective Practice:

- How did using mentor sentences change the attention of your students with regard to using conventions in their writing?
- What are some possible mentor sentences you can use? Spend some time looking through your favorite books and mark potential mentor sentences.

Always Draft with Conventions—Always!

In essence, if we want to direct our lives, we must take control of our consistent actions. It's not what we do once in a while that shapes our lives, but what we do consistently.
—Anthony Robbins

In 2007, I moved to Providence, Rhode Island, after living in Washington, D.C., and Manhattan for twelve years. When I moved, I had to drive regularly, which wasn't something I had done since I left my parents' house for college in 1995. I knew how to operate a motor vehicle, but I felt uneasy behind the wheel. I was given a portable GPS (global positioning system) as a gift to help get me through the initial shock. Even though my GPS told me where to turn and where to merge, I still had to pay attention to the road signs. I had to look carefully at signs so I knew where to yield to oncoming traffic and when to stop my car. Failing to do these basic things would've resulted in a crash. I initially relied on my GPS to keep from getting lost, but because I paid attention to the road signs, I was eventually able to drive without it.

Just as we need road signs to drive, we need punctuation to read. Without punctuation, writing becomes jumbled, hard to follow, and messy (like Interstate 95 through downtown Providence during rush hour). Therefore, we must teach our students, many of whom regularly ride as passengers in buses or in cars, that writing with punctuation is as necessary for readers as road signs are for drivers. We can teach this to our students in a few ways:

- As you're using your own writing during a mini-lesson demonstration, think aloud about where you place punctuation as you're drafting. Read a piece of writing devoid of punctuation so your class hears how writing sounds without punctuation. Then demonstrate how you'd insert punctuation to create meaning for a reader.
- Put up a model text that contains a variety of punctuation. Read it aloud and then have the students read it chorally with you. Have students notice the ways their voices change based on the punctuation they encounter in the text. You could even create a chart that records an author's punctuation intentions with your students (Angellilo 2002).

We can teach our students to become more thoughtful users of punctuation. When they realize that punctuation is like road signs, they'll be more likely to use it correctly to help their readers understand their writing.

Challenge: Plan a mini-lesson that will convey the need for consistently using conventions to create meaning. Use one of the techniques listed previously as your demonstration.

Reflective Practice:

- What are your plans for instructing your students to be more intentional about using conventions consistently in their writing?
- Have your students made the connection between using punctuation and conveying meaning for their reader?

Artful Use of Conventions Creates Voice

My attitude toward punctuation is that it ought to be as conventional as possible. The game of golf would lose a good deal if croquet mallets and billiard cues were allowed on the putting green. You ought to be able to show that you can do it a good deal better than anyone else with the regular tools before you have a license to bring in your own improvements.

—Ernest Hemingway

I've spent a lot of time examining texts closely with my students, trying to figure out why authors chose certain types of punctuation as they wrote. While it would be ideal to ask an author why he chose to use dashes in lieu of commas, that's not feasible. Hence, as devoted studiers of texts, we can surmise and hypothesize the reasons behind an author's punctuation decisions.

First, when we're teaching, we can teach our students that writers make conscious decisions about where to place punctuation as they write. We should let our students know that thinking about every mark they make on the page, as a writer, creates voice in their writing. If we tuck this idea into our teaching, it's sure to make an impression on our students.

Second, stress the importance of meaning making with your students. Conventions must be used so the writing holds meaning for the reader. For instance, we can teach students to communicate their internal thinking in writing by using italics.

Third, if you feel your class has a strong command of conventions, consider teaching a mini-lesson (or two) on breaking punctuation rules. Susan Ehmann and Kellyann Gayer's *I Can Write Like That: A Guide to Mentor Texts and Craft Studies for Writers' Workshop, K–6* contains a book list of texts that can be used to show your students how published authors break the rules. Ehmann and Gayer assert the following:

> *Young writers need the maturity to understand their audience and purpose for writing. Although it is acceptable to make these stylistic choices*

> *in a piece of creative writing, it is not acceptable in most other forms. You, as the writing teacher, will know whether your students are ready to make these distinctions, and you will guide them to knowing when such rule breaking is appropriate. (2009, 10)*

You might choose to show your students an author's writing that uses dashes or periods instead of commas in lists. In addition, you might want to teach your students the value of using fragments to convey emotion rather than writing in complete sentences. A word of caution: don't break too many rules at once. Picking one or two different kinds of rules to break might be enough to lift the level of writing for your students.

Teach your entire class how to study texts to learn more about how different authors use conventions when they write. If your students are encouraged to develop theories about *why* an author punctuates in a particular way, then they'll be able to try out their theories when it comes to their own writing.

Challenge: Get your hands on a book that breaks the rules (e.g., *Earrings* by Judith Viorst or *Fireflies* by Julie Brinkloe) and study it. Hypothesize, on paper, at least two different reasons the author chose to use punctuation in a particular way. Then push yourself to imagine how you will try the same kind of craft move in your own writing work. Once you've finished your written hypothesis, weave your writing into a mini-lesson you'd like to teach about breaking the writing rules.

Reflective Practice:

- Do you feel uneasy about encouraging your students to break the rules? What makes you feel nervous about this pedagogical decision?
- How did an emphasis on using conventions to convey meaning assist you when instructing your class about rule breaking to create voice?

Conventions During Revision

The real voyage of discovery consists not in seeking new landscapes, but in having new eyes.
—Marcel Proust

A point of confusion in the writing process for many young writers is the difference between revision and editing. Often our students will blow by (or skip altogether) the revision stage of the process and then "fix up" their spelling and punctuation before proudly announcing, "I'm done!" Upon inspection of the final piece of writing, there is little difference between it and the first draft.

We then teach students to focus on the meaning and words of their writing to help them distinguish between the two phases of the writing process. Revision is making the meaning clearer; editing is making the writing more standard. As students learn to revise more effectively, they often spend time adding or deleting words to clarify their meaning.

Another way we can teach students to clarify their meaning is through conventions. Writers often play with grammar and mechanics as part of their revision process. For me, this is one of my go-to strategies when revising. I consider where to start a new paragraph, whether to use a period or a semicolon, or whether parentheses or commas are necessary.

As we teach students the power of punctuation and usage, we can also push them to consider these possibilities during revision. Through our mini-lessons, we demonstrate how grammar and mechanics can become part of the revision process. By keeping our purpose on refining the meaning of our work, we use conventions as a means of revision. This opens the door to a new world of revision possibilities for our students.

Challenge: Teach a mini-lesson that demonstrates for students the way conventions can be used to revise writing for meaning and clarity. Look at your own writing and identify places to revise the mechanics to make your work stronger. Explain the thinking behind your decisions during your mini-lesson.

Reflective Practice:

- Were you pleased with the revisions you made to your writing? How do you feel about the revisions your students made?
- What did you notice as your students attempted to revise using conventions?
- What are some follow-up lessons your students need to refine the art of revising with conventions?

How to Edit Well

If you re-read your work, you can find on re-reading a great deal of repetition can be avoided by re-reading and editing.
—William Safire

My mother insisted on reading every paper I wrote in middle and high school before I turned it in. She proofread my work and showed me my errors, especially when I repeated the same types of mistakes. Unlike other parents, my mother insisted I sit with her as we edited my work, so she could explain its flaws and why these flaws were problematic. Her criticism drove me crazy during adolescence, but her frank and unrelenting nature made me able to edit my own writing in college and graduate school.

Once I started teaching, I quickly learned that most of my students' parents worked at night and were unable to review their children's writing work. In my first year of teaching, I'd go home at night, red pen in hand, and correct my students' writing. By the middle of the winter, I noticed their writing wasn't improving. The reason for this was clear: I was editing their work for them. Therefore, with the help of my colleagues, I began creating editing checklists to help my students learn to edit. However, that wasn't exactly foolproof because I quickly learned that explicit instruction in editing had to be provided if checklists were going to work.

Over time, I taught mini-lessons on techniques to help students edit work without depending on an adult. Some powerful techniques we can teach young writers are as follows:

Help students locate errors: Jim Vopat suggests a minimal marking technique in *Micro Lessons in Writing: Big Ideas for Editing and Publishing* (2007). Vopat suggests having the reader place a check mark on any line of writing that contains an error with punctuation, grammar, or spelling or that sounds awkward. Once the writer receives his writing back, he concentrates on editing the lines that have check marks in the margins. Most of the time, a student can correct an error once he is visually alerted to it. Vopat asserts the minimal marking technique resolves most of a student's writing errors through self-correcting, allowing you to spend time conferring with the student about "real issues." Spend time modeling how to fix errors, after it's minimally marked, in a mini-lesson.

Schedule peer conferences: Provide time for students to confer with their writing partner, and one additional classmate, for editing. Here's a rough structure of how a peer editing conference could go:

1. The writer reads her work aloud slowly to her partner.
2. The writer stops reading when she spots an error. Conversely, if the peer sees or hears an error, then she can stop the writer from reading.
3. The writer and the peer can discuss the problem, and the writer decides whether to make the change. If she doesn't think the change needs to be made, then she doesn't mark the error her partner identified.
4. This process continues again throughout the rest of the piece while both partners keep their eyes and ears open for conventional errors.

Read writing aloud: There is value to having students read their writing aloud to insert punctuation in the places their voice naturally pauses. Having writers read their work aloud also helps them fix awkward phrasing. To foster reading aloud, you can give students "phones" they can talk into so they feel as though they have an audience. You could even use a PVC elbow pipe, which allows students to read aloud softly and hear words amplified into their ear so they don't disturb others. Regardless of how students read aloud, encourage students to reread their writing with a pen in hand so they can make changes as they go along.

As a last resort, follow up with the teacher: Allow students to sign up for an editing conference with you. However, just as a college-based writing tutor would insist on the writer focusing the purpose of the meeting, ask students to set the agenda for the editing conference. For instance, the student might have trouble knowing when to use commas, so you might work with the student on when to use insertion commas, introductory commas, and commas in lists.

There are some basic guidelines we can put onto a checklist for our students, such as starting all sentences with capital letters, capitalizing proper nouns, and inserting end punctuation. When it comes to the nuances of editing, we must instruct our students on how to engage in meaningful editing so they can become the independent writers and editors we want them to be.

Challenge: Create a mini-lesson that taps into one of the strategies listed previously.

Reflective Practice:

- How did you set your students up for success at the end of the mini-lesson?
- What else do you need to do to set your students on the road to independence with regard to editing?

Taking Risks with Conventions

If you wait to do everything until you're sure it's right,
you'll probably never do much of anything.
—Win Borden

In *Bird by Bird: Some Instructions on Writing and Life* (1995), Anne Lamott writes about perfectionism:

> *Perfectionism is the voice of the oppressor, the enemy of the people. It will keep you cramped and insane your whole life . . . I think perfectionism is based on the obsessive belief that if you run carefully enough, hitting each stepping-stone just right, you won't have to die. The truth is that you will die anyway and that a lot of people who aren't even looking at their feet are going to do a whole lot better than you, and have a lot more fun while they're doing it. (28)*

I've spent too many mini-lessons teaching students the perfect, precise way of grammar. I've focused on the black and white of mechanics and usage. Things were either right or wrong, and in the case of novice writers, they were usually wrong.

I've come to realize that this approach to grammar is oppressive. It ties the hands of our young writers. Instead, by creating a safe environment where taking risks is expected and encouraged, our students will come to know grammar in a more personal way. When they take risks with mechanics and usage, they learn for themselves what works and what doesn't.

For them to know what is working, they must also know the standard. It is here we must balance our instruction between possibility and correctness. Our mini-lessons should encourage students to have fun with their writing, to attempt using conventions in new ways, and to make their writing as close to Standard English as possible. All three of these are important in helping students write well. However, too often, we only focus on making our writing standard.

Challenge: Develop a mini-lesson that will encourage students to take risks in their writing. Consider modeling for your students how you take risks with conventions in your writing. Write a sentence using parentheses or a dash. Talk through your decisions with your students so they can hear the inner workings of choosing to take risks in your writing.

Reflective Practice:

- What are some ways you can shift from perfectionism to encouraging students to take risks when it comes to conventions?
- What are your thoughts about Anne Lamott's words on perfectionism?

Fun with Conventions

No one can become really educated without having pursued
some study in which he took no interest. For it is part of education
to interest ourselves in subjects for which we have no aptitude.

—T.S. Eliot

Through the years, I've hosted six student teachers in my classroom. I was weary of relinquishing control over the conventions unit of study on which I had intensely labored. It was tough for me to step aside and allow Sarah Meserve, one of my former student teachers, to step in to teach. Halfway through the conventions unit of study I taught in 2009 I handed the reigns over to Sarah because it was time for her to teach.

Sarah wanted to shake things up a bit when it came time to teaching dialogue tags. At first, she was unsure what she could do to make it fun, so she searched on the Web. She decided to teach the students how to write and punctuate dialogue using *The Far Side* comic strip. She showed the students how Gary Larson illustrated and wrote snappy captions beneath his cartoons. Instead of having students caption *The Far Side* in a similar fashion, she found cartoons that appeared to have two characters speaking to each other. Next, Sarah asked the students to write in the dialogue they could imagine overhearing. As they wrote the words they thought one of the characters in the comic said, she taught the class how to punctuate the dialogue tag that followed the spoken words.

Sarah and I anticipated the class creating dialogue and dialogue tags for one or two of Larson's comics. For the first time during the conventions unit of study, we noticed the students thoroughly enjoying what they were doing. In addition, they were catching on to how to punctuate dialogue tags consistently. So, when a couple of students asked whether they could create and punctuate their own *Far Side*-like comics, we agreed to allow them to do so in lieu of directing them back to their writing, where they were supposed to be revising narratives to include easy-to-read and properly punctuated dialogue.

At first, I was leery of allowing the mini-lesson to last longer than ten minutes, because it seemed to be an activity that wasn't immediately applied to the students' writing. However, after the lesson, my students were more enthusiastic about writing with dialogue because they understood how to punctuate it. As a result of Sarah's lesson, the class was able to write dialogue correctly for the remainder of the school year.

Teaching conventions can be fun. We have to find ways to shake things up, just like Sarah did, to make instruction meaningful and enjoyable for our students. Not every lesson will be ingrained in our students' long-term memories, but the least we can do is strive to make our teaching more intriguing so that our students will be more thoughtful when applying the lessons they've learned to their writing.

Challenge: Look at the most boring conventions-related mini-lesson you are slated to teach. Think about ways you can shake things up to make the content fun for your students to learn. Consult a colleague or search the Internet if you're strapped for ideas or need help thinking outside of the box.

Reflective Practice:

- How were you able to create a mini-lesson that was more fun that met the same objective?
- What will you do to revamp other tired, conventions-related lessons to make them fun for your students?

Cycle 3: Making Our Teaching Stick

Repeating and Coming Back to the Teaching Point

Repetition is the reality and the seriousness of life.
—Soren Kierkegaard

I learned how to write and deliver mini-lessons from Lucy Calkins, who implored her students to repeat the teaching point several times during each mini-lesson. At first, I thought this kind of repetition was frivolous. I couldn't imagine why I had to repeat the big idea from my lesson to my students if they were listening to me for only ten minutes. But you see, that's the thing—they're only listening for ten minutes. We pack as much as we can into ten minutes of explicit instruction and hope our students will be able to use that strategy we presented independently.

Over time, I realized students internalize teaching points better if they hear them repeated, in the same way, at a few key points during the lesson. Taking a cue from Calkins, here are the times you can weave the teaching point into the mini-lesson:

- Write the teaching point in a place near the spot in which you plan to deliver the lesson. Students will read the teaching point before they even hear it.
- Insert the teaching point at the end of your mini-lesson's connection. This will connect students' prior knowledge to the strategy you're about to teach.
- State the teaching point before *and* after you demonstrate the day's strategy. Bookending your demonstration with the teaching point helps children put a name to the strategy you are teaching.
- When you've got just a minute left, summarize what you taught your students that day. It's helpful to link the teaching point and how it can be used in writing to what students might plan to do during independent writing that day and in the future.

In late fall of 2006, Tyla, one of my former students, approached our class's student teacher, Christina Rodriguez, and said, "Wow, Ms. Rodriguez. You and Ms. Shubitz are so alike! I know that a mini-lesson is about to end when I hear you say, 'So writers, today and every day, I want you to remember that writers . . .'"

Luckily, Christina didn't let her leave it at that. She said, "Why do you think we do that Tyla?"

Tyla paused and said, "I think you do that so we remember to try out what you taught us today and on other days. So we don't forget."

Ah! Out of the mouth of babes!

Challenge: Over the course of the upcoming week, push yourself to state and restate the teaching point in every lesson. Try to use the same wording each time.

Reflective Practice:

- Did posting the teaching point in writing, in advance of the mini-lesson, catch any of your students' attention? If so, how did they respond to this visual?
- How did the repetition of the teaching point enhance your students' understanding of the strategy you presented each day?

Lifting the Level of the Structure of Mini-Lessons

Let me tell you the secret that has led me to my goal: my strength lies solely in my tenacity.

—Louis Pasteur

How can I improve my mini-lessons? For an entire school year, I allowed this question to drive most of my reflective practice. To begin finding the answer, I turned to the architecture of a mini-lesson as described by the Teachers College Reading and Writing Project. I considered intentional ways to strengthen each of these parts of a mini-lesson.

In the **connection** of the mini-lesson, a reason is stated to link the new teaching point to the previous writing work. As I studied the connections of my lessons, I realized I often glossed over this part of the mini-lesson. As I considered the value of the connection, I was reminded of the importance of connecting new ideas to existing schema. By using phrases such as: *Yesterday I noticed . . .* ; *This is similar to the work we were doing . . .* ; and *Today's lesson may remind you of . . .* we can intentionally link the new teaching point to existing schema for our students.

Using all of the ways we know to teach efficiently and effectively one key idea is the purpose of the **teaching** portion of a mini-lesson. Some of the main ways to teach writers is through modeling with our own writing, using a mentor text, using an example from a student, using advice from a published writer, or sharing strategies using a chart. To make this portion of my mini-lessons more effective, I concentrated on using various ways to teach effectively. I found my go-to methods were modeling with my own writing and using advice from published writers. Therefore, I became intentional about using other methods to teach in my mini-lessons.

Like most things in life, teaching a solid mini-lesson is about balance. As I began being more intentional about using a variety of teaching methods in my mini-lessons, the teaching portion of the lesson became longer and the *active engagement* part was shortchanged. As the year progressed, I became more aware of giving students an opportunity to "have-a-go," as Carl Anderson explains this portion of a mini-lesson. Giving opportunities for students to collaborate or practice in their writer's notebook or on a current draft allowed students to engage immediately with the teaching point of the mini-lesson. I found it necessary to keep a close eye on the clock throughout active engagement to ensure my mini-lesson didn't last too long.

The final stage of a mini-lesson includes a **link** to the writing life of each student. Although embarrassingly true, initially my links went a little like this: "Now go try this in your writing today." This made me uncomfortable because I believe writers should be thoughtful and intentional about the kinds of strategies they use in their writing. I expect the writers in my classroom are engaged in work that is meaningful and being done for a bigger purpose than because the teacher said so.

Because of this defining belief about my role as a teacher of writing, I began refining my link to help students determine whether they needed a particular teaching point in their work on that day or if they should "pocket" the teaching point to use later. By using words such as *Try this in your work as a writer today if . . .* or *Writers do this when they want or need to . . .* I was able to link my mini-lessons to the big picture of becoming a lifelong writer.

I also used the link to test the relevance of my teaching point. If I wasn't able to say, *Forever, the rest of your life, you can do this when . . .* , then I knew I was only teaching writing instead of writers.

Lifting the level of our mini-lessons isn't something that can happen overnight. It takes tenacity, endurance, and reflective practice to intentionally make our mini-lessons stronger.

Challenge: Consider the different parts of the mini-lesson and choose one to refine over the next several days. Be deliberate about lifting the level of just one portion of your mini-lesson.

Reflective Practice:

- What made you decide to focus on this particular portion of a mini-lesson?
- How did you intentionally lift the level of that portion of your mini-lessons? What other part of a mini-lesson could you refine?

Using Technology in Mini-Lessons

What we want for our children . . . we should want for their teachers;
that schools be places of learning for both of them, and that such learning
be suffused with excitement, engagement, passion, challenge, creativity, and joy.

—Andy Hargraves

It was love at first sight when I laid my eyes on an ELMO. I mean ELMO, the document camera, not Elmo from *Sesame Street* (although he is adorable). I couldn't believe I could see an authentic piece of writing, on the real paper it was written on, as well as the presenter's hand, underneath the lens of the ELMO. I immediately began to fantasize about having an ELMO, rather than an overhead projector, in my classroom. I started to dream of taking writing instruction to new heights by having students revise and edit their work beneath the light of a document camera. I envisioned mini-lessons in which my demonstrations would take place in my writer's notebook, not on a transparency, for all of my students to see.

I knew I had to be proactive if I wanted ELMO in my life because I worked in a school that received ample money for books but not for technology. A document camera wasn't going to find its way into my classroom unless I made it happen. Therefore, I wrote a proposal for a document camera and an LCD projector on DonorsChoose.org. After a couple of months of waiting, my students and I received the funding for both items!

Mini-lessons became more engaging when I used technology during my teaching demonstrations. I was able to show my students the pages of my notebook, which enabled them to see my hurried handwriting, cross-outs, and additions in the margins. I was able to show my students' drafts to the entire class and could have them stand alongside me, cutting and pasting to make the revision process come alive for everyone sitting in the meeting area. In addition, when it came time to revise and edit my writing, I used the "Track Changes" feature in Word on my laptop computer to show my students my thought process. While I may not have had a computer for each student to use at the end of my mini-lessons, my students became more tech savvy because they carefully watched the way I operated the technology.

Good teaching is good teaching. However, infusing technology into the classroom engages students in a different way because it taps into a different modality. Go forth and find tools that will enhance your teaching. Once you put it into use in meaningful ways you and your students will find mini-lessons more captivating.

Challenge: In a November 10, 2009, article entitled "Technology in the Classroom: What's Good; What's Not? Selecting Tools of the Trade Requires Battery of Questions," the author interviewed Don Knezek, CEO of the International Society for Technology in Education, who asserted that the educational purpose of the technology should be considered before a technology purchase (Bernet 2009). Once you've identified the purpose of the technological tools you'd like to have in your classroom, set them alongside the writing goals you have for your students. If you can align the two, then do the necessary research to ensure that you're getting the best possible products. Finally, if your school cannot pay for technology you desire, look for technology grant opportunities so you can turn your instructional dreams into realities.

Reflective Practice:

- How will the technology you want help your whole-class instruction?
- Will the infusion of technology help your students prepare for twenty-first-century jobs? If so, how?

Teach the Skills, Not Just the Technology!

The people who resist change will be confronted by the growing number of people who see better ways are available thanks to technology.

—Bill Gates

During my senior year of high school, my English class went on a field trip to a university library. Our teacher wanted us to learn how to research and therefore needed to take us to a campus library. We learned how to find books in the stacks, locate and use microfiche, and request a resource through the interlibrary system. For the tech savvy among us, we could use a database to find pertinent journal articles. These were the tools we needed to research.

Today, I don't use many of these tools when I research. However, the lessons I learned in regards to research stick with me because my teacher also taught us the skills to research. We learned how to read through stacks of information, find the important points, and narrow our topics. I still use these skills today when I research.

Today, we don't need to leave our computer chairs to gather research. Our students are able to bring up more information than their grandparents could possibly imagine with a click of a mouse and a few seconds. The tools we use to research are different than they were a few years ago. We use search engines, wikis, and online videos. These tools will continue to change as technology evolves.

However, the research skills we teach now are the same as the skills we taught years ago. Our students still need to learn to sift through volumes of information to determine the key points, to consider the accuracy of information, and to focus the scope of their topics. These skills stand the test of time.

Our focus shouldn't be on teaching students a particular piece of technology, because quite frankly, it is unlikely they will be using the same technology in a few years. Instead, by teaching the actions of writers, we help students become independent learners. Naturally, we will tap into the power of technology, but we also must be intentional about teaching skills students will be able to use for the rest of their lives.

Challenge: Consider a piece of technology you would like to use in an upcoming lesson. Determine the skills it will help your students develop. For example, if you would like students to use a particular search engine as a research tool, make a list of skills students will need to research effectively. How does the search engine help them learn these skills?

Reflective Practice:

- Are your mini-lessons primarily focused on verbs (skills you expect students to learn) or nouns (tools you want students to use)?
- How will you emphasize the skills students need to develop to become stronger writers while also teaching specific tools to support learning?

Brain-Based Mini-Lessons

The human brain, then, is the most complicated organization of matter that we know.
—Isaac Asimov

In college I took an English course and was forced to read the course anthology cover to cover. Although there is very little favorable to say about this, one of the texts was about brain research. It changed my life. From the first paragraph, I was hooked and wanted to know more. The more I learned about the brain, the more new ideas I acquired about making learning stick. There are a few key facts about the brain that can help to guide our teaching.

- **The brain can process several activities at once:** This means that a variety of teaching strategies can be used to immerse students in learning. Physical activity, music, and visual aids can be used to engage learning.

- **The brain values meaning:** If we tap into the natural curiosity of brains by making our mini-lessons relevant and meaningful, then our teaching will be more effective.
- **Every brain wants a challenge:** When our mini-lessons present a challenge, students will be more engaged because of our natural affinity for challenges.
- **Fear inhibits brain function:** Our mini-lessons will be more effective if we create safe classroom environments. Unpredictable environments lead to students feeling anxious and nervous. Learning is nearly impossible in these conditions.
- **Learning is tied to emotion:** Our brains do not separate emotions from cognition. This means if we can generate an emotional response to mini-lessons, they are more likely to be remembered. Humor, joy, and compassion are strong emotions to connect to when learning about writing.
- **The brain connects new learning to prior knowledge:** Connecting our teaching point to information students already know is an excellent way to help new learning stick.

The more we, as educators, understand the way the brain learns, the more effective our mini-lessons will become.

Challenge: Use your favorite search engine to learn more about brain research. Try some of these key words: *brain research, brain research + education*, or *teaching + brain research*.

Reflective Practice:

- How will the brain research you are thinking about influence your upcoming mini-lessons?
- What idea is most pressing to you right now? This could be something you've already known about brain research or something you are currently learning.

Anchor Charts in the Classroom

Spoon feeding in the long run teaches us nothing but the shape of the spoon.

—E. M. Forster

"It looks like a schlock house in here," my mother would say upon entering a messy store with piles of unfolded clothes and hangers on the floor. If a store was schlocky, which is a Yiddish word that means cheap or trashy, we'd leave.

I've walked into plenty of classrooms that have looked schlocky. These are rooms where scores of charts were stapled to the walls, dangled from clotheslines, or pinned over window shades. A good deal of the time a classroom looks schlocky because of pressure from administrators to make sure the tracks of the teacher's instruction are visible around the room. A classroom might look like a schlock house if the teacher doesn't value changing the charts frequently as a means for providing students with a resource. Either way, a classroom cluttered with charts that students don't use isn't an inviting place.

Anchor charts are effective teaching tools during lessons and for students to reference independently. Some tips to maximize anchor charts in your classroom are as follows:

Create them with students: Charts made alongside students are useful because the children were part of the chart-making process. Students internalize our lessons if we involve them in chart making.

Refer to them in your lessons: If you refer to a given anchor chart in your mini-lessons, then it becomes a reference tool for students. The reference can range from reading the chart verbatim to gesturing to it as something the students can look at when they get stuck.

Record teaching points: I used to create anchor charts with each week's teaching points written on them. This visual reminded students of strategies they had learned in recent days as they were coming to the meeting area.

Hang them as long as they're needed: Only keep charts up for as long as they're useful. For instance, if you and your students created a fantastic chart for the collecting part of the writing process, it probably doesn't need to be displayed throughout the entire unit of study.

Color code: If you teach multiple subjects in elementary school or multiple classes in secondary school, then color-coding anchor charts is helpful to students who are visual learners. If your students can pick out all of the writing charts or all of their class's charts by a given color, then it will make information location faster.

I've heard people say that they keep charts posted in the classroom so visitors will know what the students have been working on. That's not only a waste of space but also a distraction to the students. If visitors want to know what's going on, then encourage them to pull up next to one of the students and ask them, "What are you working on as a writer?" Students know how to answer that question, and they do it a lot better than any piece of chart paper will! Remember, anchor charts serve as a learning tool and are worthy of displaying proudly when they have an authentic purpose for students.

Challenge: Take stock of your classroom charts. Do they all serve a purpose? Are they clear visuals that will help your students improve as writers? If your charts aren't all you want them to be, then create a new plan for chart making that will help these pieces of paper anchor your writing instruction.

Reflective Practice:

- What's meaningful about the charts in your classroom?
- How will you help students who don't regularly use anchor charts as a reference to use them more often?

Remembering Mini-Lessons

Education is what remains when one
has forgotten everything one learned in school.
—Albert Einstein

When we first transition into a writing workshop format, it feels strange to stick to a single teaching point in a lesson. At first, it doesn't feel like there is much opportunity for learning to happen because our lessons are short and focused. However, as time progresses and students have sustained opportunities to practice writing, teaching points pile up, and many opportunities for learning arise.

Sometimes I forgot previous lessons. I would look back through my conferring notes, where I had also noted mini-lesson main ideas to help determine the teaching point in many conferences. As I engaged in this act—looking back to recall specific lessons—I realized my students also needed this kind of opportunity.

Handbook notes were developed from this need. This was a separate notebook that housed the teaching points of critical lessons. Not all lessons were recorded in the handbooks. Any lesson I thought students would want to refer to, as well as the bends in the road of a study, were always noted in their handbooks.

Sometimes my middle school students would take notes from the mini-lesson; other times I would give them a handout to tape into their notebooks. If we generated a chart during a mini-lesson, I would type a copy of it later and give it to students to add to their handbooks on the following day. This allowed me to still capture their words and phrases for the charts, as well as give students a copy to keep in their handbooks.

To make the handbooks easy to use, we spent time setting up an organizational system. Students numbered each of the pages in their spiral notebooks and taped a table of contents chart in front. The date, lesson topic, and page number were noted. I found students kept this resource near during writing time. At first, I had to be intentional about referencing their handbook notes during the teaching portion of my conferences. However, this soon became second nature to me. As I modeled for students how to use their handbooks, they soon developed this habit when working independently. Students even returned later to tell me how their handbook notes carried them through English classes in later grades.

For younger students, a separate notebook to organize could be a nightmare! To make this idea more manageable, consider including handbook notes within an existing structure. For example, you could use a portion of the writer's notebook to house mini-lesson notes and mini-charts. If we believe the writer's notebook is a place to gather information to make us better writers, then collecting mini-lessons would be an appropriate use for writer's notebooks. Another idea is to use students' in-progress writing folders to keep notes and mini-charts. If students are using a two-pocket folder with brackets in the middle, then the pockets would hold the drafts, and the brackets could secure paper for mini-lesson notes and charts. For our youngest writers, we must consider how to record this information for the class. Primary writers would not need to keep this information individually. Therefore, anchor charts or class handbooks can scaffold this idea of collecting key writing ideas to return to again and again. In our conferring, we can reference previous mini-lessons with the help of these aids.

The key isn't the kind of system you establish but that students can collect tracks of your teaching. By practicing the key concepts in mini-lessons, we refine our ability to write well over the course of time.

Challenge: Determine a way to collect tracks of your teaching from mini-lessons to use as a reference during independent writing time. This could be as simple as noting the mini-lesson main ideas in your conference records and then referring to your notes while conferring, or as elaborate as developing a handbook for students to depend on while working independently.

Reflective Practice:

- What do you notice about your conferring as you become more intentional about remembering past teaching points?
- After you've used your system for a few weeks, what is working well? What needs to be refined?

Exit Slips

Follow effective action with quiet reflection.
From the quiet reflection will come even more effective action.
—Peter F. Drucker

In our hurry-up world, we rarely take the time to slow down and reflect. Yet so much of becoming more effective at *anything* is through reflective practice. For reflection to occur, a bit of quiet time must be carved out of our busiest days. I used exit slips in an effort to provide this for my students.

Each day they would engage in reflective practice by responding to two questions. First students considered the question, *What did you do as a writer today in writing workshop?* This positioned students to consider their learning as opposed to the progress of their writing.

The second portion of the exit slip was, *Write a reflection about your work as a writer today, as well as any questions you may have.* I explicitly taught students that, to write a reflection, they must include *how* they worked and *why* they feel this way. For example, *I worked well today* isn't a reflection because it's missing the "why." Instead, if a student writes, *I worked well today because I moved to a place I wasn't tempted to talk to others*, it is considered a complete reflection.

When time was limited, students completed their exit slips before the share session. However, most of the time, they completed their exit slips before transitioning to the next portion of their day. Exit slips gave me a lot of information about the effectiveness of my teaching. For example, if there were many questions about the mini-lesson, then I knew I needed to address the teaching point again.

Much of becoming a stronger writer rests in reflecting on our writing lives and then making changes to be more effective. The only way this will happen is if we, as teachers, make the time in our writing workshops for students to reflect on their lives as writers. Exit slips are one way to scaffold reflective practice.

Challenge: Develop a system for students to reflect on their work as writers during an upcoming writing workshop. Consider a few questions to guide students through reflective practice.

Reflective Practice:

- What have you noticed about yourself as you've engaged in reflective practice through this book?
- What have you learned about your students by providing time for them to reflect on their lives as writers?

Co-Teaching for Memorable Lessons

If we teach today as we taught yesterday, we rob our children of tomorrow.
—John Dewey

Some of my fondest moments from my first year of teaching were spent co-teaching writing workshop mini-lessons with Pat Werner, who served as one of my school's literacy coaches. Pat was an experienced workshop teacher from whom I learned a great deal.

Pat suggested we co-teach a mini-lesson on revision so students could understand the types of questions they could ask their writing partner when they set off to revise their pieces. We modeled a peer conversation, in which we used my writing, to help the students understand the types of accountable things partners might say to one another during the revision process. Having the two of us in front of the class talking about writing was powerful. I immediately noticed my students' peer conferences were more thoughtful as I circulated around the classroom that day. In addition, my students were doing more to nudge one another toward better revisions. As a result of that successful mini-lesson, Pat and I continued to co-teach some lessons together throughout the school year.

I was bewildered when I learned that Pat was transferring to a new school the following year. *Who would I co-teach writing workshop lessons with?* Fortunately, I had three student teachers that year, all of whom were happy to co-teach with me as the need arose.

Over the years, I sought out other teachers, student teachers, and graduate school colleagues to come in and teach lessons with me. I specifically invited people when I knew I wanted to model a peer conference. Having two adults at the helm added some variety to the monotony of having just one instructor. I used my own writing and made myself vulnerable to critique during these co-teaching mini-lessons. My students knew I was going through the writing process at the same time as they were because they saw my struggles, as a writer, during the co-teaching that took place during the mini-lesson. Perhaps that's why my students' level of engagement and follow-through was so much greater after each lesson.

Co-teaching a lesson with a colleague can seem complicated, but it shouldn't be. It's just the two of you, demonstrating the work of a functioning writing partnership. Just a little bit of planning ahead of time will make the lesson run smoothly. You'll see—you'll want to do it again and again.

Challenge: Elicit the help of another adult to co-teach a writing lesson with you. Choose a lesson where your students will benefit from seeing an accountable discussion about your writing as a model to aspire to.

Reflective Practice:

- What kind of preparation did you do for the lesson you co-taught? Was it sufficient? How would you plan differently next time?
- Were you able to sense a greater level of enthusiasm when students worked with their writing partners today? If so, can you pinpoint what engaged them the most?

Toot Your Own Horn

You always pass failure on the way to success.
—Mickey Rooney

I was in a job interview before moving to Rhode Island, when I was asked, "What have been your greatest accomplishments as a teacher?" I began to reply, but apparently the interviewer thought I was being modest. He interrupted me and said, "Stacey, I want you to toot your own horn. Toot your own horn, because no one else will." It was nice to have someone grant me permission to brag. No one had ever given me that kind of carte blanche before. It felt good to revel in my students' successes, which I connected back to my hard work.

"Toot your own horn, because no one else will" is a phrase that has stuck in my mind ever since I heard it. It's true. No one else will be as big a cheerleader for you as you. Therefore, when something goes well in your classroom, celebrate. I'm not saying that you should shout your successes from the rooftop of your school building, but you're certainly entitled to seek out your colleagues, a friend, or a significant other to tell them how well your lesson went.

How often do you hear another teacher rehash a bad day in the teacher's lounge or at a staff meeting? We listen. We respond. We feel their pain. However, it's time to break the habit of sharing the bad news with others. It's time to celebrate things going right!

Challenge: Share your success with someone whose opinion you value. Tell them how well things went with your mini-lesson. Explain the way you triumphed over adversity to reach this day.

Reflective Practice:

- Why are you proud of yourself?
- What made your mini-lesson successful?

Chapter 3: Choice

The engine of writing workshop is choice. Often students are bored, apathetic, and lethargic when it comes to writing for school. The problem is just that—writing *for* school. Too often we are caught in the cycle of preparing students for the next grade, the next school, or the next life step. If we would simply step back and allow students' current needs to drive the writing, then we would unleash a mighty power.

Empowering students to use their words to change the world is the aspiration of writing workshop. When students are given choices in their learning, they will feel in control and motivated. They will question, reason, and analyze important ideas. Most important, they will rise up and change the world for the better.

Writing for a purpose that is important *right now*, finding and choosing writing projects that are important *right now*, learning their voices matter *right now* power the engine of writing workshop. Without choice, there is little internal motivation to make the writing matter, to make the writing important for a reason other than the teacher's desk.

If writing workshop feels contrite, scripted, or driven by what students have to do "next year," then choice may be a suitable goal. Here are your options:

- **Cycle 1: Physical Choices**
  Often by relinquishing control over physical choices, it is easier to release control over bigger choices, such as audience, genre, topic, or purpose. This cycle encourages reflection on ways to provide students with choice over the materials in your classroom to lift the level of their work as writers.
- **Cycle 2: Moving Toward Independence**
  The focus throughout this cycle is encouraging students to make the writing process personal to their needs, as well as to take responsibility for their writing decisions.
- **Cycle 3: Living the Life of a Writer**
  It is a difficult jump for students to begin living as a writer outside of school as well as during the forty-five-minute writing workshop during the school day. By focusing on intentional acts to infuse living like a writer outside of school, this cycle will help you encourage your students to live truly awake lives as writers.

Although student choice is crucial to an authentic writing workshop, it is also essential to maintain structure and organization. These cycles encourage you to offer reasonable choices within defined boundaries, thus providing your students with a meaningful writing workshop experience.

Cycle 1: Physical Choices

The Culture of Having Enough

We think sometimes that poverty is only being hungry, naked and homeless.
The poverty of being unwanted, unloved and uncared for is the greatest poverty.
We must start in our own homes to remedy this kind of poverty.
—Mother Teresa

I've taught in some poor schools. My entire career has focused on serving children who usually qualify for free- or reduced-price lunches. Some students couldn't pay for field trips, while others couldn't afford to donate a box of tissues for the classroom. Therefore, when I was a classroom teacher, I was responsible for stocking the classroom shelves with ample supplies so my students never went without necessities.

By combining the items given to me by my school and the supplies I've requested through mini-grant proposals submitted to DonorsChoose.org, I created what Emily Smith, a staff developer at the Teachers College Reading and Writing Project, calls "the culture of having enough" in my classrooms. The culture of having enough essentially means that I made sure to amass enough paper, writing implements, notebooks, erasers, tape, staplers, and art supplies so that students would always have the materials they needed for writing workshop.

I explained my rationing system to my students at the beginning of each school year: "I've made sure that we have enough supplies to last us throughout the school year. This doesn't mean that we can waste what we have. We have to use our supplies responsibly. Use only what you need, but when you need something, just ask and you'll get more." Contrary to what many people might believe about the way children use and abuse classroom supplies, this system always worked in my classroom. Hence, at the end of each school year, we always divided the gently used supplies, and everyone took home the leftovers.

When you enact the culture of having enough in your classroom, kids feel wanted, loved, and cared for. They share better. They take responsibility for the things they have. When you put your trust into your students to use communal supplies responsibly, they work more efficiently, using only what they need.

Challenge: Make a list of the items you feel all students need to have access to for use in writing workshop. Talk with administration about what they can supply if your students' parents do not have the means to provide those items for the classroom. Then, for whatever your school or your students' parents don't cover, go online to DonorsChoose.org and follow the instructions to write a mini-grant proposal for the items you need to establish a classroom culture of having enough.

Reflective Practice:

- How will you teach your students to care for the supplies? Will you do a guided discovery, a class discussion, or something else?
- What will you do if you find out that students are hoarding supplies or taking items home?

Classroom Writing Center

Our brains are conditioned to know what to expect in particular spaces . . . Find a place that feels right. Get a good place to sit . . . Make sure you have what you need to start writing. These may seem like small details, but I have found they matter a great deal . . . When you come right down to it, you are the place where your words will grow. But most writers find it invaluable to have a regular writing place, a physical space, where they can water and weed a garden of words.

—Ralph Fletcher

When I began teaching writing workshop, I developed a writing center because I had read about it in a book. Little did I know, then, that when students are surrounded by the supplies of writers they begin to act like writers. Little did I know, then, that the simple development of a writing center made the entire classroom feel like a place to write. Little did I know, then, of the importance of making a physical writing space. I didn't learn these lessons until I had been out of the classroom for four years as a writing coach and experienced the inspiration from a writing center on a personal level.

When I decided to venture out of the classroom as a writing coach to see what life was like for students across grade levels, I assumed I would return to the classroom the following year. I made the same assumption for another three years. With that assumption came a hole-in-the-wall office that I never made my own. I simply plopped in my computer and my teaching license, and the hole-in-the-wall office became a place to stop, dump materials, check e-mail, and gather materials for the next classroom.

Then I realized I needed to make it my own. A place I would feel like a writer. A place I would want to write. A place I would be a writer. A place that has tracks of my life and where I could find meaning. I began by collecting baskets and containers that would become homes for writing supplies. I added inspiring words and images, photographs and books, and soon a place was created that made me want to write the moment I opened the door. Our classrooms should be this kind of place for students. The moment they walk in the door, they should itch to write. An important way to inspire this feeling is by creating a writing center. Following is a list of items that I feel motivate and inspire writers:

Calendar: A wall calendar is a useful addition to any writing center. In the primary grades, it can be used to mark publishing days and celebrations. For upper-grade writing workshops, draft due dates and upcoming project start dates can be added. Some older students may also wish to have a copy of their own so they can determine when they will finish drafting or revising to make the deadline. This is especially important as students work on independent writing projects. Calendars are a way to help students learn to manage their time to complete projects by a deadline.

Date stamp: After many headaches from attempting to help kindergarten writers date their work, my colleagues and I put a date stamp in the writing center. In the spirit of brutal honesty, it was mass chaos! Dates were stamped everywhere! The tables and chairs were covered! Stories were covered! Kindergartners were covered! Thankfully, because of quick reflexes, the teacher and I avoided being covered! We quickly regrouped and offered a mini-lesson about the date stamp the following day (and now this same lesson is given before the introduction of the date stamp), and I'm happy to report the date stamp was controlled! Older writers also benefit from a date stamp, simply because it feels official and writer-like. Today, I'm an advocate for date stamps because it is important to know when students work on a piece of writing, and date stamps are a useful way to get this information onto drafts, while helping students to develop a writer's persona.

Highlighters: These are a wonderful revision tool, when students learn to use them sparingly. Coloring an entire draft with a highlighter is not useful, yet when students use highlighters to track particular craft moves or conventions, then concrete evidence emerges about their use of these techniques. It doesn't take long for a student to realize that they've only used one ending punctuation mark throughout a friendly letter or that they have three pages of dialogue in a personal narrative. (**Colored pencils** are another option for the writing center instead of, or in addition to, highlighters.)

Inspiring words and images: It doesn't take much effort to hang an inspirational poster or photograph near the writing center. In fact, the part of the writing center that my students commented on more than anything else was the quotes that changed periodically above the supplies. I was always impressed that my students noticed when new inspirational words were posted. Finding inspirational quotes about writing is easy; just take a moment to Google "writing quotes." An even easier avenue would be to use the quotes in this book.

Mistake remover: To help prevent frustration during publishing, erasers and correction fluids are another asset to any writing center. It is shocking to see how many more conventions are corrected when students have access to correction fluid and snazzy erasers.

Paper choices: Writing centers in primary classrooms should be filled with a variety of paper choices. Different sizes of picture boxes, lines, and paper all help to inspire young writers to tell their stories well. In upper grades, a variety of draft paper is helpful. Draft paper options could include college-ruled or wide-ruled notebook paper, legal pads, or steno pads. If computers are available, students could have the option to type their drafts instead of handwriting them.

Resources: Dictionaries, thesauruses, rhyming dictionaries, and grammar handbooks are all appropriate to keep in the writing center.

Sticky notes: Sticky notes are like sprinkling magic writing dust on students. Students who refuse to revise will sing a different tune when given a sticky note. A variety of sizes are optimal. Here's a suggestion: try a jumbo sticky note. If you are considering supporting details in a letter to the editor, then use sticky tabs to flag the points to support a position. Sticky notes are a good item to put on supply lists. Look for them in discount and dollar stores.

Writing implements: Part of a teacher's job is to help students develop a sense of responsibility. Some teachers focus on whether the student has something to write with as the way to help students develop responsibility.

Early in my career, I quit fighting this battle. I decided it was most important for my students to write during writing workshop, and if they didn't have a writing implement, I would give them one. After losing hundreds (perhaps thousands) of pens and pencils, I learned a few tricks of the trade to keep them around.

I found buying pencils with a witty phrase such as "Help, I've been kidnapped from Room B34!" helped to ensure that the pencils stayed in the room—or were returned (usually by the student) within a few minutes. Another way to mark writing implements is to create a masking-tape flag atop the pen, which helps them to stay in the classroom. One year, a creative student used silk flowers and florist tape to create a "pot" of flower pens for our writing center. By wrapping a silk flower to the pen with florist tape, a unique pen was created, and students had a visual reminder that they were borrowing a pen. She filled a flowerpot with beans and stuck in the pens.

Other supplies: Staplers, staples, paper clips, scissors, tape, and glue sticks are all useful in a writing center.

Challenge: Evaluate your writing center. Make changes necessary so it inspires students to write. If you're really looking to lift the level of your writing center, enlist the help of your students to organize it. Give them the supplies, containers, and a location for the writing center. Then, step back and watch it come to life as they organize, containerize, and label the supplies. If students are invested in creating it, then they are even more empowered by it. Another idea for organizing supplies is to create "mini-centers" for each group of students. Put necessary items together that can be used by a small group of students. This eliminates some movement to and from a classroom writing center.

Reflective Practice:

- What supplies inspire you to write?
- What items in your writing center empower students to live like writers?

A Place for Everything and Everything in Its Place

Organizing is what you do before you do something,
so that when you do it, it's not all mixed up.
—A. A. Milne

Part of the success of writing workshop is organization. Our job as teachers is to help students organize themselves as writers. Yet we also know there are many ways to be organized so that each person has an effective, personal system. We must provide support so students can be organized, while allowing freedom for students to find an effective organizational system.

The four basic organizational needs for many writers are (1) a place to gather ideas, (2) a place to keep in-progress writing, (3) a place to track published writing, and (4) a place to keep helpful resources. Teachers can empower students to develop their own systems. That said, there are options we provide for each of these needs.

- **A place to gather ideas:** Writer's notebooks are the traditional place for writer's to gather their ideas. Another possibility is a blog. For the tech-savvy student who has consistent Internet service, a blog could fill the need for a place to gather ideas. Gathering potential writing ideas on an "idea sheet" (Appendix B) stored inside the in-progress writing folder helps young writers keep track of their ideas. Decorating the outside of the in-progress writing folder with pictures, as older students decorate their writer's notebooks, is another way to gather ideas. When young writers sit down to write and are faced with memories through photographs or pictures of their favorite hobbies on the outside of their in-progress writing folders, draft ideas abound. Sometimes I'm envious of the young writers who sit down, look at their folder, and exclaim, "I know just what to write!"
- **A place to keep in-progress writing:** Most students use a two-pocket folder to gather their drafts. Some may choose to organize the sides of their folder by dedicating one side to unfinished drafts and the other pocket to finished or abandoned drafts. Other students enjoy having a notebook dedicated to drafting. In this system, students don't tear out pages; instead, they use the notebook to house all of their drafts. If students have computers on which to type drafts, then they will need to consider a folder system to save their work and make it easy to locate later. Not only that, but file names will need to be developed to save work at different stages. For instance, students could save the draft as the file name plus V2 to indicate the second version. This format could be followed after each writing session.
- **A place to track published writing:** In writing workshops, when students publish their writing, it leaves the classroom and goes out into the world. However, it is beneficial for students and teachers to have a record of the published projects, as well as a place to store the feedback regarding the published work. In my seventh-grade classroom, students kept a published work folder. A published work record, as well as any drafts, grade sheets, and feedback (from me, classmates, or others outside of the class), was stored in this folder. The folders were kept in large crates according to class period under a table. Because these folders weren't regularly needed, a place out of sight was perfect for them. Over time, this record is important as students

reflect on their writing lives. They can begin to see trends in their writing and publishing, as well as growth.

Another way to track published writing is using a bulletin board. Each student could add a tag to the bulletin board indicating his or her writing and how it was shared with others beyond the classroom. These bulletin boards become especially rich when students also share the response their writing received. For instance, if a student writes a letter to the editor, then, when it is printed in the newspaper, the student attaches the clipping to the bulletin board and other writers are inspired. The feedback and drafts could be stored in a class filing system where students conveniently file this information, similar to the stored information in their published work folders.

- **A place to store resources:** Documenting teaching points on wall charts is the primary way to leave tracks of our teaching in the classroom. These charts act as resources for students, providing access to helpful information. For older students, a mini-lesson note-taking system could be established. For example, teachers could give students mini-charts to extend the resources to students' fingertips and to ensure they have access to the resources long after the wall charts have been removed.

When I dove headfirst into writing workshop, I was determined to be organized and to keep my students organized. What ensued was a system with so many rules that we spent more time organizing, or following the rules of organizing, than writing. In fact, in many instances, the system hindered our work as writers. As the years passed, I learned to look at the areas that real-world writers organized and gave students ample room to find a personal and effective system for these areas. By doing this, students developed ownership and a sense of responsibility to maintain and use a meaningful, personal system.

Challenge: Be aware of the potential for students to organize these four areas (a place to gather ideas, a place to keep in-progress writing, a place to record published writing, and a place to keep resources) in an individualized way. Empower students to take risks and try new ideas for establishing order to their writing lives. As students evaluate their systems, encourage them to make changes so the system works for them and the student isn't working for the system (like what happened in my early years of writing workshop!). Record ideas that are most effective so you can share these with your students.

Reflective Practice:

- What systems make the most sense to you as a writer?
- How does it feel to have students use different strategies to organize themselves as writers?

- Are there systems that may be too cumbersome for the students in your classroom, and should you eliminate them as options?
- In your early years of writing workshop, were you too rigid or too loose in developing organizational systems?

Choosing a Writer's Notebook

My words on an empty page
in an ordinary notebook,
The silver setting for the jewels of my life.
—Brod Bagert

Writer's notebooks are the open arms that pull students into writing. When writers spend time collecting bits and pieces of their everyday lives, they are soon enamored by the life they are living. They are motivated to find value in the regular ups-and-downs of life. As we reflect on these ordinary moments, we often find big meaning and truths about life. A writer's notebook becomes a special place for writers to create, discover, and linger in the moments of life that lead to finding meaning.

Because each life is unique, each writer's notebook should also be unique. There are many choices when it comes to writer's notebooks. The more control students have over their notebooks, the more empowered they will be to use them.

Students can select a writer's notebook based on personal preference. Medium-sized composition notebooks are popular because they have sturdy covers and sewn binding. Often this is my go-to choice for a writer's notebook. It is a workhorse that can hold many words and withstand rigorous use. Some writers prefer fancy notebooks, with sparkles and decorations on the cover. Still others prefer jumbo notebooks to accommodate large handwriting, sketches, or white space. Spiral binding, hard cover, small, thin, thick—the choices are endless.

Some schools purchase writer's notebooks for students. Never fear, students can still make these notebooks special and unique. Offering a gift-wrapped notebook to students demonstrates the notebook's importance. Because each writer's notebook documents a life, the cover should show a glimpse into the writer's life. Students can customize the covers using stickers, magazine clippings, clip art, and photos.

Students can organize the writer's notebook as they choose. Middle schoolers are quirky, and their writer's notebook habits are no exception. One of the most quirky instances I encountered as a middle school teacher was students who started at the back of their writer's notebook and wrote forward. Other students were über-organized and added a table of contents and page numbers. Allowing choice is crucial for accepting writer's notebooks. My only rule was to date each entry and to write the next entry after the previous one. (Some students wrote entries in the middle of the book, making it difficult to track their work later.)

Creating sections is another way to organize the notebook. For example, in some of my notebooks, I have a special section entitled "ephemera." Here, I keep all of the "stuff" of life that is meant to be tossed but becomes a trigger for writing ideas when tucked into my writer's notebook. I believe that the more control students have over the "guts" of their notebooks, the more comfortable they'll be with using them.

By sharing how we, as teachers, make our writer's notebooks an extension of our lives and by giving students plenty of choice about their writer's notebooks, most students find a place for writer's notebooks to fit into their daily lives.

Challenge: First, customize your own writer's notebook. If you already have a writer's notebook, personalize the inside or outside of it. Share how you've personalized your writer's notebook and then give students the opportunity to customize their writer's notebooks. This can be as simple as pictures and names on the front cover or as elaborate as each student finding their own notebook style. Often discount and dollar stores have a variety of low-cost notebook styles. If teachers gather notebooks throughout the year, then students can "shop" in the classroom for a notebook. It is imperative to give students plenty of time to shop for their new notebooks. As students customize their notebooks, encourage them to share the reasons for their choices with one another.

Reflective Practice:

- How did customizing your own writer's notebook make you feel as a writer?
- What did you learn about your students as they customized their writer's notebooks?
- How can you encourage students to share stories with you and with one another as they decorate their writer's notebooks?

Writer's Notebooks for Tech-Savvy Students

Blogs are a real force . . . They're not just for geeks anymore.
—Carlos Watson

I scoffed at the notion of starting a blog when Stephanie Jones, one of my former professors at Teachers College, suggested it as part of a class project. It sounded nerdy . . . really nerdy. Why not just keep track of my reflections on teaching in a notebook? However, when I got home, I went online and looked at a variety of blog-hosting options. Within a day, I began a blog to track my thinking about the work I was doing in Jones's graduate-level reading course. I didn't tell anyone at work about my blog for fear they'd think I was a nerd. Shockingly, a few months later, I met Ruth, who kept a blog about teaching reading and writing. She was anything but a nerd. After talking with her for a few months, we decided to start a blog, Two Writing Teachers, so we could both reflect on our practice as teachers of writing. What better way to push each other's thinking and stay in touch than blogging about the teaching of writing *together*?

Over time, I grew to realize that blogging was an excellent way to make my narrative writing public. By the middle of my fourth year of teaching, I started suggesting that my students use blogging as an alternative means to maintaining a writer's notebook. Several decided to do this and began using Edublogs, which I set up and administered for them.

I hope that all of your students who decide to keep a blog will see it as an opportunity to express themselves in ways they couldn't in a notebook. For instance, one of my former students, Rashaad, didn't like the physical act of writing in a notebook because of his handwriting. He loved using the computer to write. In addition, blogging provided an online forum for me to communicate with him by using the comments feature. We often went back and forth in the "comments" section of his blog, which led to deeper conversations in school. Rashaad was much more open to my conferring with him and critiquing his writing. Once he started blogging, he was no longer offended about what I had to say. Hence, his in-class writing became stronger.

One spring afternoon, after my students returned from lunch, we began a math unit on probability. I introduced the unit by teaching the concept of likelihood. I was attempting to teach the students the difference between impossible and unlikely. Unlikely, I told my students, meant there was about a 25 percent chance something happened. A 25 percent chance of an event occurring still seemed fuzzy to them, so I said, "It's unlikely that Rashaad will not write a blog post tonight."

He piped up immediately and said, "No, it's impossible!"

I said, "What if you have a computer problem?"

He replied, "I don't care if my computer crashes, then I'll go to my uncle's house and write it there. It's not unlikely, Ms. Shubitz, it's impossible!"

"C'mon Rashaad," I said. What if your uncle isn't home or there's a blackout?"

"Then I'll write it in my notebook!" he said with a *duh* tone to it.

"I see your point, but honestly, it's not impossible. It's just very, very, very unlikely that you're going to not write on your blog tonight, okay?" I said trying to get him to realize that there is a fine line between the highly unlikely and the impossible.

"Fine," Rashaad said, "I can live with very, very, very unlikely."

Writing on a blog, rather than in a writer's notebook, was not considered geeky if you were lucky enough to start one in my classroom. Having a blog was like a status symbol, almost better than using a Moleskine notebook. Those students who became bloggers, instead of writing in a notebook like the rest of the class, had pushed themselves as writers so much so that they were given the opportunity to go public with their daily writing.

Challenge: Identify some students in your class who might benefit from a blog. Usually these are students with excellent ideas, but who don't enjoy the physical act of writing. Talk to them about how a blog might help them express themselves as a writer. Then create a plan that involves keeping up with their daily notebook writing for a given time period. Discuss how that might transition into a blog as a means for keeping an online writer's notebook.

Reflective Practice:

- What kinds of permission do you need to obtain from your administration and from students' parents before creating blogs for your students?
- What kinds of guidelines will you create to keep your students safe once they create a blog?
- Think through independent writing time in class: How will the bloggers be held responsible for completing assignments if they're not using a notebook?

Students Need Their Own Spot

And that's the way it is.
—Walter Cronkite

My mother placed me in front of the television every weeknight as she prepared dinner in our Brooklyn apartment and later in our New Jersey home. Apparently, I would sit quietly through "The Evening News with Walter Cronkite," which afforded my mother ample time to prepare dinner before my father's arrival home from work. Hence, Cronkite became a quick companion: a voice I found soothing even in my adult years. In our home, we trusted Cronkite, as did many Americans, and accepted his broadcasts as reliable and factual, thereby making his famous phrase at the end of each newscast feel true.

As teachers, our students usually see us as the Cronkites of their lives. We are with them every weekday, delivering quality instruction that matters. In elementary school, especially, when we tell our students how to do something, they just do it.

Our words are seen, by most kids, as black and white. Because most elementary school students want to please their teachers, they do what's asked of them, regardless of whether it feels just right. Hence, as teachers, offering our students options is paramount so that they don't feel coerced.

All children need their own space in the classroom where they can focus, feel safe, and be productive, a predictable place that feels like a spot of their own.

When I taught fourth grade, my classroom was large enough to accommodate "focus spots" for each child. During the first week of writing workshop, I'd allow students to try out different places in the classroom during independent writing time. By the week's end, I'd ask each child for the top two focus spot preferences so that I could assign them (yes, assign!) to a focus spot for the duration of the year. (Later on in the year, if a spot wasn't working for a student, we'd discuss it and make the necessary change.)

Having an assigned spot chosen by the student eliminated distractions or desires to sit near a friend when a guest teacher was in the classroom. Focus spots also led to quicker transitions because all students knew where to go to start working immediately. On the rare occasion when students tried to switch their focus spots (e.g., so they could sit next to a friend for the day) without speaking with me, I'd invite them to find their spaces again. There was never an argument when it came to going back to one's focus spot because that's just the way it was in our classroom.

Challenge: Play around with focus spots on your own in your home. Don't settle for your desk. Bring your notebook or your laptop to different spots in your home to see where you sustain writing best and longest without distractions.

Reflective Practice:

- How did you write differently while sitting on the floor versus at a table versus on a piece of furniture (e.g., a couch or chair)?
- How might you help a child understand when a given spot in the room isn't working for him or her based on your own experiment with focus spots in your home?

Signal for Attention

The average American worker has fifty interruptions a day,
of which seventy percent have nothing to do with work.

—W. Edwards Deming

Picture this: You're in the middle of an important writing conference with one of your students. Suddenly, you see the figure of another child in your peripheral vision. You continue to listen to the student you're conferring with, thinking that perhaps the other student who has come up alongside you will learn something from the teaching point you're about to espouse to the student with whom you're conferring. Just as you open your mouth to deliver the compliment and teaching point to the child you're sitting next to, you see movement out of the corner of your eye. You look up and see a little boy bouncing up and down. Finally, the boy loudly blurts out, "Can I go to the bathroom?" You let him go, only to forget the eloquent wording of what you were about to say.

Interruptions like this have nothing to do with making your students' writing better. However, kids in most public schools do need to ask the teacher's permission before leaving the classroom. Therefore, I've found a way to eradicate the verbal disruptions coming from asking for water or to use the facilities. After trying out a couple of systems my first year of teaching, I quickly came to adapt the use of American Sign Language signals in my classroom. I taught my students how to signal me to ask to go the bathroom or to get a drink of water from the fountain. Then, I showed them the signs for "yes" and "no," so they would understand each response when they saw me sign back to them.

Here's another scenario: You're conferring with a student. You're sitting on the rug teaching her how to revise by physically cutting and pasting. As the student takes control of the scissors you see a pair of feet come up alongside you. You look up and see a student patiently waiting to get your attention. He signals that he'd like to get a drink from the fountain. Knowing that he's been productive so far during the independent workshop time, you signal back yes. Then, you turn back to the student who is embracing the new strategy. You think, *Ahhh! This is going to be good.*

Challenge: Go online to Baby Hands Production's Dictionary of Signs, http://www.mybabycantalk.com, to learn how to make the signs you'll need for managing interruptions in your classroom. Then think through the way in which you'll implement using the signs in your classroom.

Reflective Practice:

- Will you set up times that students may not use the symbols (e.g., during a mini-lesson or share time)?
- Will you implement a second system for signing out so that students will check a sign-out book before they come to you to silently ask for permission to leave the classroom?

One Size Doesn't Fit All

It is the ability to choose that makes us human.
—Madeleine L'Engle

Writing is hard, which is why I need to make sure I am using exactly what feels right in my hands when I'm drafting. First, I make sure I have a roller ball pen. Ballpoints don't move fast enough for me and pencils smear when I write. Therefore, it has to be a roller ball. Second, I need paper with one-inch margins so that I have room to edit once I finish, or even as I'm drafting. Third, I like to use yellow legal pads when I draft since having the paper bound at the top helps keep it from slipping and sliding.

Because I like a particular type of paper when I write, doesn't mean that my students will, or should, like the same paper. Some students may feel more comfortable writing in a notebook, while others may prefer loose-leaf paper. Some students have erratic handwriting and therefore benefit from raised-line paper, which controls how far they can push their pencil on a given line. Providing students with at least three paper options when they are ready to draft helps to honor the students' individual differences.

One size does not fit all when it comes it comes to T-shirts. One kind of paper does not work for all students either. If it did, then there wouldn't be office supply stores with large aisles filled with a myriad of paper choices. While public school classrooms cannot offer the number of choices that an office supply store does, we surely can help our students feel more human by allowing them to choose the type of writing paper that feels best beneath their writing implement when they sit down to draft.

Challenge: Price different kinds of paper at your local office supply store that you might want to offer your students for drafting during writing workshop. Buy a pack of each for your classroom. Ask students to choose what they'd like to use and ask them *why*.

Reflective Practice:

- Which paper was most popular among your students? Why?
- How can you work with your administration to get funds to keep a variety of drafting paper in your classroom?
- How do you think having a variety of drafting paper choices will help your students as writers?

Caring Enough to Revise

If a teacher told me to revise, I thought that meant my writing was a broken-down car that needed to go to the repair shop. I felt insulted. I didn't realize the teacher was saying, "Make it shine. It's worth it." Now I see revision as a beautiful word of hope. It's a new vision of something. It means you don't have to be perfect the first time. What a relief!

—Naomi Shihab Nye

How were you expected to revise when you were a student? After asking this question for many years in workshops, I find the response is predictable: *I wasn't expected to revise.*

How do your students revise? Again, the answer is predictable: *They don't.*

When thinking about revision and the answers to these questions, another question surfaces: *Why*? Why wasn't revision expected? Why don't our students revise?

Perhaps it's because for revision to happen, we have to care about the writing. To make significant revision, the writer must want to improve the writing. If the writing is terrible, writers don't revise, they begin again. If the writing isn't purposeful, there's no point in revising. If the writing won't have a meaningful audience, we won't revise; it's probably good enough as it is. So if we want our students to make significant revision, they need to have a piece of writing that is worth the hard work of revising.

This is the reason students aren't encouraged to take every single draft through the writing process. Every draft doesn't deserve the work it takes to revise, edit, and publish. So the first choice in revision is asking students to choose a worthy draft to revise. What are some other choices writers make when it comes to revision?

Writers must determine *how* they will make revisions. Using proofreading marks such as carats, writing in the margins, and using sticky notes are all potential options. Spider legs are a favorite of many primary students. In this revision technique, the teacher cuts strips of paper on which students may write the words they want to add to their draft. The student takes a single piece of tape and sticks the strip to the draft in the place where the addition makes sense. When several strips are coming off the paper, they look like "spider legs." I have found providing options like this one encourages students to revise their work.

Another choice for writers is *what* they will revise. Younger writers can add to their pictures as a means of revision. Some writers choose to add to a slim scene. More sophisticated writers choose to take out parts that detract from the meaning. Still others decide to add a particular craft technique, such as dialogue or sensory details. Sometimes writers spend time playing with language. For example, they might write a new lead to have a choice between two. Helping students determine which revision option is most appropriate for their writing is an important role for the teacher. When students have too many choices, they often feel overwhelmed and won't make any revisions. It is a delicate balance of providing choices as well as enough scaffolding so that students will feel successful as writers.

Challenge: Talk to the writers in your classroom about choosing a draft that is worthy of publishing. As a class, discuss the ways a writer would determine whether a draft is worth the work needed to revise, edit, and publish. For example, rereading all of the drafts in your writing folder would be one of the first steps in the process. Record these ideas on an idea sheet (Appendix B). Near the end of writing workshop, ask students to write a reflection about what draft they chose and why. Students could share these reflections during sharing time.

Reflective Practice:

- How did the work today energize students for revision, or did it deflate them?
- Why do you feel this way?

Develop a Publishing Center

Above all, writing is a form of communication, and it's wonderful knowing that an actual flesh-and-blood person will read your words!
—Ralph Fletcher

Writers are motivated by words. Writers are motivated by writing regularly. Writers are motivated by readers. Our student writers are no different. Publishing is crucial to the life (and survival) of all writers. Many publishing choices lie before our students.

Sharing work with an audience of their choice is an important decision for writers to consider when embarking on a writing project. Encouraging, and ensuring, that the writing is shared with the intended audience is the role of the teacher.

Students can determine what the published project will look like. Will it be a scrapbook page, a picture book, or mounted on a decorative mat? What color of paper will they use to publish? Will they type, print, or use cursive writing? Will there be original artwork, a photograph, or clip art? The choices are endless.

Developing a publishing center helps students realize the endless possibilities. A publishing center can open the doors of students' imaginations when it is stocked with art supplies (such as markers, colored pencils, crayons, and pastels) and paper choices. Other items to include in the publishing center are covers for books (construction paper, wallpaper samples, and scrapbook paper are possibilities); staples, brads, and yarn to bind pages together; and stickers, glitter, and speech bubbles to inspire students to create interesting pictures. Special stationery and envelopes help to round out the center.

By developing a system to track the different ways students publish their writing projects, increased exposure is given to different publishing possibilities. Often the final publication motivates many students to write. It is helpful to have many publishing ideas swarming around the classroom. Finally, celebrate the accomplishment of publication, as well as the feedback the writers in your classroom receive. This creates an air of excitement in the classroom. Publication fuels writers for the next writing project.

Challenge: Help students envision different possibilities for publishing their writing. Considering their audience, what kind of published project makes the most sense? For example, if the class is publishing personal narratives, there could be several potential publishing projects. If a mother is the intended audience, then the writer may want to create a scrapbook page for a family album. However, if a younger brother is the intended audience, perhaps the writer will publish the personal narrative as an illustrated children's book. If a grandparent who lives in a different state is the audience, then the student may type the personal narrative and print it on plain copy paper, then write an accompanying note to the grandparent on stationery.

Reflective Practice:

- What were your students' attitudes as they published their writing? Were they excited and upbeat? Or were they lethargic and disheartened? Perhaps they were somewhere between these extremes?
- Why do you think your students feel the way they do as they conclude their writing projects? What are some ways you can continue their excitement (or rebuild their excitement) as you begin the next writing project?

Cycle 2: Moving Toward Independence

The Proposal

Courage is doing what you're afraid to do. There can be no courage unless you're scared.
—Eddie Rickenbacker

My husband proposed to me on a humid evening in late June 2006. He stood in front of a horse and carriage he had hired to drive us around Central Park, ring box in hand, when he asked me to marry him. Although we had talked about marriage before that June evening, I know he was relieved when I said "yes." Although he was pretty confident I'd accept his proposal, he wasn't completely sure. Hence, it took courage for him to tell an elaborate story to get me downtown on that broiling June night, which was also the last night of the school year.

Our students take risks whenever they propose an idea for a project. We have the power to accept or deny their proposal, thereby leaving them euphoric or sorrowful. To set our students up to undertake an independent writing project, we need to put a project proposal form into place. They'll take it seriously and feel a little nervous, but they won't feel intimidated to even try to put their idea out into the world.

M. Colleen Cruz's *Independent Writing: One Teacher—Thirty-Two Needs, Topics, and Plans* (2004) has inspired the independent writing projects my students have undertaken through the years. Although it is not necessary to plan every detail of the project, I expect some basic information up front when students propose a project:

- **Genre:** Students explain the genre they wish to write in and why they have selected that particular genre.
- **Topic:** Students explain the idea(s) they're ruminating about so they can develop a better sense of how much of the topic is solidified and how much needs to be developed. If the idea is solidified, students should provide the teacher with the writing draft that already exists.
- **Deadline:** As the students gain a sense of the complexity for their projects, they set mini-deadlines for themselves so they can complete their work by the final deadline.
- **Additional information:** Students have an opportunity to furnish additional information that doesn't fall under genre, topic, or deadline.

Challenge: Using the information above, create your own "independent writing project proposal form" (Appendix B). If you teach early elementary grades, you might want to set it up with direct questions and space for student responses. For older grades, a prose form might work better. Regardless, create a proposal form that works for you and the students you teach.

Reflective Practice:

- How will you provide feedback to your students about their independent writing project proposal forms? Written? Verbal? Both?
- What will you do if a student puts forth an idea that is either too easy or too challenging for the time allotted?
- How will you use the independent writing project proposal forms as a means of holding students accountable for their work?

Finding a Topic You Want to Write About

Inspiration is wonderful when it happens, but the writer must develop an approach for the rest of the time . . . The wait is simply too long.
—Leonard Bernstein

Many times when I sit down to write I encounter a white, electronic expanse with nothing more than a black cursor blinking back at me. If the words don't flow quickly, I don't panic. I don't throw up my hands. I don't proclaim, "I have writer's block." Instead, I look into my toolbox of strategies—the same one I have given to my students through the years—and promptly start writing.

One of my favorite "I don't know what to write about" strategies is to go back to old notebook entries in the hope that they will spark an idea and will help me write something new. I have more than twelve writer's notebooks, which I can readily reread and consult when I cannot find a topic to write about. While the subject matter may stay the same, my approach to the topic is often markedly different because of the passage of time.

Every time one of my students finished a writer's notebook, I would ask them to turn it in to me. I immediately put his or her notebook into a hanging file folder in my classroom file cabinet. At the start of each unit of study, I would take a few minutes to retrieve all of the past notebooks from the file cabinet and distribute them if the child wished to look back through old notebooks to examine topics they'd written about earlier in the year. (This was especially useful during personal essay and memoir writing.) Therefore, during the collecting stage of a unit, when I asked my students to write new entries, they often went back to look through old notebooks to find incomplete entries to finish, or they revisited completed writing that needed improvement using the new strategies they had learned in class.

Regardless of the genre, when students write daily in their writer's notebooks, they have plenty of ideas for writing topics. Daily independent writing in notebooks only needs to last for ten minutes to give students enough writing to choose from when they need to find a topic to write about in any unit of study.

Challenge: Bring some of your old writer's notebooks to class. Review them in front of your students on the day you'd like them to come up with a topic independently, and show them how you use your old notebooks to find something to write (more) about. Having a pad of sticky notes and a pen nearby will be helpful so you can show students how you mark off pertinent entries that will help you develop your new topic.

Reflective Practice:

- Did any of your students reread their writer's notebook(s) to pick a topic independently? How did that work out for the children who chose to reread their old notebooks? Was it easier or harder for them to find something to write about using their notebook as a springboard to picking a topic?
- What kind of system can you implement in your classroom, or your school, to help keep track of old notebooks so students can revisit them any time they get stuck when deciding what to write about?

It's Okay to Say No

Unlimited choice is no choice at all.
—Penny Kittle

"You mean we can write *anything* we want?" a third grader asks while rubbing his hands together. His mischievous smile and the snicker that follows make me aware of the importance of my answer.

"You may write anything that is meaningful and challenges you to become a stronger writer." I smile, and his eyes sparkle as he considers his own writing project. His excitement permeates the room.

When giving students the choice to develop their own writing projects, it is important to think through the parameters of the projects. Giving unlimited choice and total freedom will not ensure that students become stronger writers. This is, after all, the purpose of writing workshop—to become a stronger writer. Although choice is essential, some choices should be vetoed. As teachers, it is important to position students to write well. Therefore, if students are making choices that do not lead to meaningful writing, then they should be redirected. As an editor clears articles for a journalist, a teacher should clear projects for students.

The three big choices for any writer are topic, genre, and audience, which are influenced by the purpose of the project—what impact do students want their words to make? This is the most important choice for any writer. Giving students an opportunity to use their words to effect change is a gift every person deserves. Inspiring students to use their voices to make the world better is the key to meaningful projects. When students write with purpose, they not only become stronger writers, they also learn the power of their voices.

If students are writing in ways that do not make a difference in their worlds—they do not bring happiness, inspire change, or give insight—then the drafts ought to be abandoned. When a project does not position a student to write well, then it is the teacher's duty to veto the idea.

The purpose of offering choice is to ensure students are spending time on writing that is meaningful and important to them. Choice matters only when it leads to meaningful writing for the writer. By approving choices that do not lead to meaningful writing, we are undermining the power of writing workshop and belittling the meaning of choice.

Challenge: Make a list of choices you imagine students making that would lead to meaningless writing. Then make a list of choices you imagine would lead students to powerful writing. Although the bulk of your lists will include topic choices, consider audiences and genres that will position students to write well. Finally, make a third list of possible writing projects for you to complete. Again, include the topic, genre, and audience for each of these projects. It is important to realize what moves us as writers to inspire the young writers in our classrooms.

Reflective Practice:

- What kinds of writing assignments were you expected to complete in school?
- How do your feelings about these assignments compare to your feelings about your list of personal writing projects you created in the challenge?
- How do you want your students to feel about the writing they complete in writing workshop?

Seek and Ye Shall Find

One could get a first-class education from a shelf of books five feet long.
—Charles William Eliot

When I set off on the journey to write this book, I immediately began to look at other professional texts in a new way. No longer was I reading only for the content. As I began to write, I looked for texts that would inspire me as a writer. No one actually handed me a list of books I should consult for this task. Rather, I sought out mentor texts from the books I had in my own professional library.

As an adult writer, I have to procure mentor texts that will help me grow as a writer. By sharing the way I use texts as mentors for my own writing, I encourage students to accept this practice as part of their writing persona. When we "take off the top of our heads" (as Nancie Atwell [1998] encourages) and reveal the ways we notice the craft moves mentor authors make, students learn to do this kind of work as well. With time and practice, students begin to do this work independently. As students notice an author's craft, they can be encouraged to find their own personal mentor texts. But how? Here are a few ideas to empower students to find personalized mentor texts:

- Create baskets in your classroom library, sorted by genre or by topic, which can be used by your students in class or even for overnight borrowing.
- Encourage a student to reread favorite classwide read-alouds or to try out new books by favorite authors. Goad the student to do the same kinds of reading-writing connection work you've been modeling during your read-alouds. For a student who doesn't naturally take to this work, you might need to confer with the student one-on-one.
- Facilitate share sessions at the end of independent writing time that allow a couple of students to talk about ways they used mentor texts to lift the level of their writing.
- Create a bulletin board of possible mentor texts. You could tuck mentor text possibilities into several manila envelopes. Each envelope could hold several copies of the mentor text so that students could keep the ones they like best in their writing folder. You can change the texts in the envelopes so that students always have the ability to choose from several different mentor texts during each unit of study.

When you build a classroom culture that relies on authors to be your co-teachers of writing, students peruse the classroom bookshelves with greater intentionality. They, too, will see that they can find their own mentor authors and writing teachers by reading like a writer.

Challenge: Chat with your students about ways you can work together to organize the classroom library so that it's used in writing workshop, as well as in reading workshop. Determine how baskets of books can be organized so that searching for mentor texts becomes an easy task for the students you teach.

Reflective Practice:

- How will you show your students how you use mentor texts to lift the level of your writing?
- What steps will you take to help a student who does not independently seek out his or her own mentor texts to develop reading-writing initiative?

More Than Just Talking with a Partner

Putting kids together in groups doesn't guarantee any kind of collaboration; without guidance and training, students can just as easily obstruct each other's learning instead of facilitate it.

—Nancy Steineke

One day I was working in two different classrooms with two different grade levels; however, both focused on peer conferring. In one of the writing workshops, peer conferring went well. I walked away from the workshop wishing I had filmed it because other teachers would not have believed the success of the peer collaboration without evidence. What happened in the other classroom? Let's just say the peer conferring left something to be desired. At the end of the day, a single word bounced around my brain—Why? Why was peer conferring successful in one classroom and not in the other? Because I was the common denominator, I began to reflect on the two experiences.

I realized that, in the class where peer conferring did not go well, students approached peer collaboration as a task to just get done instead of something useful. This class put away all papers—writer's notebooks, drafts, and peer conferring notes—when they were "done." Although they discussed with their partners "areas to revise" and had even jotted a few notes about this potential, when they finished with the "task" of peer conferring, they packed up and waited for more teacher direction. Not only that, but during share time, they questioned the basic procedures—*Why did we have to read the writing aloud? Why did we have to sit next to each other? Why did we have to discuss the strengths? Why did we . . . ?*

I was miffed, then disappointed, and a little guilty. As I reflected, I realized I didn't teach to the needs of the class. I didn't present peer conferring in a way that mattered to these writers. I talked about the procedures and the notes to complete, yet I never mentioned why peer collaboration was important. My explanation led to a jump-through-the-hoops-for-the-teacher kind of attitude.

With the other class, the mini-lesson focused on the reasons behind the procedures of peer conferring, as well as the rationale of completing peer conference notes. As students moved into independent work time and some ventured into a peer conference, the attitude in the room was different. Students valued the experience of peer collaboration. The meetings were an appropriate length, discussions between two writers ensued, and students returned to their seats with their conference notes and used them to continue working as writers.

We wrapped up the workshop with a share session focusing on the importance of peer collaboration. We completed a T-chart. On one side was the question, *Why is peer conferring worthwhile?* On the other side was the question, *How can I make it successful?*

When students know the rationale behind the work we do as writers, they are willing to embrace and accept it as part of their writing lives. As children reflect on an experience, they are able to determine whether it is worthwhile and how they can make it more successful in the future.

Challenge: Talk with another person about your own writing. This person could be a colleague, a spouse, a friend, or even someone from an online writing group.

After the discussion, take a moment to jot down a few ideas you have for your writing work. Share this experience with your students, providing the procedures for peer collaboration but also the reasons it is helpful.

Reflective Practice:

- How did it feel to talk with another person about your writing?
- Have you noticed that students seem to complete writing tasks just to make you, the teacher, happy?

Choose Your Own Adventure Today in Writing Workshop

All problems become smaller if, instead of indulging in them, we confront them. Touch a thistle timidly and it pricks you; grasp it boldly, and the spines crumble.

—William S. Halsey

Mr. Long, my high school government teacher, assigned our class to read *The Presidential Character: Predicting Performance in the White House* by James David Barber. Not only was it fascinating to me, since I'm a history buff, but it taught me about being passive-positive and passive-negative, qualities some of our former presidents possessed, to their and the country's detriment. I recall lengthy class discussions about the effects of a passive leader on the administration and the country. After studying the presidents in-depth, it was clear that active-positive behavior led to the greatest amount of social change, thereby allowing our country to forge ahead despite tough times.

Young writers, too, have tough times. When problems arise for student writers, they're often unsure of how to fix these problems because they're new to this type of writing situation. Even when our students know how to ask for help, they're often unsure about the problem. Hence, it's up to us, as teachers, to help our students get the help they need.

About once every unit of study, you can abandon a traditional mini-lesson for the day and offer several targeted small-group lessons based on issues your students may exhibit. Since your students may be at different places within the writing process, you will need to offer a variety of strategy lessons that will meet their needs based on the work they're doing.

When I offered targeted small-group lessons, I posted the signup sheet in the classroom with a short description of each lesson. I took a few minutes, when I'd normally deliver the mini-lesson, to explain what each small group would be working on. (During this time I put away the markers so the students wouldn't sign up for the lessons before I explained them.) I let students know what kind of work they'd likely do in the group and who (not naming names) might benefit from a given group. Then, I provided my students with a couple of minutes to talk with their writing partner about what group might be best for them for the day. Once students decided on a group, the markers came out of hiding and students signed up. Finally, before the students dispersed throughout the room, they planned what they'd work on while waiting for their small group to meet. Once plans were in place for the workshop time, students not involved in a meeting went to their focus spots while I met with the first small group in the meeting area. Afterward, the members of the first group returned to their focus spots and the next group came over for a targeted small-group lesson. This was repeated for the rest of the period. At the end of the writing workshop, a share session still took place in which a couple of students, from different small groups, presented the work they had completed that day.

Often these sessions are saved for the drafting and revision stages of writing. However, targeted, well-planned small-group sessions can find their way into any part of the units of study you teach.

Challenge: When you confer with your students or read their writing at night, write down problems they may have. Make a note of the commonalities that arise, as these make the best topics for strategy-lesson groups. After you have gathered a handful of possibilities, create a signup sheet that includes lesson topics and a short description of the teaching. Give students the responsibility of signing up for the lesson(s) that will best meet their individual needs.

Reflective Practice:

- How did the small-group settings, with clusters of kids who were having the same issues, help your students to move forward with their writing today?
- Would you try this again? If so, when is the next time you anticipate offering these targeted lesson signups?

What If . . .

Every story finds its own form. Finding that form is the great struggle of writing, for which there is no prescription.

—Garrison Keillor

"You know, I'm really more of a one-draft writer," a seventh grader once told me during a conference about his revision work. Part of me was impressed that he had accepted the persona of a writer and that he was beginning to personalize the writing process. The other part of me was a bit horrified. Being a one-draft writer wasn't quite working for him.

I had no idea what to say to him, and I was thankful I had been practicing wait time in conferences. He mistook my appalled silence as simply waiting for him to say more. "You know, the story is here. There are three scenes. I've used dialogue, lots of action, and a little bit of setting description. There's nothing more to do."

I lifted my eyebrows in response. "Seriously," he continued, "I typed it last night and it looks pretty good." He dangled the typewritten page out to me. "Not a single misspelling," he added smugly.

As the silence settled between us, I realized his misunderstanding about revision. To him, revision was something that needed to be done to *fix* writing. If he did it "right" the first time, then revising his writing wasn't necessary. This conversation gave me nightmares, especially as other students confirmed his beliefs about revision. As a result, I shifted my paradigms on how to teach revision.

Thus began my foray into understanding revision and making it matter to student writers. The crux of significant revision lies in the writer's choices. Too often students see revision as a punishment for writing poorly in the first place, not as an opportunity to make their decent writing even better.

The student's first choice is to decide which draft is worth expending time and energy to revise. The opportunity for students to write more than one draft during a unit of study allows for more significant revision. By selecting a draft that is worthy of the time and energy of revision, students are more invested in the writing and therefore will put forth the blood, sweat, and tears needed for revision. Students must be able to verbalize why their work is worth revising. Therefore, I teach that the first step of revision is to mark on the draft the part that makes the rest of the draft worthy of revision. Sometimes students identify several paragraphs; others may highlight a single line, and some may scrawl across the top of the draft, "This story matters." It doesn't matter how much or how little is singled out. What matters is that the draft is desirable.

From this point, it is the writer's responsibility to determine ways to make the writing more significant. By teaching students to ask themselves, *How could this draft be shaped into the best possible version by the deadline?* discussions in mini-lessons and conferences are more meaningful.

One endless possibility for revision lies in the structure of the writing. For example, if a student marked the lead as the reason a draft was worth revising, the student should be encouraged to ask, *What if* I wrote a different lead? *What if* my stellar lead became the ending? If a student felt the opening scenes were strong, the question could be, *What if* I spent more time on the last scene?

I often find myself encouraging students to rework entire scenes. "Find the scene that is the least developed, get out a new piece of paper, and draft it a second time," I say. I encourage students to use all they know about writing the genre well and to focus all of their energy on a single scene.

We also look at possibilities of craft. Mini-lessons and conferences focus on the craft of writing. In narrative, we may look at various character details or ways to add sensory details. Students scour their drafts, often noting which details are most prevalent and which are lacking. In a fourth-grade classroom, students used colors to mark the kinds of character details in their drafts. One student brought her lengthy draft to the share session and held it up for everyone to see. "That's a lot of green," one of her classmates announced.

"I know," she said, rolling her eyes. "I decided to see what kinds of character details I was using." She continued, "I noticed I only use dialogue. There's a ton of talking in my story! It got a little boring underlining all of that dialogue, so I imagine it would be boring to read it all too. I'm going to add some action into my story."

Finally, students may also choose to play with conventions during revision. The teaching here must be sound. We are not encouraging students to correct Standard English and call that revision. Correcting writing for Standard English is important, but that is considered editing. Students understand editing and often skip revision and go directly to the editing process; however, they could also learn how to use conventions as an art of revision. Students learn to envision possibilities in regard to conventions by asking questions such as

- Do I want parentheses or dashes to set off an aside?
- What would be the difference in meaning if I linked these sentences with a semicolon instead of using a period?
- Would a series of short sentences be the best way to build suspense, or would I rather link those sentences with ellipses?

Revision allows students a safe place to play with language, to take risks in the craft of writing, and to try new approaches without worrying about failure. After all, the drafts they are revising are already decent writing, so if they attempt a revision that isn't pleasing, they don't have to keep it. They write a second draft of a lead, and keep the first . . . this is still revision. In fact, it is significant revision, and as teachers, we honor this choice.

When we offer students the freedom to explore revision, they learn the significance of this stage of the writing process. More important, they learn that revision can be enjoyable and powerful. By asking students to envision new possibilities for their drafts, it begins to eliminate the notion that revision should be reserved for fixing bad writing. "Bad writing," I once said in a mini-lesson, "goes in the trash. Writing with glimmers of hope is deserving of revision." As students begin asking themselves, "What if . . . " when considering revision, and then making choices based on these questions, significant revision occurs. Students begin to see themselves as writers responsible for finding *one draft* worthy of the hard work of revision, as opposed to *one-draft writers.*

Challenge: Pay attention to the revision you tend to favor in your own writing life. Do you usually revise structure, craft, or conventions? The next time you write, consider how you can enhance the meaning of your writing by revising the structure. Ask the same thing of yourself by revising craft and conventions to make the meaning of your writing stronger. Share these ideas with your students by starting a chart that shows the decisions writers make when determining how to revise. As students revise, they can add their insights to the chart.

Reflective Practice:

- Do the students in your classroom see revision as endless possibilities for crafting their words, or do they view revision as a way to fix poor writing?
- As you notice students making choices that lead to significant revision, record these experiences either in your personal notes or on a class chart. This will give your students more support as you continue to open the door to revision possibilities.

Deadlines: Inspiration to Write

I have a deadline. I'm glad. I think that will help me get it done.
—Michael Chabon

"You've gotta give me deadlines," I said to Stacey as we made plans to write this book. I'm wired to meet deadlines. Stacey is wired to complete assignments as soon as possible after they are given. Although I would like to be more like Stacey, the fact remains that deadlines motivate me more than anything else when it comes to writing assignments.

Don't get me wrong, I want to write. However, taking the time to sit down and put words on paper doesn't happen for me unless I have deadlines. This is true for many students as well.

Writing workshop provides the necessary time to write well. However, if our workshops are places with time and no deadlines, there will be many writers, like me, who will dream of grand projects, capture everyday life in their writer's notebooks, dabble in drafts, play with language, and even master conventions, but will never produce a final product. Stacey makes me a better writer, primarily because she holds me accountable to deadlines.

I feel guilty when I miss a deadline, and it's not because Stacey takes away my recess, gives me a low grade, or calls my parents. Since I care about our relationship, I don't want to disappoint her. Second, I care about the writing projects we work on together. When it comes to our writing workshops, it would be wise to make these two conditions a reality for our students. When children know we care about them, and they care about the writing project, it is likely the deadline will be met.

Sometimes, however, deadlines won't be met. In times like this, we must respond with grace and second chances. The first time I missed a deadline, besides feeling like a schmuck, I also realized I needed to change my writing habits. Stacey didn't chastise me but instead adjusted the deadline with grace. I was given the opportunity to reevaluate my work as a writer. I learned to plan differently and to draft with more purpose to have the luxury to do the writing work I love the most—playing with language, crafting meaning, and experimenting with conventions. These changes in planning and drafting could only happen with the knowledge of a looming deadline, missing that deadline, and having someone hold me accountable, while extending grace at the same time.

We can help students learn to manage their time in writing workshop by helping them set their own goals (or deadlines) within a unit of study. When communicating the final deadline with students, help them think through some "mini-deadlines." Encouraging students to consider the deadlines along the journey as opposed to focusing solely on the final deadline allows them to consider their writing habits and make adjustments.

I meet deadlines because I changed the way I approached writing. If we offer extensions to the deadlines without expecting a change in the writer, then we are doing a disservice to students. All of the pieces must be present: a strong relationship, a commitment to the writing project, and an expectation to meet future deadlines. I am not proposing we offer extension after extension to a student who expects an extension. Instead, our response to deadlines provides rich teaching opportunities that will serve our students well, not only in their writing lives but also in other parts of their lives as they learn to manage time.

Challenge: Create a calendar with students to establish possible deadlines throughout a writing project. A large calendar in the writing center is useful. The final deadline should be noted, while the other mini-deadlines could be established individually or communally. Be aware of students' developing writing habits and whether these habits will help or hinder them in meeting the deadline.

Reflective Practice:

- How do you approach writing assignments? Do you complete them as soon as possible, or is a deadline necessary to inspire you?
- What habits help your students meet the deadlines? What habits hinder them?
- What are the handful of mini-deadlines that are appropriate to the grade level you teach?

Publishing Is Fuel for Writers

> Your stuff starts out being just for you . . . but then it goes out. Once you know what the story is and get it right—as right as you can anyway—it belongs to anyone who wants to read it.
>
> ***—Stephen King***

I steadied my nerves by unpacking my bag. Here I was, thousands of miles from home and from my recently adopted daughters, preparing to present at my first national conference for educators. My hands shook. I cycled through necessary items in my bag—computer, flash drive, writer's notebook, convention program, student writing

Student writing? Wait, back up. What is this? The questions tumbled through my mind as I pulled the story from where it was sandwiched between the convention program and the edge of my bag. The drawing of a smiling big person and a smiling little person with a cracked heart between them gave me pause. I'd never seen this before. Then I read the words: *I miss you Mom. I love you so much.*

My breath caught. My body stilled. Tears welled in my eyes. My then first-grade daughter had written this for me. My eyes returned to the drawing. Sure enough, that was Hannah in the picture, with me. I turned the page and was face to face with a drawing of the big person and little person with frowns and tears. Lots of tears filled the space around the people. *And I will miss you very much*, she had written.

The final page offered an image of the two of us smiling and holding hands. Hannah wrote, *I like you very much. Love, Hannah.* I sat down, not knowing whether my wobbly legs would hold me much longer. The writing moved me.

Hannah had come home eight months earlier when we adopted her from the state. Her (and her sister's) needs and well-being had consumed us, and I was hesitant to leave home. Yet Stacey and I had been accepted to present at the National Council of Teachers of English conference and I didn't want to cancel. Now here I was, sitting in a hotel room, preparing to speak about the teaching of writing, staring in awe at Hannah's writing. It had touched me in a way no other writing ever had.

Hannah's story hangs in my office today as a reminder for the mom in me of my daughter's love and as a reminder for the teacher in me of what it means to publish writing.

The final stage of the writing process, publishing, seems to carry with it many misconceptions. It is often made into a *really big deal*. Sometimes it seems like such hoopla. I've met many teachers who are so overwhelmed that they prefer to avoid the publishing process. Others mistake publishing for perfection and destroy the beauty of imperfect student writing in the name of Standard English. Others create a classroom culture where publishing is more important to students than writing, where students spend more time creating a cover than writing the words. In my own experience, we didn't have time for publishing. We had to stick to the important work of writing, not the fluff of celebrating our writing.

My stomach was in knots as I admitted this. I would have liked to change many things (and eventually I did change) in my first year as a writing workshop teacher. Yet my attitude toward publishing may have been a big faux pas.

Publishing is not fluff. It is not hoopla. It is not perfection.

Publishing is fuel for writers.

Sharing our words with an audience and using our words to make a difference in the lives of others matter. Publishing, in its purest form, is sharing our writing with another person—going public with our stories. In writing workshop, publishing is when writing goes to the intended audience beyond the classroom walls.

When Hannah slipped her writing into my computer bag, she was publishing. When our students write a letter to their aunts, they are publishing. When students submit their writing to a writing contest, they are publishing. When writing is posted on bulletin boards and in cafeterias and doctor's offices, it is published.

As teachers, it is our duty to help students find significant ways to publish their writing. When they find their voices, then breathe life into their words, filling up the blank page, it is only complete when their writing goes beyond the classroom walls.

Challenge: Create a chart or bulletin board in your classroom where students can note ideas on ways to make their writing public. A large part of any writer's life is when the writing goes into the world. Plan now for a time to celebrate the risk and dedication it takes for students to send their writing into the world.

Reflective Practice:

- What are some ideas you have to publish your own writing? Remember publishing doesn't necessarily mean submitting to editors—it simply means sharing your words with others.
- What are some publishing ideas that you think will inspire students to get their words out in the world?

C'mon and Celebrate Silently and Independently

Writing celebration is the most important part of the writing process.
—Katherine Bomer

Katherine Bomer spoke at the Teachers College Reading and Writing Project Summer Institute for the Teaching of Writing in July 2008. I had the opportunity to listen to her keynote address about celebration, something I always thought I was a pro at because I held publishing parties at the end of each unit of study. However, after listening to Bomer speak, I realized that if writers need an audience for their writing, then it's incumbent upon their teachers to provide forums so that their peers can read or listen to their writing and then respond either verbally or in writing.

During the summer of 2009, I went back to the Teachers College Reading and Writing Project Summer Institute for the Teaching of Writing and took a course with Mary Ehrenworth on breathing beauty and life into essays. On the last day of our class, we celebrated the essays we wrote during the course with a silent gallery walk celebration.

Before the celebration, Mary asked each of us to write the words "Comments for ________" at the top of a couple of blank pieces of paper. We laid our blank comment sheets alongside the essays we wrote, left them at our seats, and then stood up to walk around the room to read other people's essays. Everyone was silent. The only feedback we could give one another was in writing. Kid-like thoughts went through my head as I wondered whether anyone liked my essay and what kind of comments I'd receive. Certainly, our students have the same thoughts when they're given similar celebratory opportunities.

At the end of the celebration, Ehrenworth gave us a few minutes to connect with people whose essays we read and were moved by. I sought out one woman in particular whose essay about her son affected me deeply. Her writing was powerful, truthful, and gripping. However, two people who wrote comments on my sheets sought me out to elaborate on the comments they left for me in writing. I was so touched that they not only took time to write a comment but came and spoke with me.

A gallery walk celebration is a powerful form of publishing for both the writer and the readers.

Challenge: Brainstorm a list of things you'll want to have in place before the start of your classroom's gallery walk celebration. Then invite your students to think about how to have a successful gallery walk and what they'll need to feel safe within the classroom community of writers.

Reflective Practice:

- How did preplanning, by yourself and along with your students, help your classroom's gallery walk of independent writing projects feel successful?
- What would you do the same the next time you host a gallery walk? What would you do differently?

Cycle 3: Living the Life of a Writer

Effecting Change

How wonderful it is that nobody need wait a single moment
before starting to improve the world.
—Anne Frank

Every year, usually in January, I engaged my class in a mini-unit of study on persuasive letter writing. The purpose of the unit was to bring about change for the classroom, the school, or the community. My students wrote to a variety of people: the school principal, CEOs, CFOs, community relations departments, and even the mayor of New York City. By combining persuasion with targeting the right person at the right time, my students have been able to get a printer and paint for the classroom, DVDs for kids to watch on rainy days during recess, and even a playground! Regardless of the person to whom the letter was directed, there was one commonality among all of the letters: the desire to effect change.

When students engage in independent writing outside of the classroom, they are often writing to effect change. We must remind students each day that writing has the power to persuade, to alter the status quo, and to improve the world. The power of the pen is what turns many reluctant writers on to writing. Hence, we must make sure we empower our students' voices so they want to work to have their voices heard by others. Whether it's a letter to a parent, to an elected official, or to the editor of a newspaper, students need to know their writing has power and that one great purpose for writing is to become an agent of change.

Speaking of reluctant writers, one of the greatest motivators is to allow them to be heard. Nudging students, those who claim they have nothing to say or don't want to write, to do some out-of-class writing to effect change in either their personal, school, or community life can be a powerful exercise. Remember, even students who claim they hate to write can hold the power to change the world.

Challenge: Think deeply about the ways in which you wish to bring about change. Think small. Set your sights on something you can easily accomplish. Document the process you go through to effect change and share it with your students who are engaging in a piece of writing that seeks to shake up existing conditions or make a difference.

Reflective Practice:

- How do you think documenting the change-making process will help you coach a student to write to persuade someone to think his or her way?
- What's the next thing you want to change to improve the current state of affairs (either in *your* home, *your* school, or *your* community)?

Possibilities

Writers don't need to be given formulas; they need to be shown possibilities.
—Barry Lane

In our hurry-up-and-get-it-done society, sometimes it's tough to get our students to slow down and realize the possibilities of writing. Sometimes it's tough for us, as their teachers, to slow things down and give them time to truly live as writers. Sometimes in the quest to squeeze in all of the important teaching, we give students a formula for writing as opposed to showing them possibilities.

To find the possibilities in my writing, I found I first need to have a vision for the writing. *Who do I hope it will affect? What do I want it to sound like? Why am I writing it?* As we encourage students to envision possibilities for their writing, we should pose these questions to them.

We must be vigilant to ensure that we are offering students possibilities for their writing instead of an all-in-one formula to complete the assignment. This issue spans all grade levels. In intermediate grades, teachers feel the pressure to prepare students for middle and high school writing. Stephanie Parsons describes the struggle for primary teachers in her book *First Grade Writers:*

> *For years I thought that if I told my students to add details to their writing, I could get them to say more about their topic, tell more interesting stories, or convey information more clearly. Mostly what they did was add more words without adding clarity or substance. Details alone do not improve the quality of writing. In fact, they can detract from the quality. I needed to teach children how to start a piece of writing with a plan in mind and then add to that writing only those words or details that would help fulfill the plan. (2005, 2)*

As teachers of writing, the best way to help students envision possibilities is to engage in the work of writers ourselves. We write not to be published but to understand the inner workings of a writer's mind. More important than publishing is learning to listen to the voice in our heads that makes choices and thinks through specific writing moves. Today, when I model, I help students envision the possibilities this craft technique can have on their work. As I add sensory details to my story, I also share the reason why: "Because I want the reader to feel like they are right here in the dusty barn beside me," I say to a class of third graders. "Since I know the hope I have for my writing, I can imagine different ways to add sensory details with purpose." What a gift to give our students when we teach them to think through their writing work with a sense of purpose.

Challenge: As you confer with students, ask them about the vision they have for their writing. As you grasp the hope they have for their writing, lead them to consider what strategies would help them meet their goal. If students don't have a vision for their writing, then help them to find one by asking about the audience, purpose, and sound of their writing. If many students lack a vision, consider teaching a mini-lesson about envisioning possibilities for writing.

Reflective Practice:

- What kinds of hopes do students have for their writing?
- What do you hope for your own writing?

Living a Wide-Awake Life

There are only two options regarding commitment.
You're either in or out. There's no such thing as a life in-between.
—Pat Riley

A few years ago I struggled with how to ask kids to live like a writer when their writer's notebook was a five-subject, spiral notebook. After all, how many writers do *you* know who lug around a 200-page notebook with them all of the time? Quite frankly, I couldn't think of any, so I began to write mini-grants on DonorsChoose.org so that I could obtain the funds to purchase Moleskine notebooks and other portable writer's notebooks for my students to use to live like writers. Once the notebooks arrived and my students were able to choose the notebook that worked best for them, they committed themselves to living like writers, taking their notebooks on road trips, on the subway, and to family gatherings. *Why?* It was large enough to write in but small enough to tuck away when it came time to *live* life rather than to observe it with keenness and understanding.

About a year after I obtained the funds for portable writer's notebooks, I realized that sometimes it's not possible for kids to break out their writer's notebook on the go. However, when one notices something in the world by living a wide-awake life, it's important to write down the thought or idea that accompanies the noticing. Therefore, I began buying, and later, making, matchbook notepads for my students, which I regularly handed out. Measuring 3 by 3 inches with ten to twenty sheets of white paper in each, a matchbook notepad became the ideal place to record ideas for stories, wonderings, or noticings on the go, in the middle of the night, or while watching TV on the couch. Because the notepads are small and inexpensive, they can be placed in pockets, school bags, and on bedside tables, so that they can be reached for and jotted in quickly. Later, the sheets can be easily pulled out and taped into the writer's real notebook (and expanded on).

Using matchbook notepads and portable writer's notebooks are two of many ways we can get kids to live like a writer, so that they're constantly jotting what they notice and recording anecdotes about their everyday lives. After all, they're either committed to living a wide-awake life or they're just cruising through. There's really no in-between.

Challenge: Invest in a few matchbook notepads for yourself. Place a writing implement near each one so you can stop and jot whatever comes to mind. Do this for a week in an effort to increase your volume of daily writing.

Reflective Practice:

- How did having several mini-notebooks help you live more like a writer?
- How do you think you can implement mini- or portable notebooks into your students' writing routines?

Many Paths Can Lead to the Same Goal

If you do all that work of figuring out exactly how writing is done,
then it is available to you at any time, and you can build on it.
It's like the difference between shooting one hoop and having it go in by accident
and saying later "I shot a basket," and practicing so much you can do it whenever you want.
—Mark Salzman

Tony Phillips, my mentor teacher during my student teaching experience, taught me an important lesson: "When conferring with students, balance your time between zooming in to work individually or in small groups with students and zooming out to gain a sense of the whole group."

More than ten years later, his words still ring true. Sometimes when I zoom out, standing on the edge of the room, gaining a sense of the whole, my breath catches in my throat and goosebumps sprout on my arms. I'm in awe when students work as writers, yet they are all doing different kinds of work.

It is crucial to be intentional about leading students to find a writing process that is personal and tailored to each individual's needs. Each time I am immersed in a writing workshop, I am reminded that this is a tall order. There is a delicate balance between giving enough advice and structure to support our young writers, while at the same time leaving enough choice for them to discover their personal preferences.

The key lies in our mind-set of teaching writers, instead of writing. For example, all writers make plans for their work, but there are many acceptable avenues to plan writing. Our young writers should be expected to attempt a strategy for planning; however, after giving a good-faith effort, the freedom to abandon the strategy is extended. Our responsibility as writing teachers is to give many possibilities for completing the writing work and then to relinquish that responsibility to students as they determine what is helping and what is hindering their work as writers.

It's about letting go of what we think is right when it comes to writing and embracing the process that each individual writer forges. It's about observing what works not just for us but for the writers in our classrooms and then encouraging others in the classroom to try the same things. It's about being open and honest with our students about our successes and frustrations as writers.

Perhaps this is the key: being writers ourselves and open to the unexpected twists and turns the writing can take, thus creating the kind of atmosphere our students need to do the same. Our students all do not need to be doing the same activity as they work in a given phase of the writing process. While working with a ninth-grade class that had embraced their own writing processes, I noticed that they didn't question why everyone wasn't doing the same thing. No one questioned why Justin didn't have as many notebook entries as Elizabeth, nor why Blaine's draft was handwritten and Tyler's was typed. They were satisfied discovering and using strategies that worked best for them.

Approaching writing in this way was so natural that no one stopped to question why everyone was using different strategies to complete the process. Each writer was content because everyone was working toward the final project in a way that was logical to the individual. In our writing workshops, as we position students to discover their own needs as writers, may we boldly encourage students to forge the path that will meet their unique needs. As we bravely relinquish control, students will experience the joy of writing in ways that make sense for them.

Challenge: Choose a phase of the writing process that your students will be embarking on soon. Write down what you hope they will accomplish at this point as writers. Now make a list of all the possible ways students could accomplish this goal (e.g., outlining, storyboarding, or talking to a partner using their fingers to tick off the scenes if they're in the drafting stage).

Reflective Practice:

- Is the thought of students customizing their writing processes invigorating or stifling to you as a teacher?
- How will you push students into trying new strategies, while also creating a culture of choice in process in your classroom?
- How will you respond to a student who says, "I'm planning in my head," "I'm revising in my head," or "I'm thinking about different leads in my head," yet rarely produces the work?

Knowing the Audience

Waste your money and you're only out of money,
but waste your time and you've lost a part of your life.
—Michael LeBoeuf

A big part of responsive teaching is knowing our students. When we know our students and their strengths and weaknesses as learners, then it helps drive our instruction. We tweak originally thought-out plans based on the things we notice from the previous lesson, which is why scripted lesson plans and lessons other colleagues write for us are never just right. We always have to make something our own because we know before whom we stand.

Writing well is a lot like teaching well. No matter what, you have to know your audience: the people you're writing for. If writers are ambiguous about their audience, then it's really hard to write well because they don't know for whom they are writing. Hence, we must teach our students always to keep their audience in mind, because knowing *who* they're writing for before undertaking any type of writing is paramount. Knowing one's audience will guide young writers on a straight trajectory, helping them work efficiently and steadily even when they hit rough patches or claim they have "writer's block."

As writing teachers, we can help our students write with a sense of audience by not just asking them *who* their writing is intended for but also asking them *why* they've chosen to write for a particular audience. When students can articulate *why* they're writing for a given audience, they'll gain greater insight into that audience and will, in turn, angle their writing in a way that helps their audience better understand their piece, regardless of the genre. After all, when writing for peers, the language a student chooses will be different from the language used when writing for a teacher or for a mainstream audience in the world. In the end, knowing their audience will keep our students more focused.

Challenge: As you confer with your students, make it a priority to ask them about audience. Some questions you can use to help you initiate conversation about audience are

- What kinds of people would you like to read your writing?
- How come you've chosen to write for this particular audience?
- Why have you angled your writing this way?

Reflective Practice:

- What did you notice about your students' responses to your questions about audience? Were there any commonalities?
- If your students weren't clear about whom they're writing for, then what kind of targeted, small-group lessons can you plan to address this so they can become more focused on audience going forward?

Freedom in Topic Choice

Write what makes you happy.
—O. Henry

What wise words from O. Henry! So often we try to inspire our students to write by giving them topics we think will interest them. For me, relinquishing topic choice was one of the harder things to do when I transitioned into teaching according to the writing workshop philosophy. Looking back, I'm not sure why it was such a tough thing to let go.

Perhaps part of it was because developing topics for students to write about was fun. I enjoyed the creativity of it, the safety of it, and the ease of it. Not to mention, I was a little wimpy. If I gave freedom in topic choice, then what would they write about? What would I do when they said, "I don't know what to write about?" I was also a little egocentric. If I came up with the perfect topic, then they would love to write. I would have changed their lives.

Actually, I never developed the perfect topic. Can you believe it? Once I was brave enough to give students choice of topic, I was astounded by the results. Sure, there were the problems I expected. However, I armed myself with lots of strategies to teach in focus lessons about ways to find a topic. (Ralph Fletcher's *Writer's*

Notebooks: Unlocking the Writer Within You [1996] was the main key to my teaching students the art of finding a writing topic.) By helping students to develop their writer's notebooks, possible topics began flooding every writer.

Ironically, these were the topics that changed my students' lives as writers. When they wrote the important stories of their lives, they were changed. Suddenly writing workshop was a happy, productive, and pleasant place. Students were much happier and so was I, for they were writing more than ever before. Since they cared about the topic, they cared about the process, craft, and conventions too. These things mattered because the writing mattered.

If I had known the positive effect that would be made by the simple change of giving students the freedom to choose what to write about and teaching the strategies to find these topics, I would have made the switch in a snap. When teachers give students the freedom to write what they want to write, it is like waving a magic wand over the writing workshop. Perhaps you will even see the sparkles of the magic dust falling around your students as they settle in to write what matters most to them.

Challenge: Today, look for ways you can encourage students to write about topics that matter in their lives. Find out why students are writing the story, poem, or essay that they are working on. More important, give students the freedom and encouragement to abandon any draft that isn't making them happy. There are too many important lessons to teach for students to waste precious time writing unimportant pieces.

Reflective Practice:

- What makes you hesitant to relinquish the freedom of topic choice to students?
- What makes you excited about this possibility?
- Consider your most meaningful writing experiences. Are they times when someone forced a topic on you or when you decided the topic for yourself?

Collecting Around a Topic

Do you have any other grandpa stories?
—Carl Anderson

The hands were popping up like toast out of a toaster in an all-night diner.

"I'm done. What do I write about now?"

"I don't know what to write about"

"I have nothing to write about!"

A rookie mistake I made was thinking that students had to write about something new every draft. Naturally, they soon ran out of ideas. Now that I've been thinking as a writer for more than ten years, and reflecting on my life as a writer before my teaching career, I've learned that we write on the same topics time and time again.

Twenty years ago, I was writing about the things my brother Jeff did. Today, I'm still writing about times with Jeff. Stacey and I have been writing about the teaching of writing on our blog since 2007. Yet in our classrooms, students often think they must come up with a new topic each time they draft.

As I made this realization, my attention soon shifted from helping students come up with new ideas to helping them drill their previous topics for more ideas. Just as oil well drillers construct a rig to drill around a place that has been known to produce black gold, writers can drill around topics that have proved to produce drafts. When a student says, "I have nothing to write about," Carl Anderson teaches us to enter into a conversation about the previous drafts a student has written.

When he learns that a student has written about his grandpa, Anderson then asks, "Do you have any other grandpa stories?" Usually a student has another idea to write about when we ask him or her to drill around a topic that has already proven fruitful.

As writing workshop teachers, we can help students find their personal writing topics. One way to do this is to ask students to create heart maps. In her book *Awakening the Heart* (1999), Georgia Heard gathers students together and asks the poets she is working with to write about the things that matter most to them. We can invite students to have this same experience at the beginning of the year. As students create their heart maps, their personal topics emerge.

In 2008, I had the opportunity to participate in a workshop led by Katherine Bomer geared for educators to focus on their personal writing. Katherine encouraged us to "write close to the bones," because when we start with a topic that matters to us, our writing is more real, more genuine. Since then, I've added the option of creating a bone map instead of a heart map, so students may continue having choice when discovering writing topics. Here, students are able to write the things that are "close to their bones" directly on a picture of a bone. Once again, writing topics emerge.

We can not only encourage students to discover topics they can claim as part of their heart or close to their bones but also develop a list of audiences that are personal and common to the individual writer. Often the motivating factor for writing is not what to write but for whom to write. A list of coveted audiences often provides the perfect springboard into a writing project.

Challenge: Develop a list of your own writing topics. This can be a list or in the form of a heart or bone map.

Reflective Practice:

- What are some common writing topics among your students? How can you use this knowledge to build connections with students?
- How will you guide students to find topics that are not too general but, at the same time, not too specific?

Know Your Strengths

All imperfection is easier tolerated if served up in small doses.
—Wislawa Szymborska

I'll come clean. I always have to check three words whenever I use them: *receive*, *its*, and *generosity*. No matter how many times I ask someone, flip through the dictionary, or go to Merriam-Webster online, I still have to check the spelling of these three words each time I use them. I know this about myself. I also know that I have a tendency to use a comma splice. Therefore, if my writing will be publicized, I double-check these issues.

Part of helping students edit their writing is helping them know their strengths and weaknesses when it comes to Standard English. When students recognize that they struggle with when to use *there*, *their*, or *they're* or they write run-on sentences, then they can be hyperaware of squelching these potential editing errors. Not only that, they can seek out someone who can help them.

By helping students first define their *strengths* when it comes to editing, we are able to help them build their confidence. Before students will ask for help, they must feel like their writing is suitable for help. If students have low self-confidence about using Standard English, they may be embarrassed to ask for help. Starting with their strengths allows us to expose their imperfections little by little.

By focusing on a few editing flaws, we will avoid seeing students throw up their hands in exasperation. Instead, they will seek out someone who is able to help. Students can be encouraged to seek help in many ways.

First, we can create an "expert center" in our classrooms, with names or pictures of students along with their strengths as writers. For example, if Zach is a strong speller, this could be noted on his chart. Perhaps Samantha is an expert at sketching; this would also be indicated. A place in the classroom that can connect students according to need encourages students to seek out help to strengthen their writing.

Students can also be encouraged to find an editor outside of class. Parents, older siblings, school secretaries, other teachers, and school bus drivers have all acted as outside editors for my students. By prodding students to have someone else read over their writing, we can emphasize the importance of finding another person who is able to become familiar with their writing and help make it more conventional.

I know not only my own struggles in editing but also my brother's issues. I've been proofreading his work since I was in sixth grade. His involve paragraphing and properly punctuating his humorous asides. I know this when I begin proofreading his work; therefore, I'm able to read more efficiently than when I proofread someone else's work. As our students learn their own strengths and imperfections, they will also find people to trust in helping their writing become more conventional. By providing opportunities for students to seek out and find an editor outside of the classroom walls, we give them a resource they can use long after they walk out our classroom doors.

Challenge: Create an opportunity for your students to find an outside editor. Prepare students for this editing conference by having them identify their editing strengths as well as their imperfections to share with their outside editor.

Reflective Practice:

- How will you know whether a student has met with an outside editor?
- What procedures will you establish for a student who is unable to meet with an outside editor? Is there someone in the school you would be able to connect with a student who is unable to have anyone outside of school read his or her work?
- What are your main issues when it comes to editing?

Hey, I'm a Writer!

A desire to be observed, considered, esteemed, praised, be loved and admired by his fellows is one of the earliest as well as the keenest dispositions in the heart of a man.

—John Adams

When ten of my former fifth-grade students published *Deal with It! Powerful Words from Smart, Young Women* in the spring of 2007, they did their own public relations for the book. We had a small budget, thanks to a mini-grant we received, which was used to create full-color press kits about the book. Because of my background in public relations, I was able to teach the young authors how to write press releases, craft cover letters, and pitch the book to editors, producers, bloggers, and bookstore owners over the phone, in person, and through e-mail. Once they successfully garnered three book signings in Manhattan, they created their own posters to advertise the book signings. Proceeds from book sales went to the school's visiting author fund. Why did these girls work so hard when there was no monetary reward in it for them? I think it relates to the notion that John Adams expressed—they wanted other people to listen to their writing, to be affected by what they wrote, and they wanted to be acknowledged for all of the work they contributed in *Deal with It!* What ten-year-old child wouldn't want that?

Regardless of our students' ages or the scope of the writing project, writers want to have their work considered and admired by others. There are many ways young writers can announce that they're writers to their peers, family members, and classmates. Here are a few ways writers can publicize their independent writing:

- **Online invitations:** An electronic invitation is an excellent way to invite others to listen to writing.
- **Twitter:** Writers can update their fan base about their writing progress. A tweet can be disseminated as an announcement once a project is published too.
- **Writing groups:** Each small group of students can get together and share their work in an open-mike format, for which they post or send out invitations.

There are endless possibilities for sharing one's writing with the world. Anything that allows students to say to others, "Hey, I'm a writer!" will empower their voices and thereby lead to a greater love for the writing process.

Challenge: Help any of your students who are engaged in independent writing to find a time to celebrate their hard work, where they can be revered and recognized in a safe environment. Sit down with them and ask them what kind of celebration would excite them. Then, work with your students to coordinate a writing celebration that invites others in to celebrate their writing.

Reflective Practice:

- How did working with your students help you plan a celebration that mattered to all of you?
- Did your students suggest something for the celebration that you thought was strange, but worked? What was it?

Submitting Writing to the Real World

If you want anything to actually change or to move ahead in your life
you actually have to do it yourself, you can't sit there and wait for somebody
or talk about what you want . . . you should actually keep dreams and desires inside
and let them burn a little bit, and then they might come true.
—Russell Crowe

I was probably one of the few high school seniors who didn't cringe at the idea of the college essay. I recall getting excited about the topic of my college essay when I saw an essay question that read, "Tell about a time in your life when you took the initiative." By the age of seventeen, I had taken the initiative on several things in my life, some of which were personal and some of which affected other people's lives in my school community. As an only child, who never had the ability to rope anyone else into things with me, I knew how to make changes and do things because I had one person I could truly rely on: me.

When young writers want to be heard, they have to go out and get published. As much as we'd like our students to take the initiative, oftentimes they're too young or not quite resourceful enough to know where to go to get published. Therefore, as educators, we can provide our students with a list of writing contests and venues that regularly publish student work so that we can help our students move ahead with their writing lives.

Here are some places where students can submit their work:

- **BookHooks:** http://www.bookhooks.com (Book reviews from students of all ages from all over the world can be published on this Web site.)
- **Cricket Contests:** http://www.cricketmagkids.com/ (Special rules usually apply to students younger than the age fourteen.)
- **Kids Are Authors:** http://www.scholastic.com/bookfairs/contest/kaa_about.asp (The contest is open for students in kindergarten through eighth grade.)
- **Merlyn's Pen:** http://www.merlynspen.org/ (This is a site for teenage writers.)
- **New Moon Girls:** http://www.newmoon.com/magazine/ (This magazine is targeted to girls from ages eight through twelve.)
- **Stone Soup:** http://www.stonesoup.com/ (This magazine accepts submissions from writers up to age thirteen.)
- **The MY HERO Project:** http://www.myhero.com (This Web site encourages submissions from young people about their heroes. Students can upload images and video to accompany their writing.)
- **This I Believe:** http://thisibelieve.org/ (Students fourteen and older may submit their work without their parent's or guardian's consent. Students who are thirteen or younger must obtain their parent's consent before submitting their essay.)
- **Writers' Slate:** http://www.writingconference.com/ (This forum is open to students of all ages.)

Regardless of the venue, the most important gift you can give your students is the desire to publish their writing in the world.

Challenge: Seek out any young authors' competitions in your state or local organizations that are sponsoring writing contests. Be sure to read your union paper, teacher magazines, or literary Web sites to check for submission calls, which you can pass along to your students.

Reflective Practice:

- How can you match your students with appropriate real-world publishing opportunities without doing all of the legwork for them?
- What will you do to take the leap and get your own writing published so you can serve as a mentor for your students as they go down the path to publishing their own work?

log project picture teacher text critique student topics questions notebooks challenges interaction writing community process videotape organization organize shares published conventions genre inspiration appropriate sharing student-generated examples author file studies classmates exemplars notebook drafts publish theories books mentors

Chapter 4: Mentors

Mentor texts are the heart of empowering students to explore new possibilities as writers. Dorfman and Cappelli assert, "Mentor texts help writers notice things about an author's work that is not like anything they might have done before, and empower them to try something new" (2007, 3). As students learn to look for the writing possibilities while they read, they also develop the ability to teach themselves to write better. Using mentor texts is bigger than encouraging students to try one new technique as a writer; it's about nurturing students' independence in becoming more proficient writers. As we teach students to study writing, they see firsthand their growth as writers when they apply what they've noticed to become stronger writers.

Some people use the terms *touchstone texts* and *mentor texts* synonymously. However, the distinction is important to point out. "Touchstone texts are books, articles, short stories or poems that you use with your entire class. These are utilized during the demonstration of your minilessons and/or are read alouds that the whole class can draw on. Mentor texts can be used in two different ways. First, a mentor text can be used to lift the level of a child's writing. Second, a mentor text is not always used with an entire class of kids. Sometimes you might use a mentor text with just one or two students" (Shubitz 2009, 24). Throughout the next three cycles, we'll use the term *mentor texts* to mean a text that is used with the entire class, in small groups of students, or in one-to-one conferences.

If you would like to infuse more voices into your writing workshop, then examining a variety of mentor authors is the next step. Here are your options:

- **Cycle 1: Students as Mentors**
  This cycle will encourage you to tap into the power of unlikely mentors—the students who walk the halls of your school daily. Their writing may not be exemplary in every way, but every student has something to offer their classmates' learning.
- **Cycle 2: Teachers as Mentors**
  The focus throughout this cycle is to encourage you to become a teacher-writer who holds his or her writing up during mini-lessons and in conferences. Don't think your writing will be too advanced for your students. Don't fret if your writing isn't wonderful all of the time. Don't worry about these things because your students will respect you for your courage and willingness to share with them.
- **Cycle 3: Published Authors as Mentors**
  There are hundreds of books that line the shelves of our classrooms, many of which can be used to teach students to elevate the level of their writing. In this cycle, we'll help you learn how to pick and use quality mentor texts to teach your students various craft moves. Adopting several published authors' books as mentor texts will invigorate your students' writing and take it to a new place.

Mentor texts empower students to become independent, which is crucial because they will not always have you as their writing teacher. If students develop an understanding of how to tap into the power of mentor texts, they will be able to seek out their own mentors in the future. When they go off into the world, they will be confronted with many types of writing tasks. What a gift we give them when they know how to notice what is striking about an author's writing and develop theories about why an author writes a particular way. Then they are able to translate their observations into sophisticated craft moves on their own. These three cycles encourage you to present a variety of writing to your students to help them become stronger, more independent writers.

Cycle 1: Students as Mentors

A Variety of Sources for Student-Generated Mentor Texts

It takes all sorts to make a world.
—English Proverb

I've noticed in my work with teachers that some of the most difficult texts to come by are student-generated mentor texts. Perhaps this is because we limit ourselves to thinking that student-generated texts must come from our current students.

Although this is a nice source, it's not the only source. Former students are another place to gather student-generated mentor texts. Many times our teaching points are designed to lift students to a higher level as writers. Therefore, our current classrooms may have no students to recommend as mentors. By contrast, we had many students the year before who, at the end of the unit, were capable of executing the teaching point. By collecting and saving former students' work, we create a storehouse of possible student-generated mentor texts to use in our lessons.

Another place to find student-generated mentor texts is from other teachers' students. Talk with colleagues in your grade level or even a higher grade. Often students in the next grade are writing in ways we would like our students to write, which makes them a great source for mentor texts. In professional books, authors share student work. You can share this student work with your class, as long as you document it appropriately.

The best source for student-generated mentor texts, though, is our current students. However, we must develop a habit to have these texts to use. First, be on the lookout for wise writing moves—even moves beyond the scope of the current teaching point or unit. Notice the way students are taking risks in their writing and identify the work they are doing. After you notice these things, take the next step and collect the writing. A simple basket labeled "Copy for a Sample" empowers us to collect these samples. My basket sat near the door so I would see it when I left the classroom. After copying or scanning the works, I placed the student writing in a basket labeled "Return" so students could easily retrieve their work. The last step is to document the teaching point on a sticky note or in a computer document that is placed with the student work. File the work so you can find it later for a mini-lesson.

Using student writing is a powerful way to make our teaching points stick in mini-lessons and conferences. By broadening our search for student-generated mentor texts, we make this rich source more accessible.

Challenge: Talk with your colleagues about the writers in their classrooms. Ask to have a copy of student writing to use in an upcoming lesson. Go through the steps to collect and document the teaching point from this writing.

Reflective Practice:

- What is the easiest part of collecting student writing? Is it identifying possible teaching points? Organizing the texts?
- What is the most difficult part of collecting student writing?

Examples, Not Exemplars!

A good example has twice the value of good advice.
—Unknown

So often we look for perfection. Yet in life, perfection is rare. Sometimes what prevents us from using students' work as mentors is our desire for perfection. By shifting our perception from finding perfection to finding strong examples, many doors will be open for possible student mentors.

- **Look for risk-takers:** In high school, I was in the advanced art program, not because of an abundance of talent but because I worked hard. An important lesson I learned was when we take risks the result may not be perfect, but it is powerful. I learned art was more than a rigid set of rules. I want to give this gift to my students. When they take risks in their writing, the result may not be perfect, but it is often worthwhile. The writing is fresh, unique, and powerful.
- **Look for new structures:** Sometimes our students stumble upon interesting structures by accident. They begin writing compound or complex sentences. They use a repeating line. They attempt a flashback. They write an almost-circular ending. When we notice structures, a new world of possibilities open for gathering student-generated mentor texts.
- **Look for attempts:** After lessons, many students will attempt the teaching point. However, often many of them will not execute it perfectly. They will get close, almost, but not quite. These are excellent sources of mentor texts. When students are able to see this kind of writing, they gain an understanding of the construction of it. They see it developing. When we use this kind of writing as a mentor text, everyone benefits. The author of the text gets advice, and everyone else sees the writing develop.

- **Look past conventions:** Often our students will use sophisticated craft moves, but we miss them because we are hung up on their poor conventions. It is imperative to train ourselves to look past the conventions and into the writing. When I spot a possible mentor text through the haze of poor conventions, I will often type it to use in a lesson or conference. This way the conventions will not inhibit the teaching point. I keep this copy for teaching purposes, while the student continues to work on his or her original copy. At an appropriate time, I will confer with the student about conventions.

By opening ourselves to the possibility of examples, we will find an abundance of student-generated mentor texts. The more we use student-generated mentor texts, the more accessible we make the process of craft to students.

Challenge: Choose one of the preceding bullet points to use intentionally when looking at student writing this week. Select at least three possible student-generated mentor texts to collect for possible teaching points. Collect and file them.

Reflective Practice:

- What is easiest for you when looking for possible student-generated mentor texts?
- What is most difficult for you when looking for possible student-generated mentor texts?

Sharing the Wealth

Variety alone gives joy.
—Matthew Prior

There are many benefits to using student work as a means to clarify the teaching point in mini-lessons and conferences. Students are able to see firsthand the way the writing will look for them because someone with the same experience wrote the example. Writers are able to get an insider's look at the process because the student can speak to how the writing came to be. Students are given a confidence boost when their writing is used to teach other writers. The list of benefits is endless. However, one thing can hinder all of these benefits: sharing work from only a select few.

In any class, one or two students potentially outshine the others. When we first begin looking for student-generated mentor texts, we naturally turn to these students. Yet if we repeatedly use the same students' work, we can nix the benefits. As teachers, we wouldn't intentionally want to set one or two students above everyone else, which is why developing a system of locating and tracking whose work has been used is essential. Here are a few possibilities:

- **Mark on your conferring notes:** Indicate which mentor text is used next to the student's name on your conferring record. Be sure to include the work as well as the reason you used it as a mentor text. By using a large symbol, different color ink, or a highlighter, you can make sure it is easy to find with a quick glance through your conferring record.
- **Make a mentor author note sheet:** By using a three-column chart, you can easily track how each student is able to mentor others. In the first column, write the student's name. The second column shows the teaching point(s) derived from the student's work. The third column lists the text used for the teaching point. You can keep this chart with your lesson plans or with your conferring notes. By creating this sheet at the beginning of the year, and adding everyone's names, you can easily track who you've highlighted as a mentor author.
- **Push yourself to find two or three student examples for your teaching point:** This habit will invariably lead you to new student mentors. As you look past the more experienced writers in your class, others will rise to the surface as possible mentors.
- **Check out the affirmations in your conferring record:** If there are some students you have not used as mentor authors and you are having trouble finding a way to highlight their work, examine your conferring records. As we intentionally give specific encouragement and record these affirmations, we have at our fingertips a list of possible teaching points derived from a specific student.

To ensure using student-generated mentor texts is a positive experience, we must be intentional about sharing the wealth.

Challenge: Develop a system for tracking the student mentors you use in your writing workshop. Make sure your system includes students' names, the titles of their writing, and the reasons behind using it.

Reflective Practice:

- How will you use a system for tracking mentor authors as part of your planning process?
- How will you become more aware of finding students of different writing levels to be mentor authors?

Guest Stars

All my efforts go into creating an art that can be understood by everyone.
—Henri Matisse

Several years ago a Newbery Award–winning author visited my class. I had read her book aloud to my fifth graders, who fired questions at her for more than forty-five minutes. While some of the students asked her about the book we had read, I noticed many of their questions were about what it was like to write the book. They asked questions about how she kept herself motivated while drafting, why she crafted with a particular voice, how she worked with her editor, and what she did to get inspired when she didn't want to write. The author responded patiently to all of the questions, which I believe helped my students synthesize what she was saying so they could learn from her, one writer to another.

Because of this experience, I recognized the power of interacting with authors of mentor texts. While this was the only time a Newbery Award–winning author ever stepped foot into my classroom, I realized I was already surrounded by other authors—my students. If I were going to hold up my students' writing as mentor texts during mini-lessons, then I thought I should also provide them with the time and space to talk to the class about the writerly choices they made. This would give their peers a better understanding of why they wrote in a certain way. After all, a student can talk more knowledgeably about his or her own writing than any interpretation I might offer.

Now, when I project a student-written mentor text onto a screen during a mini-lesson, I've found it's best to have the student sitting close to me. I often introduce the text the student wrote and explain how it relates to the teaching point, but then I step back and let the student take the reins. By stepping away, I allow the students to act as the authors they are, informing their fellow writers about the decisions they made and the process they went through when creating a piece of writing. When the student finishes, I step back in to connect whatever they said to the teaching point so the rest of the class can understand the relationship between the two. Often, instead of doing a traditional active engagement where the students try to mimic what their peer did, I allot that time for questions and answers so students understand how they can learn from their peer and fellow writer.

Handing out a student's writing to the rest of the class and saying "This is good" or "I think you can write like this" seems futile when the author is in the room and can speak for him- or herself. We must tap into the power of the unlikely mentors who fill the seats in our classrooms so they can become likely mentors for their peers.

Challenge: As you confer or read student work at home, look out for writing that will inspire or will lift the level of the rest of your students' writing. Talk with the writer one-on-one and arrange for him or her to "guest star" in an upcoming mini-lesson so the rest of your class can learn a new writing trick or crafting idea from the student that they can apply to their writing. (If you'd like to preserve this student's writing for the future, then consider videotaping the mini-lesson so you can replay the excerpt to future classes.)

Reflective Practice:

- Did the student explain his or her writing and craft techniques to the class in understandable terms?
- How was the question-and-answer session? Did the dialogue help other students model their writing after that of the writer you showcased?
- What's your plan for featuring other students' writing in this forum going forward? How will you make sure that the writing of many students is used as mentor texts?

Topic Choice Mentors

We teachers can only help the work going on, as servants wait upon a master.
—Maria Montessori

The first few weeks of the school year in my fifth-grade class involved using writer's notebooks to help students discover possible writing topics. Students would learn strategies for generating ideas for writing. However, there were always a couple of students who claimed they had nothing to write about and found the strategies I gave them unhelpful. While some of this might have been "testing of the teacher," I had backup, so to speak. By backup, I mean a binder full of my former fifth graders' notebook writing ready to distribute as mentor texts. I had writing from boys and girls. Writing from prolific writers and from writers who struggled. I possessed writing about siblings, holidays, parties, city life, and family getaways. Therefore, any time a student didn't know what to write about, I pulled out a few of my former students' pieces of writing from my trusty binder and distributed them, with the hope that students would be inspired. Fortunately, they always were.

Whether students are freewriting or collecting ideas for a unit of study, it helps to inspire them by showing examples of other students' writing. It may be that students relate to other kids' experiences. It may be that I intentionally distributed texts I thought would resonate with them. Regardless, reading other students' writing inspires young writers to write about a similar topic or a different one.

Although I strongly believe in sharing my own writing with children, I always found there was something powerful about sharing other students' notebook entries. This approach started when I was teaching in East Harlem. I made great efforts to write about city life; however, I was twenty or more years older than my students. I grew up in the suburbs, whereas they were growing up in the city. I grew up as an only child. Many of my students lived with siblings. Therefore, they were more likely to relate to the writing of their peers.

Even if you don't have a cache of writing from past years, you can still collect mentor notebook entries. As students write interesting pieces in their notebooks, have them share their writing with their peers during an end-of-workshop share session. You might encourage students to use another classmate's piece of writing to inspire them to write a new entry. It doesn't have to be on the same topic; rather, the new writing can stem from anything their peer's writing made them think of. Through full-class shares and gentle nudges, new topics will be born in all of your students' notebooks.

Challenge: Look through your present students' notebooks (or your files of past students' notebook writing) and search for interesting notebook entries that might appeal to other students who don't know what to write about. Make fifteen to twenty copies of each entry. Place each entry's photocopies in a plastic sheet protector in a binder so you can pull a copy out and hand it to a student who may need some inspiration.

Reflective Practice:

- How will you familiarize yourself with the notebook entries you save? Will you categorize them by topic, genre, or something else?
- Will there be any types of entries or topics that you will not use as mentor texts?

Civilities of Conversation

Conversation should be pleasant without scurrility, witty without affection,
free without indecency, learned without conceitedness, novel without falsehood.
—William Shakespeare

Anytime we put writing in front of others we take a risk. It's tough to put yourself out there, especially in front of your peers. To drive the stress level over the top, consider what it is like when people start talking about your writing. They have questions, critiques, and hypotheses. Suddenly, you're center stage, agreeing with some of what is being said and disagreeing with other parts. Your stomach knots and you contemplate the best escape plan.

We don't want our students considering escape routes, not to mention we'd like to foster an atmosphere where being a mentor author is a positive experience; therefore, certain civilities of conversation should be introduced to our students.

- **Be courteous:** Unlike mentor texts written by professional writers, often the author of the student-written text is in the room. Therefore, the tone of voice is an important part of our responses to the text. My dad used to tell me: *It's not what you say, but how you say it*. This is a useful mantra to share with our students when using their work as mentor texts.
- **Respond as a reader:** Before delving into a discussion about craft, we should take a few minutes to discuss the writing as readers. How does it move us? How do we connect to the writer? Then we can shift into discussing the work as writers. What do we notice? What do we wonder? What would we like to try?
- **Listen to one another:** An important part of learning from a mentor text is developing a hypothesis about why the writer did something. As this conversation ensues, the student who wrote the text will need to listen as his or her classmates discuss the writing. Later, the writer may offer a response and shed light on the choices he or she made, while everyone else listens.
- **Be humble, not obnoxious:** Writing is a creative process and often people will have different ideas on how to approach it. When a student text is shared, we open the door for response. Sometimes this response comes as a critique. As students learn to navigate these conversations, help them learn tact. By teaching students to ask questions, we invite humility. As the student writer responds, we can continue to scaffold modesty by teaching him or her to acknowledge the other view, and then offer his or her response.

As students become more adept at talking as writers about a mentor text, they will also become stronger in the nuances of conversation. Teaching the civilities of conversations are lessons that will carry our students through many situations in life.

Challenge: Plan to lead students through a conversation about a student-generated mentor text. Decide how you will parallel the writing discussion with advice on how to talk with and about the author of the text.

Reflective Practice:

- How did students respond to the writer?
- What were some of the ways they used civil conversation?

Saving Student Work

Habit is a cable; we weave a thread of it every day, and at last we cannot break it.
—Horace Mann

The fall of 2008 was the fifth time I was teaching a group of students how to write a personal essay using the five-paragraph essay structure. It was also the fifth time I had a classroom of students who needed to learn about the differences between collecting narrative and nonnarrative entries in their notebooks. I had a few of my own to show them, but I realized it would have been more helpful to use former students' nonnarrative notebook entries during the initial stages of the writing process. Midway through the personal essay unit I was teaching, I began borrowing my students' notebooks at lunchtime to make copies of their nonnarrative notebook entries. It would be helpful to have copies of their writing for future classes of students who were attempting to do the same kind of work.

From my first year in the classroom, I intentionally copied students' published pieces so I could show them to future students. By my third year of teaching, I was sure to save all of the drafts that led up to the published writing so I could show other students the progression I expected them to make from one draft to another. However, it wasn't until my fifth year of teaching that I had an epiphany about saving student work throughout all parts of the writing process. By year five, I realized I had to become more intentional about saving student work consistently.

It's not possible to keep track of all students' work at all points in the writing process. Therefore, selecting three to five students you will track during a unit of study (or throughout the entire year) is helpful. Once students have transitioned from their notebooks to drafting paper, you will have the opportunity to duplicate all of their notebook entries. Then, as they go through each step of the writing process, be sure to duplicate their work so that you don't find yourself photocopying for three hours on a Friday afternoon when you want to get home and start your weekend. (Yes, I've been there before!)

It might seem like a lot of work to get in the habit of keeping examples of student work from every part of the writing process. However, once you are able to look at all of a given student's work that led up to the final piece of published writing, ideas for tweaking the unit for the following year will emerge. Most of all, you will have a treasure trove of writing you can pull out any time you teach a particular unit of study that will help you help future students. They will be able to glean ideas about the qualities of good writing from these past writings.

Challenge: Obtain permission from all of your students' parents to make copies of their work for use with future classes of students. Once signed forms are returned, select students whose work you could imagine using to teach other writers. Be careful not to choose only the top writers in your class. We can learn from every student's writing regardless of how skilled they may seem at the beginning of the year.

Reflective Practice:

- In the work you've collected, are certain parts of the writing process easier for you to document than others? What makes that so?
- Which students' work did you decide to keep track of? Why did you decide on these students?

Organizing the Work You Keep

Very simple ideas lie within the reach only of complex minds.
—Rémy de Gourmont

I used to be a paper person. That is, I used to love using the photocopier to duplicate anything and everything I wanted to hold on to. But then, I moved my apartment and my classroom from New York to Rhode Island. Seventy-eight boxes later, I realized I needed to become a digital person because I didn't have room for so much paper in my life!

Regardless of whether you prefer to have hard or electronic copies of documents and items you want to refer to, you need to have a system for filing your students' work so you can use it in the future.

- If you prefer keeping hard copies of your students' writing, then
    - Purchase sheet protectors, section dividers, and a one-inch binder for every unit of study you teach. Label each binder "Personal Narrative Mentor Texts by Former Students," "Persuasive Essay Mentor Texts by Former Students," and so on.
    - Label each section divider with the students' names whose work you're going to collect throughout all parts of the writing process for a given unit of study.
    - Start photocopying student work, placing each notebook entry or draft in its own sheet protector.
    - You might wish to duplicate extra copies of each piece you're photocopying so that you can pass it off to a future student when the need arises.
    - Label each sheet protector's contents with the stage of the writing process that the work represents.

- If you prefer storing your students' writing electronically, then
  - Create a folder on your hard drive called "Student Writing."
  - Create subfolders within the "Student Writing" folder for each unit of study you're teaching.
  - You may choose to divide each subfolder into sections either by students' names or by parts of the writing process.
  - Scan each student's work you are saving. Save it in the appropriate folder and subfolder(s) using a clear file name, which you will be able to identify easily. Example: Personal_Essay-Nurturing_Topic-Nathan-2007 or Personal_Essay-Draft_V1-Nathan-2007
  - Back up the files using Carbonite (http://www.carbonite.com) or a flash drive.

A simple system, such as those in the preceding lists, will make it easier to retrieve your former students' writing when you're preparing for mini-lessons or conferring with students in the years to come.

Challenge: Decide whether you will keep your students' work on paper or electronically. Then take the necessary steps to implement a system that works for you for safeguarding their work.

Reflective Practice:

- What makes you comfortable about the system you've decided to use for organizing student work?
- What obstacles might get in the way of keeping this system tidy?

Talking About Writing with Unlikely Mentors

Isn't it strange that we talk least about the things we think about most?
—Charles A. Lindbergh

Everyone approaches the writing process differently. What works for me, as a writer, might not work for half of the students I'm teaching in a given year. Therefore, I found it was necessary for my students to hear from more than just me when it came to how to carry out the writing process. Knowing it's financially prohibitive to invite authors into school to talk about their writing process in front of students, I often called on unlikely mentors to talk about their writing process—the students.

An end-of-workshop share session is often an excellent opportunity to have students in your class share the process they used to accomplish their work during the independent part of the workshop time. I found these types of share sessions to be exceedingly helpful to students who struggled a lot with drafting and revision. By listening to the way someone else approaches a draft and then asking questions about their process, a young writer is encouraged to either tweak or develop a new writing process for him- or herself.

If you're lucky enough to be teaching the same unit of study at the same time as your grade-level colleagues, then it will afford you with unique opportunities to look at even more student work. Whether you're talking informally after school about a student's interesting approach to the revision process or looking at samples of student work at a grade-level meeting, it is helpful to know what's going on with other students who are doing the same kind of work as your students. There were a few occasions, during the first year I taught fourth grade, that the other fourth-grade teacher and I would have one of our students visit the other's classroom to talk about how the child approached a particular part of the writing process.

It's also helpful for former students to come back to talk about how they approached a writing task once they've moved on to another grade level. One of my most successful days of workshop teaching came in the fall of 2008 when Christian, a former student who transferred to another school, came back to spend the day with me in fourth grade. My students were beginning their personal essay drafts on that day. Rather than teach my mini-lesson as planned, I enlisted Christian to talk a bit about how he had drafted his personal essay so my present class could get two different perspectives about putting their thoughts onto paper. It was fascinating to watch my students using Christian's process, which he honed when he was a student in my class the previous school year, to help them get started with their drafting.

Because it's often difficult to schedule students to come to your classroom to talk about their writing with other students, you might decide to use a digital voice recorder or a video camera to have them create a short "how-to" film about something they did well, which will easily explain their process to other students. If you have students document their process via audio or visual media, then it's easy to have them mentor many other young writers in the years to come.

Challenge: Identify past students or students from other classes who you would like to invite into your classroom to discuss their writing process with your students. Similarly, schedule some time for your students to talk about their writing process with their peers.

Reflective Practice:

- What did your students learn by listening to another young writer talk about his or her writing process? How do you think it helped to get another student's perspective?
- Did you glean anything from the student(s) who shared that you can incorporate into your full-class teaching?

Inspiration Shares

To succeed you need to find something to hold on to,
something to motivate you, something to inspire you.
—Tony Dorsett

"I was inspired by Ashley because of the way she used a repeating line."

"I was inspired by the way Ben revised his action verbs."

"I was inspired to write a flashback like Cosme."

An inspiration share is a great way to close a writing workshop. Students share how someone inspired them in their writing. Often the inspiration comes from a fellow writer in the classroom.

A few days notice is a very good thing when it comes to this kind of share. This way, students are able to consider how they are inspired by other writers, especially the writers they work alongside every day.

An inspiration share can be structured in many ways. Here are a few possibilities:

- **A whip share:** Highlight the inspiration students have found. They simply sit in a circle and each student begins with the phrase, "I was inspired by . . . because . . ."
- **An author's chair:** Students share their inspiration and then read their work aloud to highlight the way they put the inspiration into practice.
- **A two-part share:** A student goes to the source of inspiration before share time. Then the partnership shares together. The inspiration piece is read first, followed by an explanation on how it inspired the second writer. Then the second piece is read.

As students are highlighted in mini-lessons and conferences, it is natural to expect them to inspire other writers in the classroom. An inspiration share is one way to strengthen the community of writers in our classrooms.

Challenge: Plan an inspiration share for an upcoming writing workshop. Spend a few minutes in the days leading up to the inspiration share demonstrating ways students inspire you. Be specific, looking for inspiration in processes, ideas, and craft.

Reflective Practice:

- Did the way you modeled finding inspiration from your students influence the way they shared?
- Did the inspiration share increase the energy for writing among your community? Why or why not?

Finding Time to Write

Don't say you don't have enough time. You have exactly the same number of hours per day that were given to Helen Keller, Pasteur, Michelangelo, Mother Teresa, Leonardo da Vinci, Thomas Jefferson, and Albert Einstein.
—H. Jackson Brown, Jr.

Once someone asked me, "How do you balance it all?"

This question always makes me smile sheepishly. I give my standard response, "I don't." As a wife, a mother to three young children, and a full-time educator who drives more than seventy-five miles each day, my plate is full, not to mention all of the other roles and commitments I fulfill.

I'm not the only one who feels this way. We don't have to be juggling a trillion different projects and roles to feel overwhelmed. Yet the choices we make every day determine our ability to enjoy life and get the most out of each day.

Being a genuine writer makes our teaching of writing more effective. As art teachers are artists, writing teachers must be writers. This means writing more than a grocery list or a quick note to a parent.

I'm not suggesting we all set out on epic writing adventures. We don't need to write the next Great American Novel. However, we do need to be writing enough to understand the intricacies of the work we are asking our students to do. At the very least, we should be writing what we ask of our students.

If we are not active writers, how are we able to help students become efficient in their own writing processes? Sure, we can show them the beautiful words of published authors, but who is going to show them the process? Who will show them the act of collecting snippets of life, rereading notebook entries, and selecting the gem that will propel you into a draft? Who will show them the process of planning? Who will show them the act of revision? Who will model the possibilities of punctuation? Who will encourage them to keep going when the stumbling blocks come?

Who has the time to write with all of the other schoolwork I have to do?

We have the time. It boils down to choosing to write over spending ten minutes doing something else. Think about the moments that make up your day. When can you steal ten minutes to put words on the page? Perhaps by slipping out of the teachers' lounge ten minutes before lunch ends. Instead of chatting in the copy room before school, maybe you could sit in your classroom and write. For me, it involves giving up a little bit of TV. Yes, we are busy. We also make choices on how to spend our time, and a few minutes of that time can go to writing.

I find time to write because I value the insight I gain as a writer. It feels good to have filled a page in my writer's notebook. I like the feeling of coming back to something I'd forgotten I'd written, especially when the writing is powerful, and thinking, *Wow, I wrote that!* Mostly, though, I love the way writing provides me the chance to reflect on this wonderful, ordinary, perfectly imperfect life I'm living. That is a gift reserved for writing teachers who have chosen to live a sliver of their lives as writers.

Challenge: Write every day for one week. Record the time on your planner. Spend time considering the most convenient time for you to write. Make a plan to continue writing on a regular basis.

Reflective Practice:

- What will be most difficult about writing regularly?
- What were some of the benefits of writing every day?

Create Your Own Writer's Notebook

Stories have power. They delight, enchant, touch, teach, recall, inspire, motivate, challenge. They help us understand.

—Janet Litherland

Before I read a single professional book about writing workshop, I attended a weeklong training session about teaching writing. I was inspired to start a writer's notebook. I stopped at the store on the way home after the first day of the training and picked up a composition notebook. That evening, surrounded by every old magazine in the house, I began collecting pictures that represented my life. I rifled through a junk drawer in my computer desk and found things that should have been thrown away, but weren't: a scorecard from beating my husband at mini-golf; some old photos; a funny quote. That evening of collecting, cutting, and reflecting would change my life. I became a collector of stories, a documenter of life.

When I train teachers new to writing workshop, their first task is to gather a few artifacts from their lives and stick them in a book to create a writer's notebook. I receive more comments on this little task than anything else during the weeklong training. "I knew I would learn strategies for teaching writing, but little did I know I would become a writer myself," one participant commented.

Creating your own writer's notebook is transformational because it gives the stories of our lives power. We see how the lives we have lived make us who we are today. We see the way we make a difference over time. We become better writing teachers. We are transformed into people who understand the life of a writer, because we are engaged in living as writers. We are on the lookout for the stories that make up our lives.

This is possible because we have created a space, a writer's notebook, to fill with bits of life. If we are not intentional about documenting the moments of our lives, time will slip past, and we will be left wondering where it all went. We will have missed the chance to reflect on life.

The heart of a writer is reflection. As writing teachers, it is our duty to develop this mind-set. I soon found a single writer's notebook wasn't enough for me. I developed one for documenting my teaching life, another for remembering my past, another for collecting the day-to-day living I was asking students to do. With the birth of my son, I wanted a writer's notebook that would make it easy to share stories, thoughts, photos, and bits of life with family and friends. So I began an online writer's notebook using a blog.

Because I don't want the whole world privy to my photos and stories, I keep my blog private. Through invitations, I can control who is able to view this online writer's notebook. As the author of the blog, I can keep some posts private, which no one else can see. This gives me the freedom to write the stories that need to be written but don't need to be shared. My blog holds me accountable for writing regularly. People will comment if I don't post, plus my archive keeps track of my monthly posts. I've come to appreciate this different media for a writer's notebook.

There are many ways to carve out a space for a writer's notebook to document our lives. Living with the intention to collect moments from our lives today and yesterday makes us better writing teachers. More important, it makes us better people. We become the kind of people who realize the small moments in our ordinary lives add up to big meaning.

Challenge: Make a space to collect bits of your life. Consider what kind of space makes the most sense to you. Are you online regularly? Then check out some of the free blog options. Do you love your handwriting? Perhaps a notebook and a favorite pen is the choice for you. Make your space personal—collect images, words, and photos that describe you. If you already have a writer's notebook, spend time personalizing it to represent your life right now.

Reflective Practice:

- How will you carve out time to use your writer's notebook on a regular basis?
- What encourages you to write in your writer's notebook? What hinders you from writing?

Sharing Our Stories

If stories come to you, care for them. And learn to give them away where they are needed. Sometimes a person needs a story more than food to stay alive.
—Barry Lopez

As we act as writing mentors for our students, it is inevitable that our stories will surface. A bit of forethought is important when determining what stories to share with our students.

My go-to source of stories is from the time when I was the age of the students I am working with. This kind of story is powerful because it allows students to relate to me in a different way. When I tell a story from my childhood, I give a glimpse of myself before I was grown up. I also show students ordinary moments are viable options for stories. I write about playing kickball at recess, catching frogs in the creek, and riding my bike.

Since we are not only mentors for writing but also mentors in life, it is important that the stories we share are appropriate. This is another plus for sharing my childhood stories—they are appropriate and students can relate to them. Although we may be excited about the birth of a child, an upcoming promotion for our spouse, or a romantic getaway, our students won't be quite as excited to hear these tales. The point of sharing our stories with students is to lift the level of their writing, not for our personal enjoyment of sharing big news.

The other key source for stories is from my own children and pets. They are a lively crew, and I'm never short on stories about everyday life. Building snowmen, cooking dinner, and working on a frustrating homework assignment are all worthy stories to tell. These kinds of stories shine a light on family life and help students open their eyes to the daily stories living in their homes too.

As writing mentors, one of our roles is to inspire story ideas for our students. Often the hardest part of writing is starting. When we share stories from our lives we model possibilities for finding story ideas; more important, we make personal connections to our students, strengthening the community of writers.

Challenge: Make a list in your writer's notebook of possible stories you could share with your students. Consider stories from your childhood, as well as current stories, all with the intent of connecting with your students.

Reflective Practice:

- What are some of your students' interests? Do you have stories that relate to these?
- How will you determine whether a story is appropriate to share with your students?

Write in Front of Your Students

There are lots of people who give their all and have that inner glow on.
It's a shame that the majority of them are under seven years old.
—Esa Saarinen

The time I need the most courage in writing workshop is when I write off the cuff in front of students. The first time I planned to do this, I practiced three or four times in my writer's notebook. I knew this wasn't as genuine as I would have liked it to be, but it was all I had the courage to do.

Today, years later, I'm able to write impromptu in front of students. It still takes courage, and my throat catches as I'm filled with nerves to compose in front of students. However, I also know the benefits of writing in front of students.

First, they get to see first-draft writing unfold. Typically, the kind of writing our students see is polished, published, professional writing. To show students how I unfold a draft bit by bit is a lesson that sticks with them. Sometimes I talk through the choices I'm making, narrating the thoughts in my head as I draft. Other times I simply write, and at the end, I ask them what they notice. Inevitably, they notice the ebb and flow of the rate in which I write. They notice I write quickly and then slow down and select specific words. They notice the extreme amount of rereading I do. I explain my process to them; sharing how I'm the kind of writer who drafts a little, rereads, revises, rereads, drafts some more, rereads. I do this not because I expect them to write just like me, but so they see the intentional way I draft.

Writing a first draft isn't the only kind of writing we can do in front of our students. Revising and editing are important for students to see unfold. When they see another writer working through these stages of the writing process, they are able to gain a vision for what it could be like in their own work. Writing in front of students empowers them to personalize the writing process so it is most efficient for them.

When we write in front of our students, we should give it our all, allowing the joy of being a writer to become evident. Although writing is hard work, it is also fun to mold words. Our students may miss this truth if we don't model the act of writing for them.

Challenge: Make a plan to model writing in front of your students in an upcoming lesson. Be intentional about doing your best as a writer.

Reflective Practice:

- What did your students learn about being a writer from watching you write in front of them?

- What will be the next thing you will write in front of your students? What will be valuable for your students through the next demonstration?

Be the Kind of Writer You Want Your Students to Be

If you are not a writer, you will not understand the difficulties of writing.
If you are not a writer, you will not know the fears and hopes of the writers you teach.
—Mem Fox

If I wasn't a teacher who writes, then I wouldn't understand what kinds of things would get in the way of writing daily. If I wasn't a writer, then I wouldn't understand the fear one has when putting the pen to the page when the brain feels empty and devoid of anything meaningful to write. But I am a writer, so I do know what these things feel like, which is why I've enjoyed teaching writing workshop more than some of my other colleagues who are not writers.

My students rolled their eyes and raised their eyebrows at me in September 2004 when I told them I was going to publish a personal narrative on the same day they did. They seemed skeptical that I was going to do the same work as they were. However, every night, as I prepared for the next day's mini-lesson, I made sure to try out my teaching point on my own piece of writing. This way, I knew what kinds of things I could expect my students to struggle with, because I, inevitably, would share some of their struggles.

I published a new piece of writing nearly every month when I was a classroom teacher. By going through the writing process at essentially the same time as my students, my mini-lessons and conferences became more authentic because I was engrossed with the same kind of writing work they were. I wasn't just telling my students how to write in a particular way. I was showing them how to write. Show, not tell. We say this to our students constantly when we're teaching narrative writing. It applies to our instruction too. We should show, not tell, our students how to become better writers through leading by example.

Challenge: Find time to write regularly when your students are watching. This could be during the first five minutes of writing workshop or during a separate time in the school day that's solely devoted to independent writing. Regardless of when you schedule it, be sure to drop everything and write.

Reflective Practice:

- What is standing in the way of your writing with your students regularly?
- How will you make sure you drop everything and write?

Process Logs

Everything has been thought of before, but the problem is to think of it again.
—Goethe

When I took Lucy Calkins's graduate course, The Teaching of Writing, I was required to publish two pieces of writing. While Calkins advised us to write pieces we could envision using as mentor texts with our students, she put a couple of stipulations on each writing assignment. First, we had to go through several drafts for each piece of writing. She insisted that our final draft look markedly different from our first draft. Second, Calkins asked us to keep a detailed process log as we went through the writing process. Other than these two requirements, we had a lot of freedom regarding the narratives and memoirs we produced for her class.

A process log is a chronicle of the actions one takes as a writer as one goes through the writing process for a particular piece of writing. It's a document organized in chronological order that details thoughts after finishing the writing for the day. A process log allows writers to reflect on the decisions they make as they go through the writing process and serves as a written record of the steps they took to write a piece, which hopefully will aid in a greater understanding of themselves as a writer.

At first, I found keeping a detailed process log tedious. What did it really matter what I was thinking about my writing at a given time? When it was time to teach a unit of study on memoir, after writing my own process log, I was more insightful when I conferred with my students. Because I could refer to the thoughts I was having at each step of the memoir-writing process, I was able to relate to my students' struggles and was able to coach them through whatever problems they were encountering. *I had walked along the same road they were walking on*. There were even a couple of times when I pulled out my process log (Figure 4.1), which had dates attached to it, so my students could read with me the concepts I struggled with as I revised. They gained a better understanding of how I overcame the challenge, which in turn inspired them.

Process logs have been exceedingly helpful to me in two ways. First, process logs have been useful when I write in a new genre. Genres we haven't attempted before can feel tricky. Therefore, recording my process has helped me make sense of new genres and feel more at ease with them. Second, when I'm aiming to make my teaching more transparent so my students can understand how I went through the motions of a writer, a process log is useful because it records my thinking about my writing along the way. Because of process logs, I am better able to tackle new genres and teach my students about the writing process.

Here are some excerpts from the process log I kept while writing a memoir about my mother for Calkins's course:

Tuesday, October 31, 2006

I decided to accept the challenge to write about my mother. I'm in the process of using several of the strategies described in Memoir: The Art of Writing Well *to help me with this undertaking. I taught this unit last year and found that my dad was my life topic. However, I felt as though I really haven't written anything about my mom. She has worked tirelessly throughout her life to be an incredible mother to me. The least that I can do is to pay homage to her in my writing, right?*

I used several strategies, such as reflective questioning and prompts to help me figure out what I want to say about my mom. This is really hard. My dad is so much easier for me to write about. Why is it that I decided to pick such a tough subject, my mom, which should be easy for me?

I brainstormed a list of small moments with my mom that I think I can write about. Then, this evening, I drafted something about my mom.

Sunday, November 5, 2006

I revised my memoir today. I didn't actually add much that was new, but I took out extraneous things that I felt were taking away from my writing about my mom.

I need to read some memoirs so that I can learn from some mentor authors so that I can lift the level of my own writing.

Tuesday, November 28, 2006

I conferred with Heidi Hultgren and Diana Bobrow before class this afternoon. I find that I might be back to square one as a result of our conversation. While helpful, I am beginning to realize that writing a memoir on my mom is proving to be one of the greatest challenges of this semester. This is not easy work since I've been trying to find the right words and right stories that will showcase the wonderful woman who raised me. However, Heidi and Diana both felt as though my memoir was fragmented. For instance, they asked me what the big idea was of the story with the traction control. I told them I really didn't know. There's nothing that's really holding the entire piece of writing together.

Figure 4.1 (part 1 of 3)
My Memoir Process Log, Fall 2006

I went back to the first draft of my memoir when I met with them (after they asked me what the really important things were that I wanted to show). Diana asked me what the big idea was again and this time, when I read draft one to them, I said "sacrifice." I feel that my mom gave up her career to raise me. I also told them that she still comes to school and chaperones my class field trips, the kids call her Mommy Shubitz, etc. Then, Diana raised a really good point. She said, "Maybe your mother doesn't look at what she's done as a sacrifice. She continues to do this stuff for you and has no reason to. You're all grown and out of the house, but she still continues to be there for you."

Diana's comment really got me thinking. I know that I have problems with my back and neck, which is why she comes to New York City sometimes to take me to medical appointments and helps me set up my classroom. Even though I had a chaperone problem in years past, she came in more than necessary to help me out. She didn't do a halfhearted job of chaperoning, she put her all into it, breaking up a fight and even running after one of the kids up the stairs when she felt he was going too fast.

As I told these stories to Heidi and Diana, I realized that mom's sacrifice, though she might not view what she's been doing as a sacrifice, is really the topic of my memoir. Therefore, Heidi suggested that I pose some questions in the actual memoir to help me reflect more on my mom through my words. She advised me to "come to it as the reader." Finally, Heidi suggested that perhaps the narrative structure or the exposition-narrative-exposition-narrative-exposition structure might not actually be working for me. Heidi suggested that I structure my memoir as an essay with a good deal of reflection. I think I'm going to try that and see where it gets me.

Sunday, December 3, 2006

Marc just read the fourth draft of my memoir. These were his comments, questions, and concerns:

- *Do the first and last memories really connect? Are they parallel? Perhaps start out with dialogue, with talking to her about going on a trip.*
- *The writing in the beginning is fine, although it's not parallel.*
- *Didn't understand the term of "fadeless paper."*
    - *My thought: Maybe it's because Marc is a physician, not a teacher.*
- *Paragraph 3: Talking about her job. Needs more of a connecting sentence.*

Figure 4.1 (part 2 of 3)
My Memoir Process Log, Fall 2006

- *Paragraph 4: The second sentence about her wakeup call doesn't sound good. Rephrase. "During the fall of 1982 . . ." might sound better.*
- *Don't need to say when she started classes because you talk about it more later.*
- *On page 2, first paragraph: Something about the first sentence that is awkward. Don't need the phrase "so she took it."*
- *Put the word schlepping in quotes or define it.*
  - *Will your audience understand this term?*
  - *Perhaps I should do it à la Rosie Perez in* "Josie's First Allowance Day."
- *The last sentence of that paragraph should be made into two sentences. (About parents sacrificing many nights . . .)*
- *The rest is really good on that page until the last paragraph on page 2 where you talk about being fully grown and not being her problem anymore. The next sentence on page 3 is repetitive. Therefore, take out last sentence on page 2 and leave it as, "She has no obligation to do so."*
  - *Instead say, "Today, my mother plays an active role in my career even though I'm fully grown and out of the house."*
- *Liked the description/narrative of the farmer's market. Keep that. Maybe change the introductory narrative.*
  - *Might be nice to connect those two stories.*
  - *My thoughts: Want the ending to be circular. Think about parallel structure.*

* * * * * * *

I did it. I changed the story to a different one at the beginning and used Marc's comments. I'm finally happy with what I produced. I believe I have a circular ending, which Zinsser suggests. He states on page 65 of his book, "Something I often do in my writing is to bring the story full circle—to strike at the end an echo of a note that was sounded at the beginning." I believe I did that with my new lead.

I'm really proud of myself. I think the process of writing a memoir about my mom was really difficult. However, I persevered and now I have a piece of writing that I would be proud to show my mother, and the world.

Figure 4.1 (part 3 of 3)
My Memoir Process Log, Fall 2006

Challenge: Be intentional about keeping a process log for your next piece of writing. Write down what's easy, what's hard, and what you do for inspiration when you don't want to write. Also, be sure to log any professional reading or mentor texts you consult so you can refer to them in the future.

Reflective Practice:

- What made logging your process, after each time you wrote, exhausting or enjoyable?
- How do you envision using a process log as a teaching tool?

Organizing Teacher-Written Mentor Texts

Wisdom comes from experience. Experience is often a result of lack of wisdom.
—Terry Pratchett

After crafting a new piece of writing with nearly every unit of study I've taught, I have quite a few of my own mentor texts on hand, which I can pull up and share with a student in a one-to-one conference at a moment's notice. I can pull something up at a moment's notice because of a big filing cabinet and an electronic filing system.

Once you decide whether you want to keep hard copies or electronic copies (or both) of your work, here's how you can get organized:

- If you prefer keeping hard copies of your writing, then
    - Section off a part of your classroom's filing cabinet for teacher-written mentor texts. Purchase hanging file folders and manila folders. Use the paper tabs and plastic holders to label each hanging file folder with the genres you teach, such as "Small Moment Stories," "Short Fiction," etc. Label each manila folder with the title of each piece of writing you've done. Place the manila folders in the appropriate hanging file folder.
    - Photocopy each piece of writing several times so you have plenty of copies on hand when you wish to hand it out to a student.
    - Include the process log you kept for each piece of writing inside of the same manila folder.
- If you prefer storing your writing electronically, then
    - Create a folder on your hard drive called "Teacher-Written Mentor Texts."
    - Create subfolders within the "Teacher-Written Mentor Texts" folder for each unit of study you teach.
    - You may choose to divide each subfolder into sections by the title of each piece of writing you've completed.

- Save each piece of writing in the appropriate unit of study's folder.
- Save process logs in the same folder as well.
- Back up the files using Carbonite (http://www.carbonite.com/) or a flash drive.

Having an easily accessible filing system is a wise teaching move because it allows you to be ready to share your writing with a student whenever the need arises.

Challenge: Implement a filing system for your writing that suits your personality.

Reflective Practice:

- If you have multiple mentor texts per genre, how will you decide which piece to pull out and when?
- If you decided to go paperless, then how will you share your work with students in a conference? Will you print it off as needed, post it on an online classroom blackboard, or do something else?

Become Part of a Writing Community

The difference between getting somewhere and nowhere is the courage to make an early start. The fellow who sits still and does just what he is told will never be told to do big things.

—Charles Schwab

The Capital Area Writing Project (CAWP), which is my local National Writing Project site, hosts a "Teachers as Writers" group at a café on the second Saturday of each month. "Teachers as Writers is organized around the belief, supported by the National Writing Project, that teachers of writing are more effective when they spend time writing themselves" (Capital Area Writing Project 2009). In early 2010, I brought a piece of fiction writing I was working on to get feedback from other teacher-writers. It was a pleasure to gather as part of a community and talk about my in-progress writing with other adults. It helped me to move forward with my writing project.

Being part of a writing community will help you connect with other writers. It will inspire you to do your writing because it will give you an avenue to receive feedback about your writing work. Further, becoming part of a writing community allows you to engage in a writing workshop, similar to the one you lead for your students, on an adult level.

There are multiple ways you can become part of a writing community:

- Find out when and where the National Writing Project's local affiliate meets by going online to http://www.nwp.org/cs/public/print/doc/findasite/home.csp.
- Look for a Meetup Group, http://www.meetup.com/find/, near you that focuses on writing. A Meetup Group is a group of people who come together around a common interest. In many metropolitan areas, you can find a Meetup Group by the genre of writing in which you want to focus (e.g., business writing, screenplays, mystery).
- Form a writing circle with other staff members at your school.
- Become part of a virtual writing community by joining an online writing challenge. We host a Slice of Life Story Challenge every Tuesday at Two Writing Teachers, http://twowritingteachers.wordpress.com/challenges/, which encourages participants to chronicle an ordinary moment of their life in detail. Other writing challenges we've participated in are
    - Day in a Sentence: http://dogtrax.edublogs.org
    - Not Me Monday: http://www.mycharmingkids.net
    - Photo Fridays: http://flickr.com/groups/photofridays/
    - Poetry Friday: http://kidslitinformation.blogspot.com

Regardless of the type of writing community you join, becoming part of one will connect you to other writers in ways that will noticeably help to strengthen your writing quickly.

Challenge: Find a local writing community or become a regular participant in an online writing challenge.

Reflective Practice:

- What do you hope to get out of being part of a writing community? How can you become the kind of member who will encourage other members to grow as writers?
- What have you learned about yourself as a writer since you became a part of a writing community?

Publish Alongside Your Students

Achievement is largely the product of steadily raising one's level of aspiration . . . and expectations.
—Jack Nicklaus

Some of my proudest moments in the classroom have been when I have published my finished product on the same day as my students. I have always felt a strong sense of pride to be able to share my writing with my students at the publishing party (usually I would share it before or after our guests attended). Showing my final project to my students, which they heard about in many of my lessons, allowed them to see that I was willing to follow something through to the end.

There were a few occasions when I made my writing a part of the celebration. I would publish it in the same kind of manila folder, with all of my drafts stapled behind my published piece of writing, as my students did. I decorated the cover of my manila folder to resemble my students' folders. Then, when guests and visitors came into the room to listen to my students' pieces, I shared my piece too, reading it aloud to a few people and getting their feedback. Having this experience allowed me to share the joy my students felt when they read their writing aloud to a visitor.

We cannot go back and relive our childhoods, hanging off of monkey bars and playing tag at recess. However, as educators, we can enjoy some of the things our students experience. We can publish and celebrate our work alongside our students. When we aspire to make this a consistent goal, we strengthen the teacher-student relationship in the writing workshop.

Challenge: With your students, decide how you will share your writing at the next publishing celebration. Determine whether you will read aloud to them in the meeting area and elicit their feedback when you're finished sharing, or whether you will read it when they're sharing their pieces with invited guests.

Reflective Practice:

- How did your students react to your published writing?
- When did you share your writing with your students? Will you share in the same way next time or will you do something differently?

Put Your Writing Out in the World

I went for years not finishing anything. Because, of course,
when you finish something you can be judged . . . I had poems which were re-written
so many times I suspect it was just a way of avoiding sending them out.
—Erica Jong

As an advocate for doing what we ask of our students, I believe in teachers putting their writing out in the world. Since we ask students to share their writing beyond our classroom walls, it is only fair that we do the same. The following are a few ways our writing can make it out of our classrooms:

- **Write a letter to the editor:** When an issue arises that you feel strongly about, write an editorial to submit to a local newspaper. This not only makes your voice heard but also models for students how to be an active citizen.
- **Help with a newsletter:** Consider some of the groups you are associated with: professional organizations, religious groups, and political advocacies. These organizations often use newsletters to communicate. Volunteer to write an article to include in this publication.
- **Submit to magazines or journals:** If you have a favorite magazine or journal, check out the call for articles. These are often posted in the front of the magazine or online. There are many e-zines (online magazines) that have calls for articles, as well as most professional journals. National Public Radio's *This I Believe* series is another avenue to publish writing.
- **Participate in online writing challenges:** There are many online challenges in a variety of genres. A quick Google search will give you plenty of options.
- **Make an addition to your parent newsletter:** Attaching a poem, personal narrative, or another piece of writing to the newsletter you send home with your students provides an instant audience. This gives parents an opportunity to get to know you personally.
- **Start a blog:** Blogging not only forces you to share your writing with a larger audience but also is a great means of communication. You could start a blog to communicate with the students' parents, other educators, or your family members.

Regardless of the means you use to publish your writing with an audience beyond your classroom, share your experience with your students. Tell them how you feel before putting your writing out in the world, and how you feel once it's happened. Celebrate the joy that comes from finishing and sharing writing with others. Then give your students the same opportunity.

Challenge: Make a plan to share your writing beyond your classroom walls. Decide who your audience will be and take steps to get your work published.

Reflective Practice:

- What is the most difficult about sharing your writing with a larger audience?
- How do you plan to share this experience with students?

Cycle 3:
Published Authors as Mentors

Selecting Meaningful Mentor Texts

It is not peace we seek but meaning.
—Lawrence Durrell

The success of our classroom read-alouds depends on enthusiasm. If I introduced a book enthusiastically, then most of the time, my entire class loved the book. Because enthusiasm really is contagious, I played up the books I wanted to share with my students as if they were up for an Academy Award.

When you're introducing a book that you plan to refer to again and again, try the following to "sell" the book:

- Tell students up front that the book you're about to read is one they're going to see again. By the third week of school, my students usually trusted me to select books they liked. Therefore, that was usually enough to get them to listen with an open mind, even if they weren't crazy about the book's cover.
- Hook students before you read the text by giving them a preview of the book. I'm not talking about reading the blurb; I'm talking about providing them with a personal summary of the book that will get them interested so they pay close attention.
- Provide students with time to react and respond to the book as readers. This can take place in partner talks, in small-group discussions, in full-class discussions, or in their reader response notebooks.
- Tell students that the book possesses several qualities of good writing. You might want to tell them what to look out for or just make a blanket statement so they can turn and talk with a partner about what they're noticing the author did as a writer.
- Think aloud while reading. This is probably something you already do, but planned think-alouds focused on craft can help students see the greater value of the book (i.e., more than it just being an interesting story).
- Provide time, at the end of the read-aloud, to have students reflect on how they could use the text as a mentor. You might have them do this in writing or by turning and talking to a partner about it.

While students in my classroom were always free to dislike a book I used as a mentor text, it was important that they understood they could learn to write better from any text. I fondly recall introducing a picture book that I was excited about to my fourth graders. One student vehemently despised the ending of the story. While I didn't agree with her about the ending being "all wrong," I asked her, "Is there anything that you learned about writing from this text that you could apply to your own writing?"

She thought about it for a moment and said, "Well, I did like the way the author used dialogue. It made the characters feel like they were real kids talking to each other—even if the ending *was* stupid."

"So how will that help you as a writer?" I asked.

"Well, I *suppose* I could come back to this book again if I wanted to make the dialogue in my stories seem real. Actually, I *should* come back to it since the dialogue I write usually doesn't do much to make my characters feel like they're real people. Maybe this book could help me make them sound more real."

"Yes," I said. "I suppose this book might be able to help you with that."

Challenge: Talk with colleagues about books they've used successfully as mentor texts. Or scour the Kidlitosphere, which are book-related blogs authored by adults who work with children, for books you can introduce to your students for the purpose of teaching them to become better writers.

Reflective Practice:

- Did you discover any new authors whose work you really admire on your hunt for mentor texts?
- What makes a book appealing both as a text to read aloud and as a text to study for the qualities of good writing?

Shopping for Ideas

In brief, I spend half my time trying to learn the secrets of other writers—
to apply them to the expression of my own thoughts.
—Shirley Ann Grau

I sat on the floor beside Jami for a conference and glanced at her poem. It read:

Colton Colin Coil Calloon
Would never ever
Clean his room.
The more his parents
Would yell and holler,
The more he wouldn't
Even let it bother.

"Tell me about your poem," I said.

Jami shuffled a few papers and produced a sheet of poems we'd been studying. "I decided to try to write it like Shel Silverstein's 'Sarah Cynthia Sylvia Stout Would Not Take the Garbage Out,'" she said.

"How's that?" I asked, settling against the wall.

"I liked the rhythm he has, so I wanted to try it too. I didn't want to write a poem about garbage, though, but I still wanted something messy. So I thought of a little boy and his room." She looked at me, and I nodded. Then she continued, "I started with a name. I thought if I could get a name like Sarah Cynthia Sylvia Stout, then it would drive my rhythm."

Jami fully embraced Shel Silverstein as a mentor. She wasn't using his poem as a model for one, small craft move; instead, she was consumed with his poem. She knew it inside out and had read it hundreds of times. When she was ready to move on as a poet, she turned to her mentor text and asked herself: *What is Shel doing that I can do too?* As we use mentor texts, it's important to teach students how *to shop for ideas about writing well* in their mentor texts. Students may consider using the mentor text for

- **Finding a writing idea:** What writing ideas does the text trigger? What are you reminded of in your own life?
- **Envisioning structure:** How is the mentor text structured? How might you structure your writing based on the text?
- **Crafting the words:** What parts of the text stand out to you as a reader? What did the author do to make these parts strong? How did the author write the lead or the ending? What did the author do that you would like to try in your writing?
- **Using conventions:** What do you notice about the way the author used punctuation? Are there any special punctuation marks you would like to use in your writing?

A mentor text supports writers throughout their writing process. By teaching students to delve deeply into a single text, they learn the power of a mentor text.

Challenge: Using a mentor text, make a list of all the possible ways it could act as a mentor. Consider all parts of the writing process when making your list. Keep this list handy when conferring or planning lessons so you are able to model for students the power of using a mentor text throughout the writing process.

Reflective Practice:

- What are your students' attitudes about using a mentor text? What makes them willing to turn to the mentor text for help?
- Do your students view the mentor text as a support throughout the writing process? Why or why not?

Creating Theories About Why Authors Write Like They Do

> There will always be a few texts that evoke particularly strong responses within the classroom, and these become our touchstone texts, the texts we examine and re-examine, talk about, and admire and learn from. Our students read and evaluate, muse over and analyze, learn from and model themselves after texts that are like those they will write.
>
> ***—Lucy Calkins***

Nicholas Sparks has been my favorite author ever since I read *The Notebook* in one sitting in 1996, with tears streaming down my face. Sparks's books always evoke strong reactions for me when I read them. I leave each of his novels changed as a person. And, for the past couple of years, I leave each of Sparks's books wondering, "How can I get myself to write like him?" Admittedly, I've visited Sparks's Web sites to review the "Notes for Writing the Book" section to get more information about how and why Sparks chose to write in particular ways. However, this is often not enough to help me figure out how to write the next Great American Novel. While a week of picking Nicholas Sparks's brain might help, I know that's not going to happen. Therefore, I must develop hunches about why Sparks writes the way he does so I can figure out how to transfer what he does as a writer into my own writing.

Just as I have to think about how I can model myself after Nicholas Sparks if I want to write emotional works of fiction, I encourage the writers I teach how to make reading-writing connections with the texts they encounter. Young writers can be taught how to develop hunches, or theories, about what they notice writers doing in texts. Teaching students how to develop oral and written theories helps them make reading-writing connections. When students read with the intention to improve their writing, we can encourage them to notice what an author is doing as a writer and to develop ideas about why an author chooses to write in a particular way, and then we can help students figure out ways to transfer the craft they've noticed and thought about into their own writing.

Emily Smith (2009), a staff developer at the Teachers College Reading and Writing Project, has done a great deal of work in the area of mentor texts. She suggests having students talk about texts to support reading-writing connections. To foster the progression of talk around texts, Smith uses conversational prompts to help students talk about their noticings, their hunches, and their connections.

To initiate conversations about texts, students can use some of the following prompts:

- I notice . . .
- I wonder why . . .

- I picture . . .
- It seems important that . . .
- I like the way . . .
- I don't like the way . . .

To develop ideas, students need to consider why an author wrote in a particular way. Students can do this by saying

- Maybe the author wrote this way because . . .
- I think . . . because . . .
- This part makes me think . . .

Because we cannot get inside a writer's head, it's necessary to have students consider alternative possibilities. Therefore, students are encouraged to think past their original idea and develop additional insights into an author's craft. Ways students can begin talking about alternative possibilities are by starting their sentences with

- Maybe . . .
- On the other hand . . .
- Another reason the author might have written it this way is . . .

Finally, young writers should always be encouraged to consider the transfer of work from one text to another. Some phrases to help start this part of the conversation are

- This reminds me of . . .
- I've seen this in . . .
- In my writing, I'd like to . . .

Using Smith's conversational prompts has allowed me to scaffold writers when I want to teach them how to think deeply about texts they encounter. In addition, once students become adept at using the prompts orally, they can use them in their writing to develop longer theories about texts. Providing young writers with conversational prompts allows them to have the language they need to make purposeful reading-writing connections that will help them become astute writers.

Challenge: Study a portion of a favorite text. Use one of the prompts from each section to develop a theory about why an author wrote in a particular way.

Reflective Practice:

- How did the prompts take you on a journey of thought about the author's intentions?
- What's your plan for teaching students how to use these prompts to develop hunches about an author's writing?

Picture Books Aren't Just for Kindergartners!

To be well informed, one must read quickly a great number of merely instructive books. To be cultivated, one must read slowly and with a lingering appreciation the comparatively few books that have been written by men who lived, thought, and felt with style.

—Aldous Huxley

The fall of 2006 brought me the savviest class I ever taught. Nearly all thirty-two of them scoffed at me on Wednesday, September 6, when I pulled out *Nothing Ever Happens on 90th Street*.

"A picture book?" one student said disdainfully.

"Yes, a picture book," I replied. "We're going to read lots of picture books this year."

"Why?" another voice asked.

"Well-written picture books, like the ones I'm going to read to you this year, can teach us a lot about writing," I said.

I was met with blank stares, know-it-all looks, rolling eyes, and a couple sucks of the teeth.

"I mean it. You can learn to become a better writer by reading picture books. There are many amazing picture books out there. You'll see."

"Mrs. Bonner didn't read picture books to us last year when we were in fourth grade," one student said.

"Well, I'm not Mrs. Bonner. I read lots of picture books aloud to my classes. You'll come to love them."

I don't think I convinced my class that they'd come to love picture books that day. Even though I knew they would come to appreciate picture books in short order, this was a case of show, not tell. Telling my students that they'd learn a lot about writing from picture-book authors was merely lip service. It was pointless to tell them they'd come to find the value of picture books as fifth graders when they thought picture books were for babies. I knew I had to show them by reading interesting, well-written picture books. One wrong book selection in the first month of school, and I knew I'd lose them. However, I had read picture books aloud to fifth-grade classes before. My books for the first month of school were road tested, so I was confident these students would find the value of these texts and would adopt some as mentors in the weeks to come.

When selecting picture books you'll use as touchstone texts with your entire class of upper-grade students, it's important to look for books that are well written. It's a bonus if they also contain the following:

- **Quality illustrations:** Beautiful watercolor, collage, and mixed media were always a hit with my students. Anything that's sophisticated and pleasing to look at is usually a winner. If a book looks babyish, but has a great storyline, then consider reading it aloud to your students without showing them the pictures the first time around.

- **Big message:** Picture books with strong themes and thick plot structures are appealing to upper-grade students.
- **Author's note**: My students were always interested in the story beyond the story. Books with additional information in the back were often a hit with the students because they allowed the students to get inside of an author's head.

Beautiful picture books with strong writing can serve as excellent partners to enhance your writing instruction during the school year.

Challenge: Gather a bunch of picture books you are enthusiastic about. Hold a focus group with a few of your students at lunchtime or after school. Ask them what they like and dislike about each of the books so you can get a better feel for the types of books students in your class favor. You might choose to have them fill out a questionnaire about each book they view or you might go high-tech and record their reactions on video. As with any good focus group, make sure you have plenty of snacks for the group members.

Reflective Practice:

- What are some of the qualities of picture books that appealed to your students?
- How will the information you gleaned in the focus group help you pick quality mentor texts for the future?

More Than Picture Books

Nothing limits achievement like small thinking;
nothing expands possibilities like unleashed imagination.
—William Arthur Ward

Picture books are exquisite. They are often my go-to choice when working with narrative, poetry, and nonfiction in the primary grades. However, our students aren't always writing narratives and poetry. Especially as students move through the grades, the demand for expository and essay writing increases. Although there is much to learn from picture book writers, there also comes a time when we encompass other types of texts to use as mentors.

At first thought, expanding our collection of mentor texts seems a little intimidating. Where else can we go to find solid mentors? These places will get you started on creating a robust collection of mentor texts:

- **Magazines for kids:** Check out magazines targeted toward your students' age group. *Cricket*, *Highlights*, *Time for Kids,* and *Zoobooks* offer many well-written texts in a variety of genres. Check your school library or ask students to bring in copies of their favorite magazines.
- **Your favorite magazines:** Next time you're relaxing with your favorite magazine, put on your writer's eyes and look for possibilities for mentor texts. You'll be surprised at the narrative, as well as expository, writing you'll find.
- **Newspapers:** This is a classic place to find expository writing. Newspapers are filled with both hard news articles (fast-breaking stories often appearing on the front page of the paper) and feature articles (articles focused on a topic, rather than an event). I find feature articles the most useful as mentor texts because their content is timeless.
- **Collections of student work:** Publications such as *Stone Soup*, *Merlyn's Pen*, and *Teen Inc.* offer collections of student work. There are samples of narrative, expository, and poetry available. Make sure to check out these (and others) online.
- **Online collections of favorite writers:** When it comes to teaching persuasion, I have a few favorite editorialists. Mitch Albom, Leonard Pitts Jr., and Rick Reilley are at the top of my list. Before teaching a persuasive unit of study, I'll check out their online collections of articles. Find a few of your favorite journalists and check them out online. The benefit of having favorites is that you know the style of writing but also have access to updated mentor texts each year.
- **Anthologies:** Checking out anthologies of a particular genre, such as poetry or short story, is one way to have a slew of possibilities of mentor texts at your fingertips. Another option is to find a collection of short works by an author. Sandra Cisneros's *Woman at Hollering Creek* is one I appreciate when teaching narrative. Her writing is beautiful, like the picture books I love, and at the same time looks like the writing intermediate students will be crafting, with longer paragraphs and few pictures.

A word of caution: If you are unable to find the genre of writing you are asking of your students, it could be the writing doesn't exist in the world. As teachers, we must be vigilant to ensure our students are engaged in real-life types of writing, not simply completing a school assignment. As students engage in writing, mentor texts from the real world provide the opportunity to find the inner workings of craft.

Challenge: Explore some new places for finding mentor texts. Spend time online or at the local library looking for mentor texts. When you find one, make a copy and file it to use in your writing workshop.

Reflective Practice:

- What teaching points emerge from mentor texts that are not picture books?
- How will you be more intentional about finding mentor texts that are not picture books?

Using One Book for Multiple Purposes

The best kind of writing, and the biggest thrill in writing,
is to suddenly read a line from your typewriter that you didn't know was in you."
—Larry L. King

One of the many things I learned as a teacher of writing is that you can use one book for many purposes. While it might seem helpful to have many books to teach from, having a few, well-crafted texts you know well works too. During the 2008–2009 school year, there were a few texts I used for interactive read-aloud and as mentor texts for writing workshop. While it initially seemed like overkill to return to the same texts again and again, it was beneficial for my students' writing because they learned how to write better from books they had discussed in-depth with their peers.

When I took Lucy Calkins's course on reading-writing connections at the Summer 2008 Teachers College Reading and Writing Project institute, our class spent a week dissecting *Hurricane* so we could use it as a teaching tool. By the week's end, everyone in the course worked on describing the craft moves of Jonathan London, author of *Hurricane*, so that we could teach them to a student. We followed Calkins's advice when we did this:

1. Talk about your interaction with a particular part of the text step by step.
2. Point out what kinds of writerly choices the writer made and why you think the author chose to write/craft in a particular way.
3. Name the move the writer made in a way that will help the writer understand what this craft move is beyond the piece of writing you're looking at together (i.e., teach the writer, not the writing). Do this by using complete sentences, not just by using a term or some buzzwords, such as "show, not tell."

This process is similar to what Katie Wood Ray wrote about in *Wondrous Words: Writers and Writing in the Elementary Classroom*:

The Five Parts to Reading Like a Writer

1. *Notice something about the craft of the text.*
2. *Talk about it and make a theory about why a writer might use this craft.*
3. *Give the craft a name.*

4. *Think of other texts you know. Have you seen this craft before?*
5. *Try and envision using this crafting in your own writing. (1999, 120)*

In 2008, I began creating *craft tables* (Appendix C), which were my attempt to organize my thinking about books I wanted to hold up to my students as mentors. Since I'm a bit of a planner, I like to think through my teaching *before* I teach. Therefore, a craft table was an effective way to help me plan for instruction. The left column was the craft move I noticed (i.e., the buzzwords for it) in the text. The center column contained the pages where I noticed the author making a craft move. As per Calkins's advice, I only listed things I noticed the author did in two or more places in the text. In the right column, I wrote out an explanation of each craft move I noticed an author make. Essentially, this was my way of developing theories about why an author wrote in a particular way. I always made sure I was hypothesizing about what an author wrote, rather than telling, since it's not possible to know why an author makes craft moves without actually speaking with him or her.

Before I created a craft table, I developed my own process when working with texts. I found it useful to read a selected book several times. As I went through a book I liked, I marked all of the craft moves I noticed on each page with sticky notes. By the time I was through with a text, it was loaded with sticky notes. I went back to sort through the sticky notes to find the author's most important craft moves that would help a student improve his or her writing. Then, I tried to explain the craft move in-depth. If I had a lot to say about it, I placed it on the craft table.

At the 2008 summer institute, Calkins implored us to be clear when talking with students about an author's craft. She repeatedly told us, "If you want to be clear, use more words." Using more words, rather than jargon, to describe the craft moves as we teach children helps us make sure that students understand the craft moves we are teaching them. For instance, when you're explaining a craft move to a student, it's useful to explain what the author did with a paragraph of speech. Show examples from the mentor text to go along with your clear explanation. This is where solid teaching comes in. While catchy lingo is great when we talk among ourselves as adults, clarity and elaboration are paramount when we want our students to learn about various aspects of writing from one text in a clear way.

Challenge: Find a book you and your students love. Read it intently. Emulate Lucy Calkins and Katie Wood Ray as you identify all of the things you could teach your students about writing from this text.

Reflective Practice:

- What was different about reading with the intent to learn more about writing?
- What do you see as the advantages of using extra words to explain craft moves to your students?
- What do you like about the craft table, similar to the one shown in Appendix C, that you may use to create one of your own? What changes would you make?

Author Studies

If I have seen farther than others, it is because I have stood on the shoulders of giants.
—Sir Isaac Newton

If you've taken a literacy course as part of an education program, chances are you've been asked to create an author study. When I was a preservice teacher in graduate school, I wrote one about Leo Lionni. After I began teaching, and went back for my second master's, I cowrote an author study about Patricia Polacco. I intentionally wanted to work with Polacco's books because I thought they'd be interesting for my students to read. I've taught variations of that unit four times in reading workshop. However, one year, I taught a variation of an author study within writing workshop. The planning was similar to the way my former classmate Beth Rivera and I structured our Polacco author study, according to the expert guidance of my instructor, Kathy Brody.

Based on what I learned from Brody when I took her Literature for Older Children class, these are things you'll want to flesh out before you embark on a writing workshop–based author study, which is meant to strengthen your students' writing skills through the study of one author's body of work:

- **Author:** Think about one author whose writing you admire. Be sure it's accessible for all of the students in your class so all children can read the author's work independently, which will allow them to study the author's craft moves without your support.
- **Book list:** Create a list of ten titles (e.g., picture books, short stories), written by the author you select, that your students will study. Make sure you can obtain at least two copies of each text. You can borrow additional copies from your colleagues, take them out of the library, or buy them. Scholastic book orders are great for ordering multiple paperback copies. However, if the texts you want to study are hardcover, you might consider writing a mini-grant proposal on DonorsChoose.org to request financial assistance to purchase the books you'll need.
- **Biographical summary:** Learn about the author your students will study. Many authors have Web sites where you can learn more about them. In addition, you can consult books such as *Something About the Author* (Kumar 2004) or *Speaking of Journals: Children's Book Writers Talk About Their Diaries, Notebooks, and Sketchbooks* (Graham 1999), which will help you get to know a writer better. *Speaking of Journals*, which I used for a Jacqueline Woodson writing craft study when I taught in Manhattan, provided me with insight into the ways in which Woodson works as a writer. Finally, the appendix in *The Author*

Studies Handbook: Helping Students Build Powerful Connections to Literature (Kotch and Zackman 1995) is a valuable resource for learning about authors.

- **Data wall:** Make a large, in-class bulletin board display where your students can track what they learned about craft as they read each book. (A rough template can be found in Appendix C.) Check out *I Can Write Like That! A Guide to Mentor Texts and Craft Studies for Writers' Workshop, K–6* (Ehmann and Gayer 2009) if you need ideas for craft elements to study.
- **Classroom charts:** Even though you'll likely create these with your students, having a basic idea of the types of charts you want to create (and what might go on them) will help you as you prepare your mini-lessons.
- **Culminating project:** Think through the type of writing your students will do. Will they write narratives, memoirs, poetry, or something else? The final piece of writing should be similar to that of the author you're studying. Think about how you will assess your students' writing. Developing a rubric, alongside your students, based on the craft elements you study together might be one way to assess them. However, not all students will try out all craft moves, so you might choose to assess your students on the quality of their writing rather than the attempts at modeling themselves after the author. In addition, you might have students synthesize what they learned about the craft of writing from the author you studied. They can use the data wall to help them reflect on their learning.
- **Celebration:** While I've heard of many people dressing up as their favorite character from the author's book for an author study celebration, an author study celebration in writing workshop doesn't lend itself to that type of finale. The celebration I hosted provided my students with an opportunity to share their published writing, which included an explanation of how they modeled themselves after the author the class studied.

Regardless of the author you choose to study, you want to teach your students to make reading-writing connections so they can become better writers by emulating published authors.

Challenge: Decide on an author whose writing you will study with your students. Be sure this author's writing will appeal to and will be accessible for all of your students. Be sure the author you choose has enough books that will allow you to teach all of the qualities of good writing (i.e., conventions, elaboration, focus, meaning, structure, voice, and word choice) throughout the duration of the author study.

Reflective Practice:

- What are your three greatest goals for the author study you will embark on?
- How do you hope this author's writing will make your students better writers?

Make Personal Connections to Published Authors

Anything you do that you want to do well can be difficult at times.
Revising is hard. Thinking of new things to write about is hard.
And the difficulty makes it that much more rewarding.
—Jacqueline Woodson

I once saw Patricia MacLachlan (1994) hold up her baggie of prairie dirt and profess her love for the prairie. This love compels her to include the prairie in all of her writing. When writers find a topic they love, she told the audience, they must write and write and write about it.

I remember this when I'm conferring with a student who loves writing about the same thing over and over. Instead of encouraging him or her to find a new topic, I say, "You write just like Patricia. She always writes about the prairie. In fact, she carries some of the prairie in a baggie in her pocket when she's away from it." One second grader smiled sheepishly at me and pulled the tip of a Pokémon card out of his pocket.

"Like this?" he said, with glittering eyes.

"Exactly," I smiled.

Tucking the card back in his pocket, he said, "Maybe I should try a repeating line like Patricia did in *All the Places to Love*."

Professional authors are masters at the craft of writing. They spend their days refining their words and publishing incredible works. Our students' writing is lifted when they model themselves after professional authors.

However, sometimes students develop a misconception about writing when we use professionally written mentor texts. They think only a select few can master the craft of writing. They think writing is about talent or luck or the stars being aligned. By doing a little research into authors' backgrounds, we are able to use them for more than mentoring the craft of writing. We can make them personal to students, and they become mentors for living as writers. How do we learn more about our favorite authors?

The Internet is perfect for learning about famous authors. Most important, many authors have Web sites filled with information about their writing lives. Often the target audience of these Web sites is the same as the target audience of their books, which makes them kid-friendly. Even better, we gain insight into the ordinary lives of writers. We find out Jacqueline Woodson thinks writing is hard, and we can share that with our students. We say, "You are just like *Jacqueline* if you think writing is hard." This makes Jacqueline Woodson a likely mentor for our students. She's not just a supertalented writer; she also thinks the same thoughts as our students!

Besides Web sites, many authors are also in the blog world, as well as on Facebook, Twitter, and other social networking sites. These virtual spaces allow our students to connect to their favorite authors and learn they are regular people living ordinary lives.

Another place to learn about authors' lives is through memoirs on writing. Many authors write about their writing lives. Recently, I picked up Jane Yolen's *Take Joy: A Writer's Guide to Loving the Craft* (2006), a memoir of her writing life. Now when I use a mentor text by Jane Yolen, I'm able to mention bits about her life as a writer. These small insights allow students to connect personally to the author, thus making it more likely they will mentor themselves after the writer.

Memoirs also provide opportunities for read-alouds to support the teaching points in mini-lessons. I've often used an excerpt from Stephen King's (2000) memoir, *On Writing*, to show students writing is about tenacity. King shares how he nailed rejection letter after rejection letter above his desk. Eventually, he had so many he had to switch from a nail to a railroad spike!

Memoirs aren't always in novel form. Some authors share their memoirs as picture books. This gives us an easy way to share the writing lives of mentor authors with our students. As they listen to the story and look at the pictures, they make personal connections to the writer, becoming more likely to model themselves after this author.

Finally, to learn tidbits about an author, listen to him or her speak. Whenever I attend conferences, I make a point to listen to a professional author speak. I'm always thankful for the gems I discover. I'm even more thankful when I use these gems in conferences and mini-lessons, helping students feel more connected to their favorite published authors.

As teachers, we can be the bridge between students and professional writers, helping personal connections to develop. Efforts to learn a little more about the authors of mentor texts will inspire and lift the writers in our classrooms.

Challenge: Spend time researching one of the authors of a mentor text you use in writing workshop. Learn some facts about the author that you can envision sharing with students.

Reflective Practice:

- How did students respond when you shared information about an author's life?
- How will you remember what you learned about an author and use it in future writing workshops?

Teaching Conventions Through a Mentor Text

When you engage in systematic, purposeful action, using and stretching your abilities to the maximum, you cannot help but feel positive and confident about yourself.
—Brian Tracy

Often we overlook the possibility of a mentor text for teaching conventions. By considering conventions, a new door is open to students when studying a mentor text. Authors use conventions on purpose to help the reader understand the text. As we teach students this, they can then hypothesize about why an author used specific conventions, as well as the effect those conventions have on the reader.

There are a few ways to consider conventions in a mentor text:

- **The traditional use of punctuation:** Mentor texts are an excellent source in teaching students new conventions. As they study a well-known text, students build their own understandings of the proper way to use specific punctuation marks.
- **Repetition of a pattern:** Writers use conventions to add voice to their writing. Often this occurs by establishing a pattern through conventions. When students notice the patterns in conventions, they are able to develop a deeper understanding of punctuation.
- **Other possibilities:** To deepen the study of conventions in a mentor text, discuss other possible ways the author could have used punctuation. Through this discussion, students consider the effect certain conventions have on the reader. It is through a close understanding of conventions that students are able to use them sensibly in their writing.
- **Breaking Standard English:** Sometimes teachers are concerned about using mentor texts to teach conventions because many writers dispense with Standard English. Instead of avoiding this in our classrooms, we can be frank with students and encourage them to consider why a writer would break with Standard English. We can also discuss when it is inappropriate to break with Standard English.

By using mentor texts to teach conventions, students are given the opportunity to construct their personal understandings of conventions. When conventions become personal, the understanding endures over time.

Challenge: Make plans to use a mentor text in a mini-lesson as a springboard into a conversation about conventions. Anchor your teaching in one of the four areas defined earlier.

Reflective Practice:

- What were your students' insights about conventions based on the mentor text?
- How did your students respond to using a mentor text to discuss conventions?

Celebrate Mentorship

In particular, you need to readandreadandreadandread
to learn as many different ways of using language as possible.
—Mem Fox

Having a writing mentor is a key to living the life of a writer. The more we celebrate our writing mentors, the more students will be tempted to read with writers' eyes. There are many ways to celebrate having a writing mentor:

- **End-of-unit share:** Students share the way a mentor text inspired their own writing. They then share their writing aloud. Everyone inspired by a particular text shares following one another.
- **End-of-workshop share:** After talking about the possibilities for mentorship from a published writer in a mini-lesson, students share how they used the mentor text in the day's workshop.
- **Bulletin board:** Create a bulletin board by posting a mentor text and then students' work surrounding it. Students can highlight how they modeled their work after the mentor text. These notes are added to the bulletin board as well.
- **Letters to authors:** Instead of a traditional "I loved your book" letter, students may feel inspired to write to an author and share the way he or she was a writing mentor. Students can share the specific ways they were inspired by the mentor text, as well as share blurbs from their writing that was modeled after the professional author's work.

Taking a few moments to celebrate the mentorships happening in our classrooms emphasizes the importance of writing mentors. As students highlight how they learned different ways of using language, it becomes one of the norms of our writing workshops. Spend time celebrating the way students read with the eyes of a writer.

Challenge: Plan an opportunity for students to share the way they have modeled their writing after a mentor. This may be in the form of share or another alternative.

Reflective Practice:

- How does having a writing mentor lift the quality of your students' writing?
- How will you help students who do not have a writing mentor find one?

Chapter 5: Conferring

Conferring is often considered the heart of the writing workshop. It's at the center of our workshops because we spend most of our daily workshop time engaged in one-to-one conferences with our students. In these quiet conferences, we get to know our students more intimately as writers and as people.

Yet, for many teachers, conferring creates a lot of angst. It's not that talking with our students is so daunting. What's daunting is that we're supposed to sit down next to a child, listen carefully, and then come up with exactly the right thing to teach that child at that moment.

On most days, it's just you and your students in your classroom. There's no one there to tell you the teaching point you chose wasn't perfect, nor is there anyone standing over your shoulder ready to insult you if your demonstration wasn't its best. You'll know these things since that's what reflective teaching is all about.

Here's the plan for honing your conferring skills.

- **Cycle 1: Conferring Basics**
  Whether you've been teaching workshop for two or ten years, the series of discussions we created will help you think about the building blocks of conferring in a new way. While some of the discussions might seem basic, we hope you'll take the time to read through them and complete the challenges in your classroom.

- **Cycle 2: Peer Conferring**
  We've witnessed beautiful moments and exquisite pieces of writing grow out of peer conferences. This cycle will help you create a classroom climate that allows peer conferences to take place while you're conferring with students and during special "peer conferring" times.
- **Cycle 3: Lifting the Level of Our Conferences**
  When you're ready to dive deeper into your conferring practice, use this cycle to fine-tune your language, to help you reflect with colleagues, and to beef up your record-keeping systems.

Fortunately, we have 180 school days each year to refine our conferring skills. That's a lot of time to perfect the basics and lift the level of our conferences at our own pace. Be patient with yourself and remember that growth, with conferring, takes time.

Cycle 1: Conferring Basics

Talk Like a Writer

If we want to change our words, we must change our views.
—Peter H. Johnston

I used to have this misconception about writers: I thought they spent their workday in front of a computer, allowing words to pour from their souls onto the page. Then, almost by magic, their books were published, sold, and read by millions of people.

There is more than one fantastical quality to this misconception, which became clearer to me as I began studying the way writers work. The primary misconception is this: Writing does not happen in isolation. Writers live, and they pay attention to the living. They mull over their experiences; they imagine, they share, they talk to others.

When I accepted being a writer myself, the way I talked with students shifted. Our conversation didn't focus on the writing but on being a writer. Talking as a writer is one of the keys to successful conferences. Soon I noticed some common phrases emerging during conferences.

- **"Writers, consider what you will work on today."** By using this phrase before conferring, we help students shift into the role of a writer. The collective noun *writers* readily establishes the expectation that everyone in the room is a writer. As Peter H. Johnston (2004) discusses in *Choice Words*, our students must build an identity that helps them develop a sense of what it is like to belong in different social spaces. Because our students are members of a writing workshop, we must help them build the writer persona.

- **"I understand what it feels like to be frustrated with writing."** Just like other people, writers experience a gamut of emotions. Frustration, excitement, confusion, and dislike are some emotions writers feel. By validating our students' feelings in a conference and then by sliding into a teaching point, the instruction becomes more poignant.
- **"What I do when I'm not sure what choice to make is to talk to another writer."** Another way to establish a writer-to-writer tone is to share what we do to overcome an obstacle and then ask our students to try the same strategy. This places the responsibility on students to make decisions that will help them to become stronger writers. As we help students navigate these decisions, we empower them as writers.

Before I was intentional about speaking to students as one writer to another, I often focused on making the writing better. However, this instruction didn't carry over to the next piece of writing. Today, by making a slight shift in the language of my conferences, I'm able to focus on helping the writer become stronger not just in a single piece of writing, but forever.

Challenge: Be intentional about speaking the language of writers in your conferences. Share your own writing life with students to set a writer-to-writer tone in conferences.

Reflective Practice:

- How did using the language of writers help to shift your focus from teaching writing to teaching writers?
- What do you notice about your students' attitudes toward writing as you speak to them as one writer to another?

A Typical Writing Conference Is Made Up of a Few Key Parts

There should be joy in conferring when you teach kids.
—Carl Anderson

When I started conferring, it seemed overwhelming. However, now, I agree with Anderson wholeheartedly. Conferring is joyful. It allows you to spend a few precious minutes with a child, connecting to them and teaching them something they can use as a writer, not just on that day but every day. Conferring in my classroom was sacred. I taught my students how to work out their own issues during writing workshop so I wouldn't be interrupted while I conferred. A student can interrupt me during conferring for an emergency. Otherwise, the time I spend chatting with students about their writing is sacred. It is joyful!

There's talking about writing and *there's talking about writing!* According to Don Murray in *A Writer Teaches Writing*, conferences are supposed to be dialogues:

> *[Conferences] are not mini-lectures but the working talk of fellow writers sharing their experience with the writing process. At times, of course, they will be teacher and student, master and apprentice, if you want, but most of the time they will be remarkably close to peers, because each writer, no matter how experienced, begins again with each draft. (2004, 148)*

Regardless of which student you're talking to, the conference needs to have structure so that your time, as well as the students', is efficiently used. Like any other conversation, a writing conference has an expected structure. Here are three distinct elements to a writing conference, similar to the conferring structure I first learned about at the Teachers College Reading and Writing Project's Summer Institute for the Teaching of Writing:

- **Investigate:** When we walk up to a student, it's important to pose a few open-ended questions to discover the work they're doing as a writer. During this stage of the conference, we invite the student to do most of the talking, as we listen to the student and gently probe to gather information about the independent work. This way we can decide what the student is doing well and what needs to be taught.
- **Compliment:** Based on the probing we did in the first part of the conference, we find something the student is doing well and compliment the student on it. As Jen Serravallo, a staff developer for the Teachers College Reading and Writing Project, taught me, the compliment you give a student should be "about a paragraph of speech." Don't skimp on the compliments because they build students' confidence, making the teaching point more accepted in the next part of the conference.
- **Instruct:** The third part of the conference is where you kick it into high gear and teach the writer in front of you how to do something better as a writer. The instruction you give the child during this time can be demonstrated by using your writing or a published author's writing. The demonstration should be short and explicit, allowing enough time for the student to try out the strategy you've taught him so you know he or she can do it independently.

An investigate-compliment-instruct conference should take five to seven minutes per student. To be efficient in conferences is to think through a variety of teaching points as possibilities while conferring with students, so you can "diagnose and treat" while remembering to recognize students for the amazing work they're already doing along the way.

Challenge: Practice conferring with a teacher-friend to make your conferences as fluid as possible. During your practice conferences, you might want to keep a timer that is *counting up* alongside you so you can pace yourself through all three parts of the conference. Make sure you've researched for a long enough period of time, but not for *too* long—you want to have ample time to compliment and instruct. Role playing with another adult will make the actual conferences with your students run smoother.

Reflective Practice:

- How did you balance the time in the three parts of the conferences you held?
- Were your compliments about a paragraph of speech? If not, how will you strengthen the compliments you give, without making them syrupy or repetitive?
- Were the demonstrations during the "instruct" part of the conference effective for making your teaching point clear to the writer?

Conference Types

I think we all have a little voice inside us that will guide us. It may be God,
I don't know. But I think that if we shut out all the noise and clutter from our lives
and listen to that voice, it will tell us the right thing to do.
—Christopher Reeve

When I look back on my conferring notebook from my final year in the classroom, I realized I held a variety of conferences. Although the frequency of each type of conference varied from student to student, I noticed I didn't confer with my fourth graders in just one way.

Here's a look at your options before you confer. (These conference types are an outgrowth of my work as a student at Teachers College.)

- **Coaching conference:** This type of conference can be used to support a writer who is struggling with a concept and needs help through a particular part of the writing process. Just like a coach helps players from the sidelines without stopping the game, you pull up next to the writer and provide them with lean prompts to support the writing work he or she is presently doing.

- **Investigate-compliment-instruct conference:** This is the most frequent conference I had with my students. These conferences are usually five to seven minutes long and provide an opportunity to offer explicit instruction, similar to a mini-lesson targeted to the needs of one particular student.
- **Mentor text conference:** This type of conference is particularly useful in the nurturing and revision stages of the writing process, when you've read a student's notebook or draft and pinpoint a strategy you can teach the student to lift the level of his or her work. You come into this conference with the agenda and the mentor text set, giving the child a chance to study a text with you. Once an element of the text has been studied, you invite the student to find ways to weave those elements into their writing repertoire, first in the writing they're working on and then by asking them how they can use this strategy in future pieces of writing.
- **Sticky note conference:** This conference doesn't involve talking—just writing. Essentially, you notice something quickly that the student is doing well or needs to work on immediately and you write it down on a sticky note. Then you gently place it in their notebook so they can read it and follow through on your suggestion, or keep doing what they're doing, immediately. This type of "conference" allows you to check in with a large number of students in a short amount of time, thereby leaving a lot of students with a boost or a suggestion on how to improve their work as a writer. (I've often found this kind of conference to be useful on a collecting day, at the start of a new unit of study.)

It's hard to know exactly the right conference for each student at any given time. However, if you trust your instincts, and listen to the little voice in your head, then you're certain to make the right decision.

Challenge: Pinpoint one of the previously mentioned conferences that you've never tried before, and try it out in your classroom with each student. (This might mean that you're delivering the same conference several times, but that also means that it gets better with each pass.)

Reflective Practice:

- What worked about this new conference structure for you or for your students?
- How could you tweak this new structure to make it a regular part of your conferring repertoire?
- Will you track the types of conferences you hold with each student?

The Teacher's Role in a Conference

One looks back with appreciation to the brilliant teachers, but with gratitude to those who touched our human feelings. The curriculum is so much necessary raw material, but warmth is a vital element for the growing plant and for the soul of the child.

—Carl Jung

Repeatedly, I've heard that our job as teachers in a writing conference is to be a researcher first and then a teacher. We ask many open-ended questions to get our students to talk about the writing work they're doing. Then, once we've figured out what they're doing well, we compliment them and then offer specific instructions to help students make the next leap as writers. It sounds basic, doesn't it? Not so fast! According to Jen Serravallo, who taught me a lot about the art of conferring during a Teachers College Reading and Writing Project Summer Institute, it takes two full school years to refine conferring.

In *How's It Going? A Practical Guide to Conferring with Student Writers*, Carl Anderson writes:

> *It's all too easy to focus so intently on the work students are doing as writers, and teaching them how to do that work better, that we see only their work, and not the young writers who are doing the work. The reason that many students are willing to take on the difficult challenge of outgrowing themselves as writers is not because we ask just the right questions about their writing work, or because our feedback is right on the mark, or because we teach them brilliantly. In the end, the success of a conference often rests on the extent to which students sense that we are genuinely interested in them as writers—and as individuals. (2000, 20—22)*

Anderson's advice is true. The better I know my students, the easier conferences flow. The easier a writing conference flows, the deeper my rapport with a student. The deeper the rapport with a student, the tighter the writing becomes. The tighter the writing becomes, the more the writer's skills build efficiently.

Yes, it is true that you should listen keenly, at first, and then teach a student the next concept needed to help him or her become a better writer. However, no amount of listening or smart delivery of teaching points can take the place of nurturing the student you're meeting with by caring deeply about his or her heart, soul, and writing.

Challenge: Figure out which students you don't know as well as you'd like. Spend some time getting to know them by either reading their writer's notebooks more carefully or by inviting them to join you for a special lunch.

Reflective Practice:

- How did the time you invested in getting to know your students help your conference during writing workshop?
- What steps do you need to take to show a greater interest in other students whom you don't know as well?

The Student's Role in a Conference

I know that you believe you understand what you think I said,
but I'm not sure you realize that what you heard is not what I meant.
—Robert McCloskey

Natalie, who was one of the most thoughtful students I've ever encountered as a teacher, understood exactly what I meant when I asked her, "What are you working on as a writer?" when I sat beside her for our first-ever writing conference in September 2008. Natalie literally pondered the question for about sixty seconds rather than telling me about her writing like most kids do during the first few weeks of school. Finally, after a minute of silence, and me worrying whether the wait time was going to lead to something, Natalie said, "I'm working on adding lots of details to my writing so I can publish it." *Wow!* She didn't tell me about the story she was writing about her trip to Boston with her aunt. She didn't talk about her writing. Instead she spoke about the work I found her doing in her writer's notebook when I sat down to confer with her.

Carl Anderson (2000) asserts that students set the agenda for the writing conference when the teacher sits next to them. However, the child's role shifts once the teacher takes over in the second half of the conference. The student responds to questions, listens to the teacher's instructions, and tries to implement what he or she has learned into his or her writing that day and thereafter.

Every year that I taught full time in the classroom, I spent a day or two reviewing my expectations. This meant that the student was responsible for informing me about his or her work as a writer, and I was responsible for listening and teaching him or her something based on that information. However, the event with Natalie occurred before I even taught my students about conferring roles. This instance with Natalie, and all of the conferences that followed, shows the importance of listening to a question someone asks you and responding accordingly.

Challenge: Talk about your expectations for your students when they're conferring with you in writing workshop. Then hold some mock conferences in front of your class, allowing the class to observe how each student set the agenda for the conference and followed through with the suggestions.

Reflective Practice:

- How did your students respond to the conferences you held in front of the class?
- Were they able to recognize when the student strayed from talking about his or her writing?
- Was your class able to recognize what they should say and do in a writing conference?

Record-Keeping Systems That Make Sense for You

It's pretty hard to be efficient without being obnoxious.
—Kin Hubbard

I'm less than neat with my conferring notes, and I don't try to hide it. They were never a work of art. I recall trying to hide my writing conference notebook from my colleagues early on in my teaching career for fear that someone would glimpse the messy handwritten pages, the sticky notes that were plastered everywhere, and the papers haphazardly stapled in with photocopied student writing samples that I wanted to revisit in my next writing conference.

Over the years, I realized that the appearance of my conferring notes didn't matter as long as I could quickly locate student information, as well as see the tracks of my teaching right before heading into a conference.

To keep track of who I met with, I used a basic system in a notebook, which has its advantages and disadvantages (Appendix D). Essentially, my conferring notes were a three-column chart with a space for the date, compliments, and teaching points. Each column had an organizational purpose. The date allowed me to track how frequently I met with each student. The compliments column helped me to refrain from doling out the same accolades every time I met with a student; therefore, I was pushed to consider different affirmations. Finally, recording teaching points allowed me to look for trends in my teaching with each student. A record of what you taught during the previous conference helps to monitor the child's progress with previously covered skills.

Conferring notes ensure accountability for the teacher, but they also hold students accountable for what they're taught. So use a system that works for you.

Challenge: Examine your conferring notes to determine whether your present system of record keeping works for you. If there are pieces that are working, then keep them! Try to figure out what doesn't work for you so you can tweak your current system in ways that will help your conferring notes drive instruction. Look at the conferring notes of willing colleagues, and record what you like about them. Then incorporate them into a format that works for you.

Reflective Practice:

- What do you love about your present record-keeping system? What works for you?
- How will changes to your record-keeping system help you streamline your conferring notes so they become a more useful teaching tool?
- Will your new system help with efficiency so that record keeping doesn't become burdensome?

Balancing Our Roles

Try to remember that tenderness is more important than technique.
—Ralph Fletcher

Writing workshop teachers are a bit like guide dogs. We travel alongside our student writers while providing safety, comfort, and encouragement. At the same time, we block them from any paths that may not be in their best interest. This takes both a kindred heart and a no-nonsense approach. Even more important is learning to balance the two roles.

In the beginning of the school year, I tend to err on the side of a kindred heart. I empathize with students as they struggle with living the writing life. I know that it is difficult to find topics to write about, to put words on the page can be tedious, and to run out of steam is easy. I also share my excitement in observing the world with the eyes of a writer, my passion for writing about the things that matter most to me, and my joy when I write well.

However, a point comes when it is necessary to nudge students away from choices that hinder their best work as writers. In writing workshop, students are expected to become stronger writers. When the choices they make do not support this goal, it is our responsibility to redirect them. As with guide dogs, this can be a gentle nudge or an abrupt change of course. At times, both are appropriate.

For example, when students think or plan in their heads, yet have no evidence of their plan, we must make a choice whether to nudge or insist. Thomas was one of my students early in my career who was a sophisticated seventh-grade writer.

Thomas planned most of his writing in his head, which meant he needed gentle nudging. The first time I watched him stare out the window I thought he was daydreaming. As I conferred with him, I realized he was considering his writing and making plans for how it would work. I encouraged him to jot down his thinking so that he would be able to pick up where he left off the next day.

By contrast, a few years later when I saw Jordan, another student, gazing out the same window like Thomas, it was evident that Jordan was daydreaming. Therefore, I insisted that he write his plan in his notebook to ensure he was focused on his writing work. The teaching point was no-nonsense and direct.

Writers in our classrooms have varying degrees of writing experience, as well as different personalities. It takes time to learn how to respond to the individual and specific needs of everyone. By dedicating ourselves to active listening and to responding to the individual, we can meet the needs of all the writers in our classrooms.

Challenge: Take the time this week in conferences to ascertain whether the writer you are conferring with needs a kindred spirit or a no-nonsense approach. Be intentional about balancing these approaches as you work alongside students.

Reflective Practice:

- Are you more of a kindred spirit or no-nonsense when you work with the writers in your classroom?
- What are some ways you can become either gentler or bolder when helping students as writers?

Encourage Them

If you want to teach me to write, first you must love me.

—Avi

I grew up in a home where children were showered with unconditional love, encouragement, and acceptance. As a teenager, I thought my parents were overzealous, overprotective, and overbearing. Today, I understand two more adjectives for their parenting style: solid and rare.

I also remember that home was the only place I wanted to go at the end of a tough day. Home was the one place where it was okay to be me. Today, I strive to make my home the same kind of place. All those who cross our threshold are good enough just as they are.

It doesn't take long to realize that many of the students in our classrooms do not have this kind of safe place. They deal with hunger, drug-addicted parents, or homelessness. As teachers, we aren't able to right the injustices of the world; yet we can make a small impact by providing a safe place for our students to be themselves.

How can we provide a safe place for students as massive curriculum standards loom overhead? We do this by encouraging students in their journey to become stronger writers. By infusing our writing workshops and, specifically, our conferences, with the language of encouragement, we can provide both a safe place for students to be themselves as well as meet standards. Here are ways to infuse the language of encouragement into our conferences.

- **"I'm sorry to hear that your dad moved out last night. That must be difficult."** When students are invited to write about the pieces of their lives that matter most and then trust us enough to share these bits, we ought to honor them by responding with genuine kindness. When the writing teacher inside of me responds before the caring human, my priorities are out of balance. Until our students know we care about their lives, they won't care about our instruction.
- **"I noticed you have been using ending punctuation."** When we first respond to our students by acknowledging the positive work they are doing, they are more open to listening and accepting a teaching point. Because we are working with inexperienced writers, we must also acknowledge their approximations of writing well. For example, when a first grader puts a period at the end of every line, we respond with excitement at the student's knowledge of ending punctuation. In addition, acknowledging the hopeful work of our students encourages them to take risks and to grow as writers. One solid, genuine compliment can sustain a writer for a long time.
- **"I noticed you revised by adding dialogue. It really makes your character come alive. Let me help you punctuate it correctly."** Building on strengths is one of the best ways to make a teaching point. If we identify what our students are approximating as writers, we can often acknowledge their work and then encourage them to do it even better by focusing our instruction on a specific strategy or skill. When we encourage our students to do what they are attempting, but not quite achieving as writers, we nudge them to grow as writers.
- **"I'll check back and see how that is going for you."** We are given another opportunity to encourage students as writers by being intentional about checking back with them after conferences. When students make a good-faith effort in regard to the teaching point, affirm their effort and achievement. Checking back also gives us insight into additional instruction the student may need.

When we infuse our conferences with the language of encouragement, we provide students a safe place to be themselves. By accepting students as they are, recognizing their strengths and approximations, and encouraging them to improve as writers, we create a rich, safe environment that helps students lift the level of their writing.

Challenge: Intentionally use the language of encouragement in your conferences. Record the ways you encourage the writers in your classroom, as well as how you use this encouragement as a way into your teaching point.

Reflective Practice:

- Who encourages you the most? What are some of the things this person says to encourage you?
- Is it natural for you to use language of encouragement with your students? Why or why not?
- What do you notice about your students as you affirm the work they are doing as writers?

The Art of a Compliment

I can live for two months on a good compliment.
—Mark Twain

"Well done," are words that no one can hear enough. Our writing workshops include writers of varying strengths, wide experiences, and many personalities. The single common thread is our appreciation of a compliment. Taking the time to notice an attempt at writing well and then spending a few seconds encouraging the writers in our classrooms are central to an authentic writing community.

Encouragement isn't difficult to do, but it is often overlooked. With the push for standardized teaching and rigorous classrooms, we often rush past encouragement. For some teachers, looking past the grammatical errors to find something a writer has done well is difficult. Still other teachers offer contrite, canned compliments. It takes dedication and attention to detail to offer meaningful and powerful compliments.

- **Check out your previous teaching point:** By consulting our conference notes, we can readily find the teaching point from the last conference. With a quick glance through the writing, we can ascertain whether the student has mastered the previous teaching point. If so, validate the learning by noticing the improvement.
- **Respond with emotions:** If the writing tickles our funny bones or makes us blink back tears, we should share this with the writer. Powerful writers tap into

readers' emotions. When our students evoke emotions, let them know. That way, they'll do it again and again.

- **Consider the mini-lessons:** When students use the mini-lesson as inspiration to write well, we should respond positively. When we notice how our students apply the mini-lesson to their writing, we are able to support their application of the lesson. However, we shouldn't compliment a student on this every time, because it is expected that students should follow through on the teaching point from the mini-lesson. If we always praise this work, then it undermines this crucial expectation.
- **Look for what students are almost doing, but not quite:** This is my go-to compliment because it leads nicely into a teaching point. Just like learning anything else, learning to write is full of approximations. Often, as teachers, we see these approximations as errors. By shifting our mind-set slightly, we can look to approximation as the basis for a compliment. When students are approximating to write well, it tells us they have a new understanding of how to write well. When we offer encouragement in these new understandings and then help students make their approximation more conventional, we are developing stronger writers.

When we encourage the writers in our classrooms, we are changing lives. For many of our students, we may be the only adults in their lives who offer encouragement. For others, encouragement may be the substance they need to put forth the effort to learn to write well.

Finally, the benefit of offering encouragement isn't only for our students. The unexpected outcome of encouraging others is that we feel encouraged ourselves. When we notice the strengths of our students' learning, they are empowered. Pausing to offer a compliment before moving into a teaching point only brings benefits to our writing workshops.

Challenge: Jot down these four ideas for offering encouragement on a sticky note, and place it on your conference record sheet. As you confer, keep a tally of the types of compliments you offer. (Don't forget to write the compliment on your conference record sheet as well.)

Reflective Practice:

- Is offering encouragement natural for you or do you need to make an intentional effort to encourage?
- How can you make the compliments you offer more meaningful to your students?

Highlighting Teaching Points in Conferences

A teacher is one who makes himself progressively unnecessary.
—Thomas Carruthers

"Writers, find a place to wrap up your work for today and put away your writing. If you had a conference today, please bring your work with you to the share session." Thus begins the transition from work time to share time. In this case, the share session consists of highlighting the writing work that surfaced during the conferences.

As students make their way to the author's chair, their eyes sparkle. In this type of share, the writer's work is highlighted by first acknowledging the strength of the writer and then discussing the student's work following the conference. When students' strengths are highlighted, they sit a little taller. As they speak about their learning, it becomes a part of their repertoire. It is most effective when the writer does most of the talking. However, the teacher helps the student share the most important parts of the conference by asking unobtrusive questions to help guide the share, while honoring the student's words and work.

Another way to honor students who are sharing is to encourage them to hold their own work. This helps increase a sense of ownership. Sometimes, though, students are animated when discussing their learning, and holding their own writing becomes cumbersome. Often young writers want to point out parts of their pictures or drafts, or older students want to talk with their hands. At these times, I encourage the writer to ask someone to help hold the draft for the class to see while the writer points out the parts needed to share the learning with the class.

As teachers, it is our duty to scaffold the share so students shine as they share their learning. When smiles emerge and energy levels increase, it is clear the share is successful. As time progresses, we expect students to become more sophisticated in their ability to share so we can provide less direction while the share session is sustained.

The payoff of this type of share is the opportunity for another whole-class teaching point. Sharing the teaching points from conferences enables the class to try the same kind of work as their classmates who are sharing. Even more important, over time each individual's strength is highlighted and everyone has the opportunity to be commended for their work. By the end of the school year, students are able to lead and respond to this type of share without teacher help, thus making teachers "progressively unnecessary."

Challenge: Plan to include this type of share session at the end of an upcoming writing workshop. Make plans about where the writer will sit during the share session and where you will sit. Make sure the writer is in the bigger chair so he or she is the point of attention. Plan to sit in a smaller stool or on the floor to support the writer during the share session.

Reflective Practice:

- Were the teaching points detailed enough on your conference record to help you guide each writer's sharing time?
- Did your students need a lot or a little scaffolding during the share session?
- How can you encourage your students to take more control of the share session as time progresses?

Cycle 2: Peer Conferring

Expectations of Peer Conferences

Working together, ordinary people can perform extraordinary feats.
—Unknown

When it comes to hitches in writing workshop, peer conferring seems to be at the top of the list. After talking with teachers at many grade levels, it seems the main issue is the difficulty for students to offer sound writing advice to one another. Because writers in our classrooms are amateurs, it makes sense that they won't offer sophisticated advice to one another. This leaves me wondering: *What is it that we, as teachers, expect out of a peer conference?*

Peer conferring should be more about the process of talking to other writers and less about the outcome. Talking with others is a worthy way to spend time as writers. As we learn the art of conversation, many doors open to us. This gift is too important not to give our students. Peer conferring is successful when students leave our classrooms with the social skills needed for a conversation.

Nancy Steineke, in *Reading and Writing Together: Collaborative Literacy in Action*, shares the in-depth process she uses to teach high school students the social skills to collaborate effectively. She writes, "Humans, though instinctively social, are not born with collaborative genes. These behaviors have to be learned, so if students are not using an important interpersonal skill, it needs to be taught directly" (2002, 56). Peer conferring provides an opportunity to teach social skills.

Before any other skills can be taught, a culture of encouragement and support ought to be established. This structure is too important to be left in fate's hands.

We can help mold this environment by modeling respect, encouragement, and support. When teachers respect their students, then students are more likely to reflect this attitude with one another.

According to Steineke, we must explicitly teach students how to get along. She suggests making a T-chart with one column dedicated to *the things we hear* in an environment of "friendliness and support." The other column collects *the way students look* when they are in an environment of "friendliness and support" (61). In Sue Price's sixth-grade writing workshop, we applied Steineke's ideas. On the "sounds like" side of the chart, students added phrases they could say, such as

- "Way to go"
- "Good idea"
- "Please"
- "Maybe you'll get it next time."

On the "looks like" side, we collected:

- Sitting together, but away from other groups
- Thumbs up
- Taking turns

Before students moved to partner or small-group work, Sue asked them to look at the chart and then choose one phrase and one action they would use during the course of the conversation. At first, being intentional about using these phrases and actions feels contrived and robotic; however, as students become more familiar with creating an environment of friendliness and support, it becomes part of the culture of the classroom and feels natural.

Learning to listen is another critical social skill. Too often people are so eager to add to the conversation, that we forget to listen first. When we listen to students in conferences, allow their words to soak in, and take advantage of wait time, we model for students how to listen. When supporting students in peer conferences, we can encourage them to practice these same strategies. By teaching students how to listen to and focus on the speaker, make eye contact, and consider the response before speaking, we help them establish the conditions needed for an effective conversation.

The more people learn how to ask quality questions, the better conversationalists they become. Teaching students to ask open-ended and follow-up questions are valid teaching points in mini-lessons.

Listening to the responses to quality questions is important, but so is offering help. An excellent resource for offering advice is anchor charts. By teaching students to use all they know about writing well when offering advice, we help them lift the level of their suggestions in peer conference.

When we take the time to teach social skills during peer conferring, we not only lift the level of peer conferences but also provide students with a base of important skills that will open doors for them throughout their lives.

Challenge: Make a plan to teach a mini-lesson with a focus on social skills. Consider your class of students. Don't be afraid to teach the basics. Which social skill would lift the level of their collaboration? A lesson with a focus on ways to encourage other writers has the potential to lift the quality of writing among your students.

Reflective Practice:

- What are some of the behaviors in your classroom that shows students respect and encourage one another?
- What are some behaviors you would like to see change in order for students to be effective collaborators?

The Recipe for a Powerful Writing Partnership

Do whatever you do intensely.
—Robert Henri

Francesca and Tyresha were assigned to be writing partners in September 2006. Every time I announced I was thinking of changing up some of the writing partnerships in my classroom, these two girls would beg me not to change their partnership. During the school year, I realized these girls relied on each other to do solid writing work. They listened intently during mini-lessons, formulated quality plan boxes, worked industriously during independent writing time, and always had constructive writing partner sessions. Hence, Francesca and Tyresha remained writing partners throughout fifth grade because they worked fervently together, thereby making each other stronger writers.

Francesca and Tyresha's partnership flourished for many reasons. First, both girls wanted to be better writers. They entered fifth grade with a good grasp of conventions but with little experience writing genres other than fiction. Second, both girls had a strong work ethic. They understood that the phrase "Off you go!" at the end of a mini-lesson meant they should get started on writing work immediately. Third, Francesca and Tyresha understood the importance of being present in both body and mind. If one girl was absent, the other would take extra materials and would subsequently explain or reteach the information the following school day. Finally, the girls used each other's feedback during all stages of the writing process from planning to revising to publishing. They were always honest with each other, providing accolades for a job well done and constructive criticism when one missed the mark. These techniques worked in concert to create a dynamic writing partnership. Every teacher should have the opportunity to witness this in his or her classroom.

We cannot expect all students to have writing partnerships like Francesca and Tyresha's. However, when we notice successful partnerships, it's important to compliment the duo so they can continue to build on the foundation they're developing together.

Challenge: Study your students when they work in partnerships. Whose partnership is full of intensity? Spend some time talking with the partnership to investigate what makes their partnership successful.

Reflective Practice:

- How can you replicate what's working well with the partnership you studied to benefit other writing partnerships?
- Can you record or videotape the partnership at work so you can study their conversation with the rest of your students?

Writer to Writer

Do you really listen or do you just wait for your turn to talk?
—Unknown

"I'm not sure I understand what you mean," Bailey said to Amy.

Amy paused for a moment, looking over her draft. "Well, my brother left for the army and I miss him."

Bailey looked over Amy's shoulder at the draft she was holding. "Where in your draft did you write about him leaving for the army?"

"In the second part." Amy shuffled the papers and began skimming. Bailey's eyes were moving across the words too.

"I don't see it," Bailey said.

Amy's eyes were shifting down the page. She turned to the next. "It's supposed to be here, but I think I forgot to include it."

"If you'd add that part about him leaving, it would have made a lot more sense to me," Bailey smiled.

Amy made a note on her draft and pulled out a clean sheet of paper to write her revision. Bailey shifted her attention back to her own writing. If you watched them over the remainder of the day's writing workshop, you would see them put their heads together over a single sheet of paper, have a quick conversation, and then move back to their own writing.

I wish I could say all of the peer conferences I observe are as strong as Amy and Bailey's. In my early years of workshop teaching, I thought if I gave students a smorgasbord of options to suggest for the writer to do after the peer conferences, then their conferences would become more valuable. In reality, this led to busy-work for students. Peer conferring became a hoop to jump through to publish writing for school. I noticed what was happening, but I wasn't sure how to stop it and still provide opportunity for peer conferring. That is, until I witnessed Bailey and Amy's conversation.

Very little about their conversation was formal or scripted. They weren't at the "peer conference table," nor did they use a "peer conference form." They were simply sitting next to each other, talking about their writing. Their conversation centered on the meaning of Amy's writing. From this point on, my teaching about peer conferring focused on meaning. *Meaning* is the heart of all conversations between writers.

For useful peer conferences to occur in our classrooms, it is critical for students to talk, putting their heads together, trying to find the best way to make the writing more meaningful. As teachers, there are specific conversational moves we can teach students to help them learn to talk as writers.

- **Position ourselves to respond:** One of the reasons Bailey was able to give Amy effective feedback is because she gave Amy her undivided attention. Bailey's eyes were on Amy's draft; her hands were empty; and her focus was on helping Amy make her draft stronger. By teaching students to sit close and huddle together over a single draft, we position them for effective peer conferences.
- **Respond as a reader:** Young writers must learn to shift into the role of a reader when responding to the draft. Although this is a subtle change, it is an important one. Some of the most valuable feedback I can get in response to one of my drafts is how it affected someone as a reader. Often, as writers, we're too close to the writing. We know what it's supposed to say, so it takes an outsider to tell us what it really says.

  In some classrooms, teachers help make the partner roles concrete by providing a "reader" tag and a "writer" tag for students to clip onto their shirts when having a peer conference. This also allows the teacher to know, at a glance, whose draft is the focus of the conference.
- **Ask questions (and follow-up questions):** Teaching students to ask open-ended questions about the writer's drafting choices is one way to make peer conferring more valuable. This shifts the focus of the conference from finding

something more the writer should do to helping the writer consider new possibilities for the draft. By speaking as one writer to another, focusing on the meaning of the draft, and learning specific conversational moves, the quality of peer conferences will be lifted.

Challenge: Schedule a mini-lesson that focuses explicitly on teaching students to speak as one writer to another. Consider the best way to approach this instruction based on the needs of your students. Options for a mini-lesson of this nature include modeling a peer conference with another teacher who you are able to talk with as one writer to another; asking two of your students who speak as writers to model; or creating an anchor chart highlighting key conversational moves writers make when responding to one another.

Reflective Practice:

- What common phrases do you use in your conferences when responding to students' writing that could be useful to your students as they respond to one another?
- How can you help students focus on the meaning of their writing rather than the "stuff" of revision?

Purposes for Peer Conferences

There is no such thing as a worthless conversation, provided you know what to listen for. And questions are the breath of life for a conversation.

—James Nathan Miller

The more I write, the more I need to talk to others about my writing. Collaborating with Stacey on this book helped me realize the importance of peer conferring. My writing is lifted when we talk. I asked her to address questions or issues in my drafts. By cracking open the writers' common questions when looking for feedback, students are able to respond more effectively in peer conferences.

- **"Does this make sense?"** When writers spend a lot of time writing a draft, they become attached to it. A pair of outside eyes often provides the insight needed to determine whether all of the important parts are included for the draft to make sense.
- **"Do I need this part?"** Pruning writing is one of the most difficult feats for a writer. Young writers especially become attached to their words. It is hard

work getting words on the page. Peer conferences provide an opportunity to discover what words can be pruned to make the meaning clearer.

- **"What is the big idea in my draft?"** The heart of all writing lies in creating meaning with our words. When another writer offers feedback on the big idea in our drafts, we find out whether our purpose is clear.
- **"Will you help me think of another way to say this?"** One element of revision is playing with words. When we invite another writer to help us take this risk, we stretch our imagination, creativity, and writing skills. Fleshing out a new lead or a different ending with another writer is a great way to hone our writing.
- **"Will you listen to me tell my story/talk through my research?"** In the initial stages of a draft or before drafting, many writers benefit from talking with another person. Talk solidifies our ideas as it reveals new ideas. Talk helps us find the main idea and organize our thoughts. Telling a story we are planning to write or talking through our initial plan for a draft is never wasted time.
- **"Will you help me edit?"** This is a natural question when writers want to publicize their writing. Another set of eyes looking over conventions is crucial for our writing to be its best.
- **"Is this good?"** I used to cringe when I heard this question, and as a teacher, I rarely answer it. Yet, as a writer, there are certain people I turn to when I need to hear that my writing is "good." I know my mom will always tell me that I'm a good writer. Sometimes I need a confidence boost, so I ask Mom, "Is this good?" Our students need this same boost. Writing is hard work, and I've come to accept that it's okay for students to simply respond with "good job." These words have never hurt any writer.

Creating a chart about the purposes of peer conferences documents the important ways students collaborate as writers. It also gives value to the natural talk of writers and helps our writing workshops become even more authentic.

Challenge: Propose to students that writers meet to talk for different purposes. Invite them to have a peer conference when they would like feedback from another writer. Then track the reasons for their peer conferences on a chart.

Reflective Practice:

- What is the main reason the students in your classroom talk as writers?
- How will you open the doors to different kinds of peer conferences?

Space for Peer Conferences

Everyone needs their own spot.
—Mary Engelbreit

In most writing workshops, students find comfort in having their own personal space. As creatures of habit, they often migrate to these same places each day. The reasons for their focus spot choices are varied: some prefer the quietest corner of the room; others like to be at their desks; still others want to hunker down beneath a table. Therefore, defined spaces for peer conferring are needed.

Writing workshop can be personalized according the needs of the teacher and the class. Defining space for peer conferring should not be excluded from personalization. I have established many different structures for peer conference spaces. Some of the more successful systems follow:

- **Establish peer conference stations:** Identify three places in the classroom where peer conferring is expected. This allows students who prefer quiet when writing to avoid these spots. It also allows for only three peer conferences to occur at a given time. If all the spaces are filled and two students want to have a conference, they need to wait until a space opens.
- **Create peer conference kits:** Collecting the needed supplies for peer conferring in a single bucket reminds students of the work expected in a peer conference. Items such as sticky notes, colored pens, and highlighters could be included in the kit. A limited number of kits restricts the number of peer conferences occurring at one time.
- **Encourage students to talk with writers near them:** When students sit near one another, it is natural to talk as writers. By inviting these conversations when needed, we can facilitate a natural peer conference. Students often appreciate this type of informal conversation. When they speak with someone near them, there are fewer interruptions and their work isn't put on hold until a meeting area becomes available.

The procedures established in regards to peer conferring can potentially scaffold students to have productive conversations. A basic routine is to know where to have a peer conference.

Challenge: Create a system for your students to use when having a peer conference. Consider how many conferences you would like to occur at once, as well as the needs of your students.

Reflective Practice:

- What about these locations helps or hinders the work of writers? If you haven't established peer conferring locations, what are some possibilities in your classroom?
- How formal do you envision the peer conferences in your classroom?

Peer Conference Notes

Accountability breeds response-ability.
—Stephen R. Covey

Ten girls came upstairs to my classroom four mornings a week, for forty minutes a day, to work on independent writing projects as part of New York City's extended day program in the fall of 2006. For their first round of independent writing projects, the girls worked in a variety of genres: personal narrative, short essay, playwriting, and fiction. Even with a student teacher in the room, it became necessary to create partnerships according to genre, and teach the students how to confer with one another. At first, this was messy. After all, I had to teach them how to confer meaningfully. However, once they became skilled at complimenting and instructing one another, I realized I needed to know what they were talking about each day, in case I wasn't within earshot of their conference. Hence, a simple note-taking device to track their conferences evolved.

I have now taught many students how to track things they confer about with a writing partner. First, students think about their notes in terms of tracking: saying one thing that celebrates the smart work their partner did as a writer (i.e., the compliment) and one thing that will help their partner be a stronger writer (i.e., the instruction). Second, I provide students with a simple T-chart. On the left side of the T-chart is space to write down the compliment for the writer, while the right side of the chart provides space to record the instructional tip. All I ask is that the student write a sentence or two in each column, detailing the essence of the conference. This simple snapshot holds the student accountable both to me and to his or her partner. Because there is a written record, I understand what's been discussed and can remind the student of what he or she worked on with his or her writing partner.

Finally, because students are honest about what they discuss in peer conferences, these notes allow me to learn when a peer conference is out of balance, meaning that there are more instructional items given than compliments or vice versa. Hence, the peer conference notes can often become a teaching tool to help partnerships engage in more balanced, thoughtful peer conferences.

Challenge: Design a student-friendly peer conference note system, which will also help you. Further, determine where the peer conference notes will live (e.g., on a new sheet of paper each time, in a notebook, in a binder) and how often you will monitor them. Finally, be sure to get your students' input on the system before you implement it.

Reflective Practice:

- What was your students' response to the note-taking system you developed?
- What will you do to teach your students how to take thoughtful notes at the end of their peer conferences?
- How do you envision this system evolving from year to year?

Adult Conferences

It takes a village to raise a child.
—African Proverb

A twist on traditional peer conferring is to invite students to get feedback from an adult. By taking the draft, along with a simple adult conference form (Appendix D), students are able to gain insight into how to revise their drafts. The key to the success of adult conferences is to keep them manageable.

Before requesting an adult conference, writers give direction to the adult by asking for specific feedback on their drafts. In a mini-lesson, brainstorm feedback that would be valuable to obtain from an adult. *Is the writing clear? Are you able to picture scene two in your mind?* These are examples of ideas that might grow out of a brainstorming session.

Once students complete this section of the adult conference form, they take the form and their draft and ask a trusted adult to read it and offer feedback in response to the question. When the adult has a few minutes to spare, he or she reads the draft and then provides written feedback in the space provided on the adult conference form. The form also encourages a conversation between the writer and responder; however, this isn't a requirement.

Speaking of requirements, the adult conference was never a requirement in my classroom. It would be unfair to require students to complete an assignment that depends on someone else's work. In writing workshop, I asked students to have at least two conferences over the course of a unit about the work they were planning to publish. One option was an adult conference. I also use the term "adult" loosely. For my seventh graders, anyone in high school or beyond qualified. The point of the adult conference was for students to talk with a person outside of the classroom about their writing. Who they chose was up to them.

I also made copies of drafts for students to give to their adult responder. This made it convenient for parents who worked the night shift and needed the day to read and respond to the writing. Students could leave their drafts with an adult for a couple of days yet still continue to work on it (without worrying about misplacing it).

Students were encouraged to think ahead and give the adult responder plenty of time to provide feedback. If the due date neared and the adult had yet to offer feedback, then the student writer was responsible for making other plans for a different conference.

Because of these structures, the response to adult conferring was positive. Students often approached adults within the school for feedback. The faculty appreciated seeing students in the process of writing and enjoyed helping them become stronger writers. Parents also commented about seeing writing in process. One mother said, "It makes me realize how much work goes into the revision and editing when I saw his first draft compared to the final draft."

Challenge: Provide students with the opportunity to have an adult conference. Provide a simple form for the student and adult to complete. Plan a mini-lesson or a series of mini-lessons, which would provide students with the ability to plan, to initiate, and to use feedback from an adult conference.

Reflective Practice:

- What are some of the structures you plan to implement for adult conferring?
- What are some of the necessary items to include on your adult conference form?

Online Conferring

The more I want to get something done, the less I call it work.
—***Richard Bach***

Remember the days when we'd call our friends on the phone to study (i.e., gossip about who liked who and then do some work)? I remember, in high school, my mother even drove me to friends' houses so we could work on projects or prepare for exams. Collaboration, over the phone or in person, usually helped me get ahead in school. In the twenty-first century, phone conversations or study dates aren't the only ways to collaborate, thanks to the availability of technology that allows us to communicate at a faster speed.

Whether you're in a school where writing workshop is taught twice a week for forty minutes or daily for an hour, it's possible for writing workshop to continue outside of class. All your students need is a computer with Internet access and a desire to continue in order to make their writing stronger. A strong writing partnership can easily have an electronic peer conference in a variety of ways:

- **Instant message (IM):** AOL, Facebook, and Gmail are three of many IM providers. Students who worked on something during the school day can go back and forth at night, continuing their peer conference electronically.
- **Google Docs:** Ruth and I learned firsthand that it's possible for two people to work on the same document at the same time when we were writing this book. It helps to have an IM window or a phone conversation going at the same time to enhance the changes that might take place on a piece of writing.
- **E-mail:** Back-and-forth e-mail correspondence is a simple way to give and receive feedback between partners. In addition, one writer can attach writing in a Word document and have his or her partner track changes and add comments before updating the document and sending it back.
- **Wikis:** A wiki is another fantastic tool that allows multiple users to edit content in real time. PBWorks and Wikispaces are two reliable options that provide fee-free wikis for students.

It might be useful to set up a time to show students (and their parents) how these online tools can be used for online conferring.

Challenge: Try out one of these tools, preferably one you haven't used before, to confer online with one of your students. Once you feel comfortable with the technology, you can introduce it to your class.

Reflective Practice:

- How did your online interaction help the student with his or her writing?
- What kinds of online etiquette might you need to teach your students before introducing online conferring as an extension of peer conferences to them?

When a Peer Conference Goes Bad!

I'm not concerned about all hell breaking loose,
but that a *part* of hell will break loose . . . it'll be much harder to detect.
—George Carlin

Regardless of how meticulous I was when my students returned their writing partner questionnaires at the start of the school year, I would inevitably match up some students who never should have been paired. In addition, there'd always be those one or two kids no one in the class wanted to work with because they were known to mess around, didn't care about doing their best work, or were just plain mean. Regardless of the reason, everyone in my writing workshops was required to have a partner. As a result, there have been a few times in my teaching career when I've witnessed peer conferences go bad—and I mean really bad!

Based on the bad peer conferences I've been privy to, I've come up with ways to handle different types of sticky situations you might encounter in your classroom.

- **The "she didn't do her work" situation:** When one partner falls behind, it can make a peer conference tough to do. I often remind partnerships with this problem that students are in different places within the writing process, and therefore can still work with each other, even if one's writing partner isn't in the same place.
- **The "he told me my writing is bad" situation:** One of your students is clearly going to be more upset than the other in this scenario. Before you can teach into this situation, have students spend a few minutes apart to write down what happened and how it made each of them feel. (Prepared sheets that go something like "I felt ________ when you ________. I would like you to do __________ when we work together in the future." are useful to have available in case a situation like this arises.) Then, give the students a few minutes to talk things out. If necessary, jump in with some words about giving constructive criticism.
- **The "she's not helping me with my writing even though I helped with hers" situation:** Certainly there will be students who feel their work is more important than their partners' writing. Encouraging students to take turns with who goes first each day is useful. However, for chronic situations where one student doesn't want to help her partner once she's received feedback, a private conversation with the student about give-and-take might be necessary to change how she views the peer conferring process.
- **The "he's not my friend anymore" situation:** Every now and then kids who weren't friends until they were writing partners, become friends. When the friendship goes awry for even a day, it's likely the partners will not want to work together. A gentle reminder to put their personal differences aside during class, so the focus is on their writing, is often all one needs to do to mitigate this situation, which can be solved with a peer mediator during lunchtime.
- **The "she's talking to other kids" situation:** Changing where a writing partnership sits is the quickest way to resolve this situation. If one member of the partnership is easily distracted, then providing students with some sort of physical barrier to block distractions might be the best solution.

Do not give into initial demands to change a writing partnership. After all, students need to learn to work with all kinds of people. Even if you find yourself siding with one student, try to refrain from taking sides. Using a calm tone, reassuring words, and neutral body language will go a long way at managing peer conferences when they go astray.

Challenge: Think about foreseeable problems you face with students in your classroom. Brainstorm ways you might solve predictable problems now.

Reflective Practice:

- How can you be proactive by working with the students whose situations you envisioned, who are at risk for having a bad peer conference experience?
- How will you respond if a parent demands to have a child's writing partner changed after a particularly bad peer conference?

Sharing the Fruits of Their Labor: Debriefing About Peer Conferences

Amazing things are all around me, appearing ordinary at first,
until I really look at them closely.
—Joanne Ryder

At the end of writing workshop time, before I invited my students back to the rug, I took the time to listen to at least one peer conference. If the conference was going well, I couldn't help but linger there, listening to my kids, feeling proud of the quality of their talk as well as the substance of their writing. If I overheard really smart work happening, I would usually ask the partnership to share what they were talking about in their peer conference with the entire class during the whole-class share. (Admittedly, this would often make my workshop go a little longer, especially if two students were already lined up to share that day, but it was always worth the extra time.)

I insisted on two things when students shared discussions or writing work during their conference:

- **Both students talk:** One partner cannot do all of the talking. If I noticed one student was talking the most, I would either ask a question to the silent partner at the end of the debrief or I'd quietly encourage the student to engage his or her silent partner.
- **Work is shown:** I usually had the document camera on during share time. Having students show the places in their writing they discussed with their partner or changed because of their peer conference is exceedingly helpful. (If you don't have a document camera in your classroom, have the student show his or her work to the class in the circle. If you'd like, he or she can pass it around so peers can take a closer look.)

Other than insisting that both students speak and share their writing work, I let the students take control of presenting to the class. When we refrain from imposing a structure on the students, something enlightening is usually said, thereby inspiring other partnerships to challenge themselves more in their peer conferences.

Challenge: It's easy to highlight a well-functioning partnership in a full-class share. However, consider boosting a run-of-the-mill partnership. If necessary, spend some extra time working with them, noticing their strengths. Then encourage them to share something interesting they did together with the full class.

Reflective Practice:

- What made it challenging to highlight a partnership that you didn't regard as stellar?
- What did you learn about the highlighted partnership when they shared?
- What do you think your other students learned about peer conferring by watching this partnership present the work from their conference with the rest of the class?

Cycle 3: Lifting the Level of Our Conferences

Enjoy Conferring

All children wear the sign: "I want to be important NOW."
Many of our juvenile delinquency problems arise because nobody reads the sign.
—Dan Pursuit

The heart of everything we do should lie in the relationships we develop along the way. Developing relationships with the people in our classrooms should be more important than standards or testing. Before writing workshop, I felt I never had the time to get to know students by talking with them. We were too busy flitting from one activity to the next to pause and converse.

Once I understood that a writing conference isn't anything magical or programmed but a predictable conversation, the level of my conferring dramatically increased. My enjoyment increased, leading to a desire to want to confer. With more practice, I refined conferring even more. I've come to believe specific attitudes are necessary to intentionally lift the level of our conferring.

- **Don't make it more complicated than it needs to be:** Sometimes I get so caught up in the right steps, the right teaching point, the right conferring notes that I forget it all boils down to having a conversation. All I expect of myself is to talk with students about their writing, let them know what they are doing well, and nudge them to try a strategy that will help them become a stronger writer. It's not brain surgery! It's talking with students.
- **Listen, and then listen more:** When I first began to find my footing in conferences, I wanted them to be efficient. I thought the faster I could determine a teaching point, teach, and move on, the better conferrer I would be. Today, I listen more. I look for the meaning beyond the words. I've become comfortable with wait time and allow silence to linger in a conference. Often it is in these moments that the most thinking occurs. Through listening, we develop a deeper understanding of the young writers in our classrooms.
- **Smile:** It can be a little nerve-racking when someone older—someone who is a better writer and is asking lots of questions about you and your writing—wants to converse with you. Because this defines us as we confer, remember that a small smile has mighty power when it comes to settling nerves.
- **Build on strengths:** Nothing makes a conference more enjoyable than focusing on the strengths of the writer. When these strengths springboard into the teaching point, the experience is even more enjoyable. For example, when students learn to punctuate dialogue, quotation marks pop up everywhere. When we say to students, "I notice you are adding dialogue to your narrative, and it is making your characters come alive. I also notice you know quotation marks are necessary when writing dialogue. Let me show you their proper placement . . . ," we help them become stronger writers by building on their strengths.

By shifting our attitudes to enjoy conferring instead of dreading it, we are able to become stronger conferrers. When this happens, writing workshop is not only lifted to a new level but relationships are also forged and students know they are valued because we have taken the time to talk with them.

Challenge: Choose one of the aforementioned attitudes to adopt over the next several days. Your choice may be an element that you have believed in for a number of years; however, over the next few days be purposeful in accepting it.

Reflective Practice:

- Which of the attitudes are easiest for you to accept?
- Why are some of the attitudes difficult for you to accept?
- What have you found enjoyable about conferring?

Monitoring Our Language

Children grow into the intellectual life around them.
—Lev Vygotsky

Dimitres Pantelidis, the principal at P.S. 171 in East Harlem, sent me to a slew of Calendar Days, sponsored by the Teachers College Reading and Writing Project, when I taught fifth grade. One of the most significant Calendar Days, which we talked about a lot after I returned, was led by Peter H. Johnston. One of the most important things I learned from Johnston, author of *Choice Words: How Our Language Affects Children's Learning* (2004), dealt with phrases that undermine resilience in children. While I never used phrases like, "I'm disappointed in you," "You're not good at this," or even "You're a good boy/girl," I used the phrase, "I'm so proud of you" all of the time. Johnston explained this phrase undermines resilience in children because children depend on you to be proud of them. Instead, saying something like, "You should be very proud of yourself," is more effective and increases resilience in children. Therefore, I eradicated "I'm so proud of you" from my repertoire of compliments. Instead, after I attended Johnston's February 2007 workshop, I began saying, "You should be proud of yourself."

After attending a Responsive Classroom institute in 2006, I eradicated phrases such as "I like the way __________ is doing . . ." or "I love the way you're __________ . . ." when I conferred with my students. These statements make children depend on the teacher's praise. To give my students a greater sense of agency, I borrowed several phrases from Johnston (2004, 31—34). They are as follows:

- How did you do that?
- What problems did you encounter as a writer today? (This phrase alone makes students think strategically about problems.)
- How did you figure that out?
- Tell me about your challenges . . . So, what did you do about that?
- Where are you going with this piece of writing?
- What are you going to do with this piece?

After attending the Responsive Classroom institute and Johnston's seminar, I immediately wanted to begin changing my language. I realized I couldn't try all of these statements at one time. However, by consciously trying to infuse one statement into my conversations with students each week, these phrases became commonplace in my speech and subsequently helped students develop a greater sense of agency when they were working as writers.

Challenge: Grab a digital voice recorder before your next round of conferences so you can examine the language you use when you're conferring with your students. As you play back your conferences, write down frequently used phrases on a sheet of paper.

Reflective Practice:

- What phrases do you repeatedly use with your students? Are your statements undermining their resilience or are they creating a sense of agency?
- What can you do to create a greater sense of agency when you confer with the writers in your classroom?

Role-Playing with Colleagues

Education is not the filling of a pail, but the lighting of a fire.
—William Butler Yeats

Pat Werner, my ever-patient and brilliant literacy coach, often suggested we confer about reading and writing in front of students as part of the mini-lesson. I'd usually play the role of the teacher and Pat would often take on the student's role. We'd have a short, mock conference during the demonstration part of the mini-lesson. We'd unpack what we did or elicit from the students what they noticed us doing. Inevitably, when my students heard the way Pat and I talked together, their conferences always improved.

Role-playing worked so well with Pat that I tried it when I had student teachers in subsequent years. My student teachers would role-play with me in a mini-lesson when I wanted to demonstrate a point. It's one thing to demonstrate how you'd go about changing your own piece of writing, but it's more helpful for a child to watch two adults interacting over one piece of writing. When children listen to adults discuss their writing moves publicly, it often helps them relate what they see us doing to their own work. Furthermore, watching two adults have a quick conference during a mini-lesson can subsequently lift the level of peer conferences.

Don't have a literacy coach or student teacher who can role-play with you? Don't be bashful. Ask another colleague to help you! You can ask another teacher, one of your administrators, or a support staff professional to assist you with the demonstration in front of your students. It's a good idea to elicit their help a few days ahead of time so they can clear their schedule and plan alongside of you. Chances are they're more nervous about the role-playing than you are about asking them, so if you find a colleague to agree to this, be sure to equip them with the tools they'll need to be successful. You might want to inform your colleague about the genre you're working on and basic language you use during a writing conference.

Challenge: Look through your next unit of study. Locate a mini-lesson that would benefit from an adult role-play. Then enlist someone to help you with the role-play conference in front of your class.

Reflective Practice:

- What was it like to "share the stage" with someone else during your mini-lesson? Would you do it again?
- Describe the conferences you had with your students after they watched the adult role-play. How were they similar or different from conferences you've had in the past?

Analyzing Conference Records

Get in the habit of analysis—analysis will in time
enable synthesis to become your habit of mind.
—Frank Lloyd Wright

I was told to keep detailed conference notes when I began teaching. Arriving at a system that worked for me was a long journey. I found myself spending a lot of time, in-between conferences with my students, writing down the details from a conference. At another point, I rebelled and didn't keep notes at all because I didn't want to waste time. This wasn't the answer either. I had to find an in-between solution, because once I stopped keeping conference records I needed some way to prepare to confer with a student so that I could remember what we last discussed. There was no way I could remember what I talked about the last time I met with each student! I tried a variety of note-taking systems that colleagues and staff developers showed me through the years and eventually found a system that was perfect for me.

Once I found a note-taking system that worked for me, I began using it diligently. After each conference, I quickly recorded the compliment I gave to the student, as well as the teaching point I demonstrated during the instructional portion of our conference. Over time, I stopped writing the compliment and teaching point in complete sentences. Rather, I wrote enough words to help me remember the gist of the conference (instead of writing down "Writers unfold the heart of their story bit-by-bit-by-bit," I started writing, "Unfolding heart bit-by-bit") so that I wasn't burdened with laborious note taking.

At the beginning of each writing workshop, I spent two or three minutes looking over my conference notebook as my students settled in their focus spots. Reviewing my notebook helped me recall with whom I met recently (to keep an eye out for things I might need to check on with a student) and who needed to have a conference with me. Once I selected my students, I analyzed my notes from the previous conferences to ask myself questions to prepare for the conferences:

- What did I compliment the student on the past few times? While I'm perfectly content to have my husband tell me I have a nice smile, I don't want to hear him tell me that I have a nice smile day after day after day. Young writers need to hear they're doing a variety of things well. Knowing what the student did well in the past can help you look beyond the same compliments during your upcoming conference.
- What did I teach the past few times? Reviewing the past few teaching points helped to hold students accountable for previous learning. This helped ensure that I didn't teach the same thing to a student who already has a particular understanding or provided me an opportunity to reteach an important writing skill.

I also analyzed my conference notes at the end of each unit of study, which allowed me to determine how frequently my conferences focused on process, craft, or conventions. In addition, I was able to determine what my class, as a whole, was doing well as writers (by taking stock of all of the compliments I doled out) and what they needed more help with as writers. Looking at the class as a whole helped me to determine mini-lessons I might add into a future unit of study based on the needs I found classwide. Finally, studying the frequency I met with each student allowed me to see who was monopolizing my time and therefore helped me strategize ways to help that student. (For example, at one point, I was meeting with one of my students two to three times a week. Once I moved his rug spot to the front of the meeting area and changed his writing partner, our conferences went back to once a week since he was more focused during class and had a reliable partner whom he could consult when he was confused about what to do next as a writer.)

When you keep conference records for yourself, rather than for someone else who mandates how you keep them and what they should say, you'll notice that they become a useful tool to guide instruction in your classroom. Find a system that works for you, and don't be afraid to tweak it. Finally, remember to examine your conference records frequently, until it becomes a habit, so your conferences truly become the heart of your workshop.

Challenge: Schedule a time (at the end of each mini-lesson, day, week, or month) to analyze your writing conference records. First, look through them and note what your students are doing well. Then go back and find commonalities regarding instructional needs.

Reflective Practice:

- What are your students doing well as writers?
- What do your students need to work on as writers? Can these things be addressed in small instructional groups or do some of them need to be addressed during full-class mini-lessons?
- Are you meeting with all students equally? If not, what steps will you take to make your conferring more equitable?

Small-Group Conferences

The writer's energy for writing must go up, not down.
—Don Murray

It's rare to find all students in the same phase of the writing process at all times in a writing workshop. Some writers move at a faster pace than others, thereby causing all of our students to be in different places at different times. When I noticed this happening, I often allowed my students to sign up for small-group conferences based on their needs.

When offering small-group conferences, I suggest offering four to six sessions (whatever you can reasonably manage within a given period). The topics can be based on

- strategies for lifting the level of a particular genre;
- different parts of the writing process (e.g., drafting, revision, editing);
- the qualities of good writing (e.g., meaning, focus, elaboration, voice, word choice, structure, and conventions).

While students don't always sign up for the small-group conference I would have chosen for them, giving them the choice of what to sign up for allows them to have some power in their education. In addition, it's more likely that the writer's energy for writing will increase at the end of the small-group conference because he or she chose to work on a particular strategy. Therefore, his or her enthusiasm as a writer should be higher at the end of the session.

Challenge: During your mini-lesson, introduce the small-group conference options to your students. Give it an enthusiastic plug so they get excited about being empowered to choose the conference that works for them. Invite them to talk over the conference group they'd like to be in with their writing partner. Partners will also create a verbal plan (for the time they're not meeting with their group) before they sign up for their small group.

Reflective Practice:

- Did the small-group conferences help your students' enthusiasm for their writing work today?
- What did you enjoy about these conferences? What was challenging about moving around from conference to conference?
- How will you touch base with students about the work they did today? Is there anyone in particular you need to meet with the next day to reinforce small-group exercise?

Setting Goals to the Point of Need

The writing world, by its very nature, is differentiated.
—Colleen Cruz

When I first began conferring, I was ecstatic to find a teaching point that didn't involve grammar. As I learned more about writing and my students began writing more, I felt overwhelmed by how much my students had to learn about writing well. My conferences lengthened as I noticed several teaching "opportunities." Yet the mantra, "teach one thing," had been drilled into my head. To conform my conferring to this belief, I began to write down my teaching point when I decided to stick to a single topic in a conference. As I did this, I noticed my teaching points weren't always the most pressing matter. Determined to become more effective in my conferences, I decided to become more selective with teaching points.

In the beginning of the conference, I became an intentional listener. When I noticed a teaching point, I jotted down one or two words to remind me of it in my conferring notes. As the conference shifted into the teaching portion, I consulted my brainstorming list and chose the teaching point that would affect the writer the most.

Later I reviewed other possible teaching points and began to use those to set goals for students. As I knew my students better as writers, I also knew their most pressing needs. This allowed me to be intentional about teaching. Because I had already thought through the priorities for each of my students, the teaching point was easily pinpointed during the conference.

Another advantage to setting goals is being able to meet students at their point of need. When I realized Nolan never reread his writing, I met with him during critical rereading times—at the beginning of writing time when he was working on a draft, before revision, and before he found a peer editor, which forced him to reread for conventions on his own before enlisting the help of another student. Because of these goals and by intentionally conferring with him at a point of need, I was able to help Nolan to become a writer who reread his work. As Nolan began rereading independently, I added a new goal to his list of needs. As we meet students' needs and adapt their goal list, we make certain each student is pushed to become a stronger writer.

By setting goals for students, we become intentional in our conferences. From week to week, the teaching points build on one another, making the differentiated instruction in conferences effective.

Challenge: Create a place on your conferring notes to list two or three possible goals for each of your students. Set aside some time to consider the most pressing needs for each of the writers in your classroom. Plan to be intentional about meeting students at their points of need.

Reflective Practice:

- How did your conferring change when you set goals for each student?
- What were some common goals among your students?
- How will you monitor growth and achievement of the goals you've identified for students?

Listen More

Children will not remember you for the material things you provided
but for the feeling that you cherished them.
—Richard L. Evans

My students always knew when I was armed and ready for conferring when they saw me walking around the classroom holding my black spiral notebook. In the beginning of the school year, they usually raised their hand, hungry to get my feedback. By midyear, they learned that I'd stop by when I knew they needed something or, more important, when I saw they were writing diligently.

Some of the most glorious times I spent in my classroom were alongside a child conferring. In these quiet conferences, I learned of baby brothers who died and were no longer talked about, of mothers who devoted an afternoon a week to one of their children for special bonding time, and of grandfathers who taught their kin about "needs versus wants." I listened to the stories with keen interest knowing my students were sharing the stories of their lives. As they shared their personal stories, I listened as their writing teacher and found a way to help them write their life stories better—not just that particular story on that particular day.

The first time I heard Carl Anderson speak he said, "It's the details of a writing piece that make it special and beautiful." When we listen to the details of our children's lives, we honor their stories. By honoring their stories and showing them respect for what they already know about storytelling, we help ourselves become better teachers of writing. This happens because when we are aware of what our students are capable of, we can teach them the next big thing to help them become better storytellers or, rather, better writers.

Challenge: Research a little longer for the next few days when you confer with your students. Linger with them and let them talk just a bit more than you normally would. Listen carefully to what they say so you can connect with them on a personal level and on a writerly level.

Reflective Practice:

- What did you learn about one of your students today by listening to what they had to say during your conferences?
- How can you listen to your students in conferences a little longer so that you can understand what's working for them and what's important to them, while still maintaining an efficient conferring schedule?

Recording and Reflecting with Colleagues

It's in the act of having to do things you don't want to
that you learn something about moving part of the self.
—bell hooks

When I first began learning about writing workshop, I had the opportunity to be part of a study group of about twenty teachers through the All-Write!!! Consortium. I agonized over the lengthy application; however, the reward was worth it: I would be part of a study group of twenty teachers who would meet twelve days throughout the school year. The icing on the cake? Carl Anderson would be leading the group.

In the foreword of Anderson's book *How's It Going? A Practical Guide to Conferring with Student Writers*, Lucy Calkins describes Anderson's work as "sprinkling Miracle-Gro on [teachers]" (2000, xiv). This was certainly the case for me. I grew leaps and bounds that year, nothing short of a miracle, as my paradigms and beliefs changed and as I refined my practice.

Since conferring is the heart of writing workshop, and one of Anderson's specialties, we were expected to lift the level of our conferring skills throughout the year. Under Anderson's tutelage, we began to learn the art of conferring. My most uncomfortable experience was transcribing a conference. Ironically, this facilitated a crucial turning point in my development as a writing workshop teacher.

To transcribe a conference, Anderson encouraged us to record ourselves. *You've gotta be kidding*, I thought, picturing myself recording a conference with one of my students using the old tape recorder left over from my college lecture hall days. My cheeks flushed as I recalled my pathetic attempts at conferring. However, Anderson said he would be checking in with us during the next session and the thought of not having a transcript was even more humiliating than the actual recording and transcribing of the conference.

Mustering courage, along with my old tape recorder, I explained to my students Anderson's assignment. I knew if I confessed my "homework" to them, they would hold me accountable. (There is nothing sweeter to an adolescent than a teacher's pain from an assignment.) I recorded my conferences over the course of a few days. I resisted the urge to tape over the really awful ones. After I recorded several conferences, the tape recorder sat on my desk for over a week. I didn't want to listen. As the next session neared, I reluctantly took the recorder with me on my drive home.

Finally, I pushed play. As I listened, I began to make important realizations about my conferring. First, I always gave positive feedback to students. Sometimes this feedback was specific; sometimes it was general. I also realized my conferences were short. I replayed the conferences in the privacy of my car. Listening a second time, I realized I wasn't teaching in most of my conferences. I was complimentary and encouraging, but I wasn't teaching.

As I transcribed the conference, even more was revealed. I realized I had picked up effective key phrases from Anderson. I made a note to use these phrases regularly in my conferences: "I'm noticing"; "What some writers do is"; "Try it and I'll check back in a few minutes." These phrases lifted the level of my conferences.

Taking my transcripts to the next study group was nerve-racking. I didn't want to share my flawed conferences with other teachers, let alone with "The Conferring Guy"! However, this proved to be a crucial point in my learning and an experience that has stayed with me over the years. As we shared our transcripts and analyzed the conferences, two things happened. First, I realized I wasn't as bad as I thought I was when it came to conferring. The other teachers in my small group gave me hope. They were able to affirm some of my strengths in conferring. At the same time, I was able to identify their strengths, not only affirming them but also seeing ways to improve. Second, I realized the missing pieces of my conferences and ways I could improve. The teachers in my small group helped me process ways to move into the teaching portion of a conference. When I returned to my classroom, I had specific goals to improve my conferring. Through the work with transcripts and colleagues, my goal changed from *learn to confer* to *use the strength of the student as a springboard into the teaching point*.

Being part of a small group led by an expert in writing workshop isn't an opportunity we all have. However, recording our conferences, reflecting on and transcribing them, and then using the transcripts as a point of reflection and goal setting with colleagues is possible. When we are intentional about our growth in conferring, it is inevitable that the level of our conferring ability will improve.

Challenge: Plan to record several of your conferences. Listen and reflect on your conferring skills. Then choose at least one conference to transcribe. Finally, take the last step and analyze your transcript with someone. This may be a trusted colleague or a teacher from an online community.

Reflective Practice:

- What is your strength when you confer with student writers?
- What are a few of your conferring goals after recording, transcribing, and discussing your conferences?

Document a Successful Conference

The reward of a thing well done, is to have done it.
—Ralph Waldo Emerson

One of the best gifts we can give ourselves as teachers of writing is to document the good stuff of our writing workshops. It's no secret that conferring is hard. Yet I'm sure there have been conferences you've walked away from feeling good. There are times when you just know you nailed it. When we remember these conferences and then spend time reflecting on them, we grow as teachers.

I was working with third-grade classroom teacher Tony Miller, launching writing workshop, when Meg looked at my conferring record and said, "You've not met with me. Look, my box is blank. Let's talk." The freckles sprinkled across her cheeks, coupled with her big brown eyes, melted my heart.

As I pulled up a chair beside her, she began telling me about her dog Lilly. "Well she's like 10 percent my dog. She's actually my piano teacher's dog," and she launched into telling me a Lilly story. I was so entertained by her that I didn't stop her as she told about another Lilly memory.

As she took a breath and gathered her thoughts, I interrupted her by asking, "So why did you want to talk to me about your writing?"

Meg shrugged. "Well, nothing. I just wanted to talk about my story." She smiled and started in again, "Lilly is really funny, like the time she . . ."

"Wait, a minute." I smiled at her and touched her shoulder with the eraser of my pencil. "Meg, you just discovered something really important about yourself as a writer." She smiled, and I continued. "You know that you can collect ideas about a topic in your notebook, plan a draft, write a little, and then you need to talk about your story. After talking, do you feel like you can write your story better now?"

"Oh, yeah." She grinned at me.

"Do you still need to talk a little more?"

"Yes, just the last part, the funny part about Lilly."

"Well, the good news is you don't have to talk to a teacher, you can talk to any writer in the room. Is there a writer in your group that you feel would be a good listener?"

She pointed across the table to Jeff. "Just ask him if he has a few minutes to listen to you while you tell him a funny story about Lilly," I encouraged.

As Meg directed her request to Jeff, who joyfully accepted, I couldn't help but smile. Not only did Meg have more energy for writing but so did I.

As I reflected on this conference, I realized a telltale sign of a successful conference: the energy level increases. I considered my conferring choices when I first started writing workshop. As I recalled, I knew I would have stopped Meg when she said she didn't really have any questions about her writing, she just wanted to talk. I would have "taught" her that when she requests a conference, she should have something she wants to talk about as a writer.

Today, I trust students more. I listen more. My first response is often as a writer instead of as a teacher. In this case, Meg reminded me of me. Often, when I'm working on my writing, I get my husband's attention and ask him to listen to this or that. As a writer, I need to "just talk." As a teacher, I need to just listen.

Challenge: Recall a time when you walked away from a conference feeling good about your ability to confer. Set a timer and write for fifteen minutes, recalling the details of the conference. Then push yourself to reflect on the experience and develop a big idea about your conferring.

Reflective Practice:

- How do you feel about your conferring abilities after completing the challenge?
- What are some telltale signs of a successful conference you have noticed?

Helping Others Become Stronger Writers

Appreciation is a wonderful thing:
It makes what is excellent in others belong to us as well.
—Voltaire

"Excuse me, Sarah," Joe says after Sarah shares about her story, "how does what you said help us become better writers?"

"Thank you, Joe," Sarah responds. "I thought some of you may get an idea for a story by the things you do after school too."

"That makes sense," Joe says. "Thanks."

"Does anyone else have something to share?" Sarah asks the class.

Meanwhile, Cathy Laker's eyes twinkle as she rejoices in the language of her second-grade students. After nearly six weeks of participating in this type of share, her students are developing not only the language of civility but also a purpose behind their share time. Her students come to the circle at the end of writing workshop expecting to learn more about writing from their peers. When they do learn something, they express gratitude. This is a common practice when writers share their work.

This type of open forum share takes tenacity to develop, yet the results are well worth the dedicated work. First, students are nudged during conferences to share their learning during the share session with their peers. Cathy often coaches her students in what they will say during the share session. At the end of writing workshop, students are asked to find a place to stop writing and to bring anything to the share circle that would help other writers in the classroom.

Cathy opens the share session with, "Does anyone have anything to share today that would be useful to other writers?" Because she has encouraged students to share during conferring, there are always volunteers. After they share, she encourages them to answer the question, "How does that help the rest of us as writers?"

In an open forum share, one purpose is to help other writers in the community. Another purpose is for the community to help the writer who is sharing. In Barb Bean's third-/fourth-grade multiage classroom, a student asks to share: "I need help with my ending. The first one is supposed to make you think, but it might be confusing. The second ending seems really boring."

As she reads her two endings, the rest of the community is listening intently, while some even jot on sticky notes. When she finishes she asks, "Does anyone have feedback for me?"

The success of an open forum share rests in the language our students use. When they learn the nuances of discussion, as well as the specific purposes of the share (to teach or to gain feedback), their language reflects these understandings. As they begin talking as writers, they accept the persona of a writer and the share session becomes even more powerful.

Challenge: Plan to host several open forum shares in the upcoming weeks. During conferences, be intentional about using the language of writers as well as encouraging students to share their learning during the open forum share. The success of this type of share depends on our language and encouragement in conferences. As students become accustomed to this type of share, it will evolve and become more natural over time.

Reflective Practice:

- How will you encourage students during conferring to share?
- What did you like most about the open forum share?
- How will you continue to improve this type of share session during the school year?

Chapter 6: Assessment

Assessment is an integral part of writing workshop. Without it, writing workshop becomes stagnant. Therefore, it is important to develop an attitude of assessment. An attitude of learning the strengths and seeing the growth of the writers in our conferences. An attitude of defining a writer at a specific point in time on a specific piece of writing. An attitude of encouraging students to assess themselves as writers.

When Carl Anderson is around writers, he is in a state of assessment. Assessing writers is now second nature to him. We can all aspire to develop this habit. Like all attitudes, assessment can be altered and refined. If you'd like to adjust your attitude regarding assessment, consider the cycles in this chapter:

- **Cycle 1: Formative Assessment**
  This is the most critical type of assessment we engage in as writing teachers. The focus of this cycle is on assessing students intentionally in their daily lives as writers. In a sense, we are forming our opinions of each student's strengths and needs.

- **Cycle 2: Summative Assessment**
  Just as professional writers have deadlines, so do our students. At the end of a unit of study, students will turn in a final copy to be graded. In this cycle, we wrestle with issues about grading and balancing different perspectives during summative assessment.
- **Cycle 3: Standardized Tests**
  Like it or not, standardized tests are a part of our students' writing lives. This cycle offers practical ideas to align preparation for a writing prompt as close to an authentic workshop experience as possible.

Like any habit, developing a habit of mind toward assessing writers will take time and patience. Through the ups and downs of establishing this new habit, our assessment practices are strengthened. When this happens, writing workshop becomes an even better place for writers.

Cycle 1: Formative Assessment

Inviting Formative Assessment

First we make our habits, then our habits make us.
—Charles C. Noble

Habits are an important part of developing sophistication in any craft. The art of teaching is no exception. If there is any habit I have intentionally developed as a writing teacher, it is formative assessment. When I began to refine my assessment practices intentionally (which I feel is an ongoing process), I listened to Carl Anderson speak on the topic. I remembered being jarred when I heard him say, "When I'm around young writers I am constantly assessing them."

At the time, I couldn't imagine being in a constant state of assessing writers. Today, I have also developed this habit. It is a habit that serves me well as I work with a variety of writers each day. Establishing a habit regarding formative assessment is difficult and even uncomfortable. Yet there are ways to encourage this habit.

- **Conferring notes:** I created a space on my conferring notes labeled "What I'm Noticing About This Writer" as a reminder to assess students intentionally as I met with them in individual conferences.
- **Observation lists:** I added a sheet to my clipboard underneath my conferring record titled "What I Know from Watching Writers." Although the remainder of the page was blank, it was a different color from my conferring notes and a visual reminder to spend time assessing my students through observation.

- **Observe another classroom:** I developed the habit of constantly assessing student writers in other writing workshops. When I went into a workshop besides my own, I no longer felt pressure to do something else, nor did I know the students personally. I was forced to assess writers solely on observation.
- **Response basket:** Creating a basket for students to drop off their in-progress writing for feedback was one effective way to create a formative assessment habit. As I spent time reading and responding to student writing to help students grow as writers (instead of evaluating them), I became the kind of teacher who naturally assessed young writers simply by being around them. Although it took more out-of-class time, I appreciated the luxury of spending time with a piece of writing and thinking deeply about the student as a writer. Initially, this was a large amount of time; however, as I became more proficient at formative assessment, I also became more efficient with reading and responding to student writing. The response basket has always been optional, which helps me manage the amount of student writing to take home.

As we train ourselves to assess student writers naturally, we develop a habit that will make us stronger writing teachers.

Challenge: Develop a method to invite formative assessment into your writing workshop. Create concrete reminders to help develop this habit.

Reflective Practice:

- Why is it important to develop a habit of assessing student writers when you are around them?
- What have you noticed about the way you think about the writers in your classroom as you've become more intentional about assessing them day in and day out?

On-Demand Writing

Too many of us now approach a blank page not as an occasion for discovery, but as a minefield to be traversed gingerly. We inch our way from word to word, concerned less with clarity and precision than with sheer survival.

—Joseph M. Williams

By the time students reach upper elementary school, they already know a lot about writing personal narratives and fiction. While writing samples from previous years are helpful, often the writing we receive inside a student's portfolio is a piece of published writing, which has been honed over the course of a few weeks. I'd rather find out what a student is capable of doing when they're in my classroom because it helps to know what students know about a given genre before we begin a unit of study. One way to garner this information is to give students an on-demand writing assignment.

Some students find on-demand assignments anxiety provoking because producing a piece of writing without any assistance in a short amount of time is out of reach for many young writers. Therefore, stress that this task is a way to help you, as their teacher, understand what they do well when writing in this genre. It's crucial for students to know their writing will not be graded but, rather, will be assessed by you so you can work with them in conferences or in small groups.

I provided students with a sheet of paper that outlined my expectations for the writing exercise (Appendix E). I always reviewed the sheet with my students *before* they started working on a piece of writing so I could answer their questions, because their on-demand writing was to be completed in silence and without teacher assistance. Therefore, I spent ten to fifteen minutes answering questions about the expectations for the assignment so students were clear about writing independently.

On-demand writing assessments are useful when students have been exposed to a genre in at least one previous school year. However, regardless of the genre, include the following items on the assignment sheet as points of reference:

- **Task:** A short description of the task students need to complete.
- **Time:** The amount of time all students have to work on their on-demand writing. (Students with modifications should be given extended time to complete the assessment.)
- **Checklist:** A list of details for students to remember as they complete their on-demand writing. The checklist might include mundane reminders like putting a name and date on each page or more specific reminders like making sure a new paragraph is started whenever necessary.
- **Requests:** This is a place to ask students to do certain things. I found that "requesting" students to do things like skipping lines or proofreading their work, rather than mandating it, actually led to most students taking the time to make sure they were turning in their best work.

At the end of each on-demand writing assessment, I included three reflection questions so I could gain a better understanding of how things went for my students. Typically, I would ask students variations of the following questions:

- What about this task was simple for you? Please explain.
- What felt challenging to you about this task? Please be specific.
- This assignment made me feel like I was (circle one):

an accomplished writer	a good writer
a fair writer	a writer in need of improvement

Students' responses about their experience each time they completed an on-demand assignment allowed me to have a better understanding of what was going on inside their heads, as well as what they produced on the page. Having both their writing and their reflections allowed me to form a consistent opinion about my next teaching moves at the beginning of each unit of study I taught.

Challenge: Create an on-demand writing assessment for your next unit of study. Make sure the assignment scaffolds your students as they attempt to write in a new genre. Be sure to draw from the writing skills your students already have so they will feel successful as they complete this task.

Reflective Practice:

- How did the preassignment discussion with your students go? What did you do to make them feel at ease about this task?
- What did you learn about your students' writing as a result of this assignment?
- What was your students' stamina like during this assignment? How did they pace themselves? What did early finishers do? Did any students not finish the assignment in the time provided?

Driving Full-Class Instruction

It is our attitude at the beginning of a difficult task which,
more than anything else, will affect its successful outcome.
—William James

Exasperated, a teacher threw up her arms and lamented, "Will you just tell me what to teach next? Give me a list of lessons and I'll teach them."

I smile as I remember the feeling from so long ago, yet it resurfaces each time I work alongside a teacher new to writing workshop. Therefore, I share my story.

When I first started writing workshop, there weren't many resources dedicated to lessons or units of study. Within the books I was reading, there were many ideas for lessons and units of study but few that were scripted or outlined. At the time, I didn't know any better. I was new to the profession, and as the saying goes, ignorance is bliss. In a case of survival, I found lessons in places other than a teacher's manual.

Over the years, I learned that formative assessment is the best way to know what lessons to teach. When we pay attention to the ways students are working well as writers and the ways they ought to improve as writers, we have a gold mine of lesson possibilities.

In their article "Inside the Black Box: Raising Standards Through Classroom Assessment," Black and Wiliam (1998) assert that, "For assessment to function formatively, the results have to be used to adjust teaching and learning; thus a significant aspect of any program will be the ways in which teachers make these adjustments." The key is to review our conferring records with the intent to adjust our whole-class instruction. Over the years, I've trained myself to review conferring notes with this mind-set, looking for

- **Approximations:** As with learning anything new, we make approximations when we grow as writers. The approximations students make can be excellent starting points for lessons. For example, students often approximate paragraphing by starting a new line and indenting on a whim. This approximation leads us into a lesson on when to start a new paragraph.
- **Common teaching points:** When I use the same teaching point multiple times, I know this is an essential idea that should be taught in a mini-lesson so everyone is privy to the information.
- **Misunderstandings:** If I am clearing up confusion for students, this indicates a potential mini-lesson.
- **Strengths:** Some of my favorite lessons are derived from student strengths. When one writer is competent in a technique others are not, then that is a potential mini-lesson.

Today, many resources are available for mini-lessons and units of study. No longer is there a challenge to find a mini-lesson idea. The challenge has shifted to finding the best mini-lesson for your students. By using conferring notes and considering possible mini-lessons, we can adjust our teaching to meet the students' needs.

Challenge: Spend some time with your conferring notes, looking at them through the lenses identified earlier. List potential mini-lessons you could teach.

Reflective Practice:

- Which "lenses" worked the best for you? Why do you think this "lens" generated the most ideas?
- How will you determine which lesson from your list you will teach?

Checking Back After a Conference

It is our responsibilities, not ourselves, that we should take seriously.
—Peter Ustinov

I caught the flu when I was a junior in college. My internist was also sick so I saw Dr. Dunn, another doctor in her practice. Even though I had received a flu shot, I was diagnosed with the flu. Dr. Dunn suggested how I could combat my aches, stuffiness, and fever. By the end of the Friday morning appointment, we had agreed on an at-home treatment plan. Dr. Dunn told me he'd call me over the weekend to see how I was doing. I left the office and purchased my medications but doubted he would call. I went back to my apartment and wallowed in misery for the next two days.

On Sunday afternoon, the phone rang. I expected it to be a friend. However, I was shocked to hear Dr. Dunn's voice. He wanted to check in with me to see how the over-the-counter medications were working. He was pleased to hear I was feeling better and recommended one other thing to aid my recovery. I thanked him profusely. I hung up in disbelief because that was one of the only times in my life I've ever had a doctor follow up with me, on a weekend nonetheless, after a medical appointment.

If we think of writing conferences as medical appointments, then we should treat our students the way we'd like our physicians to treat us. We should agree on a plan for their writing. Based on what we have taught in the conference, we can ask our students, "How do you plan to use this?" This will help us understand whether they're going to use our suggestions meaningfully. In addition, we should follow up with students after a conference to see how they're applying the strategy we taught. Just as Dr. Dunn wanted to make sure I was following through with the medications and getting better, it's necessary for teachers to make sure students are applying the techniques from the conference to become better writers.

Checking back with students after a conference can often feel time consuming. However, if we want to be practitioners who make a difference, we will find nuggets of time, either at the end of a share session or the following day, to follow up with our students.

Challenge: Make an effort to check in with all of the students you confer with this week. Create a checklist (Appendix E) to help keep track of your check-ins.

Reflective Practice:

- What were your students' moods when you checked in with them?
- How do you think your check-ins helped reinforce your teaching?
- Did you find yourself reteaching during any of the check-ins? Why do you think you had to reteach what was taught in the conference?

Reading Notebooks Leads to Responsive Teaching

And in the end, it's not the years in your life that count. It's the life in your years.
—Abraham Lincoln

My students used their writer's notebooks for two purposes. The first was to write anecdotal pieces about their daily lives. The second was to develop pieces of writing for each unit of study. As a result, each week, when I read each student's notebook during lunchtime, it was important for me to look at both his or her in-class and at-home writing so I could get a better sense of what was happening for each student. I often took notes about what the student was doing well as a writer and what he or she was struggling with. Many times, my notes became the basis for individual or small-group conferences for students with similar instructional needs.

Mark Overmeyer's book on formative assessment reminds us that we have many avenues to help direct our teaching. He asserts, "As teachers of writing, we can monitor student progress during all parts of the writing process, even during the initial, idea-gathering stages, by thinking of assessment as something that can inform our instruction—formative, rather than summative, assessment" (2009, 4).

One way to give yourself the space to allow your students' writing trends to inform your instruction throughout the school year is by building in a couple of "buffer days" for each unit of study you plan to teach. My former fourth-grade colleagues and I did this so we could be responsive to problems we noticed on our students' drafts as well as in their notebook writing. Having a couple of days of unplanned teaching points allowed us to look at our whole classes and consider what our students needed to learn to write better. I could examine my students' notebooks and discover a gap in my teaching. When I noticed my students weren't writing deeply during an essay unit of study (judging from the shallow writing I read in their notebooks), I used one of my buffer days to teach a mini-lesson on strategies for writing longer, more meaningful pieces. Having ample time to change instructional plans as needs arise helps us transform our instruction to meet the needs of all learners.

When we read our students' notebooks deeply, looking beyond whether they've used Standard English, we honor our students by noticing what they've mastered and what they still need to learn. And in the end, it's not whether we read our students' notebooks—it's what we do with the information we glean when we peruse their notebooks that counts.

Challenge: Figure out how to make the time you spend reading through your students' notebooks more meaningful. Think about using a checklist (see Appendix 2 of Carl Anderson's [2005] *Assessing Writers*) or taking anecdotal notes to help you keep track of what your students are doing well, as a group, or what you need to focus on more during your instruction based on your close reading of their notebooks.

Reflective Practice:

- What do your students, by and large, do well as writers? What's challenging for them as a class?
- How has the checklist or anecdotal note taking helped you assess your students' needs and plan for instruction that responds to what you've learned about them from reading their notebooks?

Responding to In-Progress Writing

Feedback is the breakfast of champions.
—Ken Blanchard

Formative assessment doesn't have to occur during writing workshop. It can also happen as we read student writing outside of writing workshop. As we form opinions about student writers, we should take time to read their in-progress writing. The purpose of this reading isn't to grade the writing but to offer feedback.

As much as I like teaching writing, it doesn't mean that I want to spend all of my free time reading student writing. Here are some ways to respond to in-progress writing and still have time for your favorite hobby.

- **Read a portion:** Just as tapas portions for each course make dining out more enjoyable, so do small portions of student writing. It isn't necessary to read entire drafts to gain insight.
    - *Read the same element from everyone.* This is managed by reading the same part of everyone's draft. For example, after studying leads, collect everyone's writing and read only the leads. By reading the same portion from each student, we are able to give feedback quickly and assess the effectiveness of our mini-lessons on a particular element.
    - *Read writing from a single writing period.* By reading drafts written during one work period, we are able to gain insight, without drowning in piles of papers. This technique enables us to assess the writing fluency of students in addition to the way students use craft and conventions.
    - *Ask students to identify a section to read.* When we ask students to identify a section of writing they would like us to read, we are able to respond directly to their needs. Often we gain powerful insights about the student as a writer based on the section we're offering feedback about.
- **Check out the revisions:** One way to determine whether students are growing as writers is to analyze their revisions. As we understand their writing

process, we can see ways they are improving their works, as well as help them to refine this process
- **Read for a purpose:** When I read student work, I often establish a purpose ahead of time. Other times, I ask students to set the purpose. They can do this by jotting a note at the top of their drafts to orient me as I read.

By reading in-progress writing, we are able to gain valuable insights about our students that are often overlooked during conferences and observations during writing workshop. Intentionally reading portions of writing will make this critical practice manageable for writing workshop teachers.

Challenge: Plan to collect student writing this week. Consider how you will make reading and responding to your students manageable.

Reflective Practice:
- What did you learn about the writers in your classroom that you didn't know before?
- Were you efficient when reading and responding to your students' writing? If so, what made you efficient? If not, what else could you have done to be more efficient?

Kid-Watching

The camera is an instrument that teaches people to see without a camera.
—Dorothea Lange

When students are working as writers, I like to think of myself as a camera. Sometimes I zoom in on the details of an individual. Other times I zoom out and try to see as much of the picture as possible. It is this nuance of zooming in and zooming out that drives my formative assessment.

When I'm working closely with a student or a small group of students, I'm noticing their work as writers. This work allows me to gain a sense of the personalized needs of the writers in my classroom. It grounds me in knowing that each writer is an individual with a unique process.

Sometimes I get stuck on the zoom-in feature. I feel pressure to confer with as many students as possible. However, when this happens, I miss an opportunity for a different kind of formative assessment. By zooming out and observing the class as a whole, I'm able to learn new information about the writers in the classroom.

When I observe the big pictures, I assess the effectiveness of the procedures. Are students self-sufficient when they need supplies or resources? Through this vantage point, I'm able to learn whether students know how to redirect themselves and one another when they are off task. I notice whether students have found a space where they can work effectively. Most important, I can assess the writing community as a whole. I see firsthand whether they support one another in their work as writers.

We spend too much time engrossed in watching the big picture, and as a result, our conferring suffers. Just as a proficient photographer trains her eye to take photographs from many vantage points, as writing workshop teachers we must train ourselves to assess through many vantage points. Zooming in and zooming out gives us a more well-rounded view of the way students are working as writers.

Challenge: Intentionally zoom in and zoom out on your next writing workshop. List your observations from the different vantage points or from places you stand in your classroom.

Reflective Practice:

- What are some of the differences in your lists based on the two vantage points?
- How will you use your observations to inform your teaching in writing workshop?

Studying Writing Partnerships

What you don't see with your eyes, don't invent with your tongue.
—Jewish Proverb

Many of the writing workshops I led in my classroom ended with time for writing partnerships to meet with one another. I always provided students with a lens to focus their sharing so partner time didn't turn into socialization time. The focused sharing provided students with an opportunity to share their work with one another to reinforce that day's, or a previous day's, teaching point.

It is helpful to watch the way partnerships function during share times. It's useful to observe the way students interact with one another at the end of a writing workshop. Just as we spend several moments observing our students as they settle into independent writing time, we must take time to read our classrooms as students work with their writing partners. During this time, keep these questions in mind as you closely observe your students:

- **Balance of time:** Do both students have the chance to share their writing and give feedback or is one student monopolizing the share session?
- **Commenting:** What kind of feedback do partners give one another? Are students complimenting and providing one another with constructive criticism?
- **Focus:** Are both students focused on the lens you provided them? Do students know when and how to shift from the lens you give them to setting their own agenda for a partnership talk?
- **Pacing:** Do students come to their partnership ready to share their writing? How do students use the allotted time? What does the partnership do if they "finish" early?
- **Questioning:** Do partners ask one another focused questions to improve their writing?

Once you've watched your students from afar or by sitting in on their conference, you will be able to glean more information about how to confer with partners as you plan future instruction. Any time we attempt to understand a partnership's true needs, we increase our ability to make a writing partnership into a dynamic team that will motivate each writer to do his or her best.

Challenge: Take some time to observe partnerships throughout this week. Take anecdotal notes about what you witness. At the end of the week, review your notes and determine your next teaching steps for each partnership. Plan to focus teaching on what you noticed when you meet with each writing partnership the following week.

Reflective Practice:

- How did your close observation of a given partnership help you gain a better understanding of how that partnership functions?
- Was anecdotal note taking an effective way to capture what you noticed? If not, could you use technology (e.g., a digital voice recorder or a video camera) to capture a partnership's meeting?

Talking Shop During Downtime

If it is to be, it is up to me.
—William H. Johnson

There is not much downtime when you're teaching. When I started teaching, I often felt rushed to cram everything into the school day. As the years went on, I became more adept at fitting everything into every school day. By my fifth year, I was able to find pockets of downtime during the day when students could have a—gasp!—break. I quickly realized spare time could be used for informal discussions with students about read-aloud books, math troubles, or writing. If I talked about school in a less academic way, then it was possible to talk shop during interludes in the day.

Reluctant writers, proficient writers, lackluster writers, and superstar writers need to talk about their writing with someone. I found it useful to talk with all of my writers outside of conferring time in writing workshop. For many students, the format of a writing conference can feel like a performance; they know they have to be on. Conversing with your teacher about your writing on the way back from lunch feels more like talking to a peer. I often found students were excited to work on their writing after an informal conversation with me. Therefore, there are a few times during the school day when you can make an effort to talk about student writing away from writing workshop:

- **First thing in the morning:** If your students trickle into the classroom, then let them know they can come to you to talk about the writing they did the previous night once they've fulfilled their morning responsibilities, such as unpacking and turning in their homework.
- **During snack:** Students who receive a five- to ten-minute bathroom or snack break can spend some of the time talking to you about their writing. Conversations that happen during this time of the day often revolve around the writing work students have done or are planning to do during writing workshop.
- **Before and after lunch or recess:** Many of my students took their writer's notebooks down to lunch and recess with them. Often, students wanted to chat about their writing. Taking just a minute to stop and listen can really help writers who want to push themselves.

Talking shop is something adult writers do with one another. Allowing your students to discuss their writing with you during downtime can increase their enthusiasm and their desire to write.

Challenge: Strike up a writerly conversation with at least one reluctant writer and one proficient writer in your class this week. Keep the conversation casual so it doesn't feel like a writing conference. Let your student take the lead for discussing his or her writing with you.

Reflective Practice:

- What kind of writer was the most challenging to talk with during downtime? How did you keep the conversation going without seeming like his or her teacher?
- How can you use downtime to learn more about the writing work your students are doing or hope to do?

Assessing Share Time

We can create classrooms where words matter, where words make a difference, where words make an effect.
—Lucy Calkins

When students share, they find the value of their words. If we are not actively engaged in a writing community, it is easy to forget how important our words are and how they can, indeed, make a difference. Stacey and I host a writing challenge every March on our blog. One of the powerful things about this challenge is the writing community that ensues. Within days, writers begin connecting to one another through stories. I'm often honored when someone shares an important story with the writing community—my life is richer because of it. At the same time, I'm touched to know my writing influences others. March (as well as every Tuesday throughout the year) reminds us about how stories bind people because our words matter. As teachers, it is crucial to remember that stories matter.

By assessing students as they share, we can help them connect as a writing community. Just like when we confer individually with students, we can determine what they are doing well when they share and what they could do differently to become more proficient. We must record our observations and share them with students. I've found it is best to share these teaching points with individual students outside of the share session.

Since the purpose of the share session is to celebrate our work as writers, it can be undermining to use the time for a teaching point. To honor the student as well as the purpose of the share, jot a note to the student with feedback about share time. Another way to communicate this information is during conferring time the following day. As long as we make notes in our records and refer to these notes, we will be able to improve the strength of the writing community.

When I assess students during share sessions, I notice the following:

- **The confidence with which a student speaks:** When a student speaks with poise during a share session, he or she usually gets higher-quality feedback than a student who doesn't speak as boldly. Helping students to become more self-confident when they speak about their writing strengthens our writing community.
- **The response students offer the writer who is sharing:** By increasing the feedback the writing community gives, as well as the usefulness of the responses, we can support one another even more.
- **The specificity of our conversation:** When students ask for specific input from the community or the community gives specific examples when responding to a writer, the share session is strengthened.
- **The energy level of the writing community:** At the end of a share session, the energy level should be high. When writing workshop closes on high energy,

it is more likely to open the next day with a sense of hope and delight in the writing work that lies ahead. Helping students to be deliberate about increasing the energy level of a share session goes a long way toward strengthening the writing community.

As our share sessions become more proficient, students will see how their words matter to the writing community. When students realize the power of their words, then our classrooms become places where writing makes a difference and the voices of our students can make the world a better place.

Challenge: Purposely assess a share session during an upcoming writing workshop. Offer specific feedback to some writers with the intent of strengthening the writing community.

Reflective Practice:

- What do your students do well as members of a writing community? What are some things they could do to strengthen their community?
- How will you offer feedback to students regarding their participation in the share session?

Cycle 2: Summative Assessment

Providing Guidelines for Writing Assignments

When I examine whole files of papers that have been marked and commented on by teachers, many of them look as though they have been trampled on by cleated boots.

—Paul Diederich

I am a left-brained person. I approach things logically. I like lists. I crave clarity. Therefore, if something is unclear, I strive to make it straightforward. Hence, I have often provided guidelines for writing assignments so my expectations for students would be 100 percent explicit.

I've handed out guidelines for published writing in two particular units of study: persuasive letter writing and short fiction/picture book writing. I provided students with guidelines for these assignments because these were assignments that were going to be shared beyond the classroom. Students were to mail persuasive letters to decision makers within our school and in the community. Students whose fiction picture books achieved the agreed-upon grade on the rubric we co-created sent their picture books to a Manhattan publisher. Therefore, to help my students work up to their potential as they entered the publishing stage of their writing, I found it necessary to specify how to make their published writing robust.

Guidelines always came in the form of checklists in my classroom. I used a checklist format because it held each student accountable for making sure their work contained all of the necessary elements for publication. Further, the checklists were usually created after the rubric, which meant that completing the items on the checklist usually ensured a good grade on a given assignment. Often, students worked with their writing partners to ensure they could honestly check off all of the items on the checklist before they turned in their final published piece of writing (Figure 6.1).

Persuasive Letter Checklist

Name: ______________________________

Check these items off as you complete them. Turn this sheet in with your completed persuasive letter. Thank you!

_____ I have a captivating introduction that makes the recipient of my letter interested in what I have to say.

_____ I have at least three well-explained reasons that make a compelling, persuasive argument.

_____ Each of my reasons has two or three facts or examples to drive home my point.

_____ I have clearly demonstrated how the reader/recipient of the letter can help me with the issue I'm trying to persuade him/her on.

_____ My tone is polite.

_____ My letter contains the following properly punctuated items:

- _____ a heading with my contact information
- _____ the recipient's address (inside address)
- _____ a proper salutation
- _____ an introduction that states my reason for writing
- _____ an appropriate closing
- _____ my signature and full name

_____ I included a properly punctuated return address and the sender's address on an envelope.

_____ I included information on how I can be reached (through Ms. Shubitz) at our school (i.e., I listed the school's phone number and Ms. Shubitz's e-mail address).

_____ My handwriting is legible or my letter is typed in an easy-to-read font.

Figure 6.1

Students are more successful when we communicate our expectations clearly. If we want to witness achievement in our classrooms, then it's prudent for us to make sure our students know exactly what they must do to succeed.

Challenge: Use the rubric you co-created with your students and your knowledge of all the necessary elements students' final products should contain to create guidelines or a checklist for the next published piece students will turn in. Take five to ten minutes to review the checklist with your students so you can clarify ambiguities.

Reflective Practice:

- Did the published writing your students turned in fare well when you graded it? Were these pieces stronger or weaker than past student work in this genre?
- How did guidelines help you clearly communicate your expectations to your students?

Quick Publish Assessments

The truth will set you free. But first, it will piss you off.
—Gloria Steinem

Lucy Calkins was leading a talk about assessment during her evening graduate course on the teaching of writing. She encouraged each of her students to give our own students a short writing assessment in September and, if possible, at the end of each unit of study so we could observe their growth as writers. I ran with Calkins's suggestion and began having my students complete "quick publish assessments," which were assignments they completed independently in one period, without any assistance from a teacher or a peer, to assess what they learned about a particular genre of writing.

The day after Calkins's suggestion in September 2006, I asked my fifth graders to take forty-five minutes to write a true, one-time story. My students had never been asked to produce a piece of writing like this without assistance, so their writing was mediocre. However, the September writing sample was valuable because I had a baseline for what my students could accomplish in one writing period. By the time they completed their personal narrative unit of study in November, I asked them to write another quick personal narrative. The level of their writing had improved from the September true, one-time stories. On each student's paper, I made a small T-chart with a plus and a minus as the column headings. On the plus side, I wrote, "This is what the student already knows about the qualities of good writing," and on the minus side I wrote, "This is what I need to teach the student next." I listed only one thing on each side so I could focus on what they were doing that was at the top of their game and one thing that was critical for them to learn immediately the next time I conferred with them.

Over time, I transformed my notes on the T-charts into letters to my students, written on 8.5-by-11-inch sheets of paper. I wrote a compliment and a teaching point about the writing they did on their quick publish assessment. In the letters, I also provided students with suggestions about next steps to help lift the quality of the writing.

Quick publish assessments can be uncomfortably revealing about flaws in one's teaching. During the first year I administered these assessments at the end of a unit of study, I quickly noticed weaknesses in my teaching. As I read my students' writing, I noticed there were topics I hadn't covered well enough during full-class instruction. As humbling as this may sound, finding out what students are missing as writers can help to drive future writing instruction. First, by revealing the holes in my teaching, I was able to make changes to future units of study, making sure to include ideas originally omitted from previous instruction. In addition, discovering what I may have missed teaching my students in a given unit helped me as I revised a unit of study for the following school year. To become a better teacher of writing, we often have to humble ourselves by learning what we didn't teach well so we can better instruct our students in the future.

Challenge: Set aside a period to administer a quick publish assessment at the end of your next unit of study. You might choose to write up the task on a sheet of paper, in addition to explaining your expectations to your students, so you can effectively communicate your expectations to all of your students. (An example of a task sheet for a quick publish assessment is contained in Appendix E.) You might choose to discuss with them the important things you hope to see in students' writing so they're clear about the qualities of good writing they should demonstrate.

Reflective Practice:

- What did your students show you they understood about the genre of writing that the quick publish assessment covered?
- Were there any holes in your teaching? Can you fix these gaps by reteaching strategies to your students as a whole class or in small groups?

Writing Analysis

I love the man that can smile in trouble, that can gather strength by distress, and grow brave by reflection.
—Thomas Paine

Bo sat in the back of my seventh-grade classroom, shelled up in a black hoodie. It was clear that English was not his version of a good time. He began making his judgments of me, just as I had of him, and, like his, mine were all wrong. I had him pegged as a kid who didn't care, a kid who wouldn't try. Perhaps he thought the same of me: another English teacher who didn't care, who wouldn't try.

We began our first unit of study on memoir. Bo wrote a little in his writer's notebook. His final piece was about the death of his hamster. I was surprised to read about this moment in a tough guy's life. He also completed a analysis of his writing process. I was again surprised to read that he didn't have confidence in himself as a writer. With these two writings, Bo let me in.

A writing analysis is an opportunity to learn the behind-the-scenes work of a writer. It asks students reflective questions about their thinking and choices leading up to the final draft. We are able to have a more complete understanding of each writer when we assess the writing process of our students, making our summative assessment more accurate.

During the year, I decided to analyze Bo's writing process. As we wrote daily, Bo gained confidence in himself as a writer, while at the same time I grew stronger as a teacher of writing. The writing analysis at the end of each unit of study became a key to my improvement. We learn ways to empower students when we learn about the choices behind a piece of writing. I find the more I learn about students' processes, the easier it is for me to nudge them to grow as writers.

Since a writer's process makes a difference in the final draft, it is worth considering it during summative assessment. I've found that these questions lead to useful information:

- **How did the idea originate?** The more significant a topic is to writers, the better they write. This allows us to see whether students are writing with meaning, as well as whether common themes emerge over time.
- **What did you do to write your best first draft?** Writing a first draft with intention is important, and it pushes students to think about how they write well initially.

- **How did other people help you with your writing?** Collaboration with other writers is essential for lifting the level of our own work. Therefore, it is important to gain insight into this process.
- **What kinds of significant revision did you complete?** Adding in a handful of adjectives doesn't qualify as *significant* revision. Tapping into the revision process and pushing students to consider worthy and meaningful revision is honored in the writing analysis.
- **Why did you make these revisions?** Revision is most effective when there is a purpose behind it. Reflecting on the heart of the revision choices and giving insight into the effectiveness of the revision process helps assess students' process.
- **What was difficult about editing for you?** When students answer this question, they reveal their needs when it comes to the editing process.
- **If you had more time, what would you change about your final draft?** The answer here often sheds light on the final draft and gives me insight as I assess it. Sometimes students attempt a revision at the last minute that doesn't quite work. This helps me more accurately assess the final draft.
- **What is the best thing you did as a writer?** I'm often surprised to discover a students' best is often a risk taken as a writer. Typically, the "best thing" noted isn't something they executed perfectly. I've avoided many broken spirits by shifting my comment to encouragement instead of a teaching point by knowing the answer to this question.

The reflective nature of a writing analysis gives both the teacher and students insight into their unique writing processes. As we discover the choices behind a piece of writing, we assess the writer more accurately. The summative assessment shifts from simply a grade at the top of a paper to a means of empowerment and growth.

Challenge: Create a writing analysis for the current unit of study in your writing workshop. Consider four to six questions that will be most meaningful to you as you gain insight about the decisions your students make as writers. (See Appendix E for two examples, as well as Aimee Buckner's *Notebook Know-How: Strategies for Writer's Notebook* [2005] or Sharon Davis and Judy Hill's *The No-Nonsense Guide to Teaching Writing: Strategies, Structures, and Solutions* [2003].)

Reflective Practice:

- What surprised you about your students' writing process?
- What was most useful about the writing analysis?
- What changes will you make on the writing analysis next time?

Allowing Space for Self-Assessment

Never be afraid to sit awhile and think.
—Lorraine Hansberry

Sometimes the difference between mediocre writing and high-quality writing is when students take the time to review their final drafts before handing them in. One way to encourage this review is to allow students to self-assess their writing based on the scoring rubric. Consider the following formats to support students as they review their final drafts.

- **Mark on the rubric using a specific color:** Students assess themselves on the same rubric the teacher will use. To tell the students' input, it is helpful for students to write in a different color for their self-assessment from the teacher.
- **Copy the same rubric on both sides of a paper so the student can complete one side and the teacher the other:** This is similar to the first concept, except it allows each person to use his or her own rubric.
- **Designate a column for student assessment and one for teacher assessment:** Next to the criteria on the rubric, leave a space for students to show their assessment. Following the self-assessment space, there can be space for the teacher's assessment.

These formats allow students to assess themselves using checkmarks on a rubric. Although this is a place to start, I appreciated knowing students' thoughts behind their choices. Therefore, I pushed them to assess themselves as well as to support their stance. These setups helped me to understand their decisions:

- **Leave a space for students to write their support for their decision:** By leaving a large box on each row of the rubric, students were able to write their self-assessment for each indicator on the rubric. An alternative to this method is to number each indicator and have student's write their reasoning for each number on a separate sheet of paper.
- **Have students make notations on their final drafts that demonstrate their performance for each indicator on the rubric:** When students justified their choices on final drafts before turning them in, I was able to gain valuable insight into each individual. Although this system takes longer, I have found it is worthwhile as it allows me to have a more accurate understanding of each writer.

We help students become intentional writers of high-quality final drafts when we provide concrete ways for them to self-assess their final drafts. It is essential to encourage students to sit awhile and think.

Challenge: Develop a system for your students to self-assess their final drafts. Connect their self-assessment to the rubric you will use as a summative assessment.

Reflective Practice:

- How will you encourage students to take their self-assessment seriously?
- How did the self-assessment help students to turn in higher-quality work?

Creating Rubrics with Students

> Evaluation is embedded in all we do. Every time we make a choice—
> cereal or toast for breakfast, the black skirt or the black pants . . .
> each decision involves evaluation. We're all pros at it.
> ***—Jane Fraser and Donna Skolnick***

I discovered Rubistar, the online rubric creator, when I was student teaching. I loved how easy it was to create one's own rubric. For my first two and a half years of teaching, I used Rubistar whenever I wanted to create a rubric for a writing assignment or a project my students were working on. Fast to create? Yes. Meaningful for my students? Absolutely not. My students had no say in the rubrics I created on Rubistar. I just created them based on the English language arts standards and handed them out to my students. Even though I took a few minutes to review each rubric with my class and provided time for student questions, most of the students' interaction with the rubric had to do with clarifying what I had put on it. In hindsight, I realize that handing them a rubric I created was meaningless. No wonder many students didn't get 4s, a grade that demonstrated excellence. They were unsure of what I was asking of them!

I didn't realize that the way I was creating my rubrics was problematic until I read "Assessing with Heart" (Spandel 2006, 14). I learned that when we work to develop rubrics and checklists *with* our students, rather than *for* them, assessment becomes more meaningful for students. Spandel stated: "Checklists and rubrics are not complete until they are backed by samples of writing. Students have a right to see samples of what we want from them as writers. If we cannot produce them, we ought to take another look at our criteria to see if what we are asking of our students is realistic" (2006, 16).

Once you reach the halfway point in a unit of study, it's smart to sit down with students to talk about the piece of writing they're going to publish. You can create a rubric with your students in many ways. However, you should know a few things *before* you begin the rubric-creation process with them.

- **Know what you want to assess:** Think about the mini-lessons you've taught to your entire class. Much of the full-class instruction will be items you should consider assessing on the rubric.
- **Keep the standards in your head:** If students must master certain state-mandated skills in a particular genre, then you'll want to consider holding students accountable for these skills when you're grading them.
- **Elicit what students think is important:** Ask students to think about the writing work they've done in the unit of study. Have them determine what's been important and what they think is worthy of assessment. Often students will name things that are too small to assess, so you can guide them toward the bigger picture during class discussion.
- **Bring writing samples:** If you have examples of graded student work from your past students, present it. Black out any identifying details from the piece so you can share past students' exemplary work with your class, which will help you discuss concrete expectations.

Once you and your students have created a list that represents quality work in a given genre, offer to turn the list into a rubric, using a template that you like or that your school requires. So that the rubric remains a cooperative effort, I always came back the following day to show students how the items and the rubric aligned. Occasionally, small changes were requested, but mostly they were satisfied with the final rubric.

Going through the rubric-creation process with students is time consuming. It might take up to thirty minutes of instruction time to generate a list and to review the final rubric in its appropriate format. This exercise is worthwhile because students' expectations are clearer when they have ownership of how their writing will be assessed.

Challenge: Set aside time to create a rubric with your students for their next published writing piece. Come prepared to the rubric-creation session with the items you want to assess so you can guide the discussion, if necessary.

Reflective Practice:

- How did your students respond to creating a rubric with you?
- Did you bring any samples, or finished products, of writing to the rubric-creation session? If so, how did that shape the rubric you created?

Writer's Notebooks and the Overall Workshop Grade

Honest criticism is hard to take—especially when it comes from a relative, a friend, an acquaintance, or a stranger.
—Franklin P. Jones

I rarely ate lunch in other teachers' classrooms or in the faculty lounge when I was a classroom teacher. I ate lunch in my classroom because I spent most of my lunch periods reading over my students' writer's notebooks. I relished the time I spent peeking into my students' daily lives by perusing the pages of their notebooks. I kept a pad of sticky notes beside me when I read notebooks to jot down questions or comments for students about their writing. I always jotted a longer note to students when I finished reading their notebooks, with overall thoughts I had about their writing. I tried to be positive, even when the writing wasn't very good, because I know it's hard to have your writing judged.

For the first few years, I assessed my students' writer's notebooks each week. I used a rubric adapted from Aimee Buckner's *Notebook Know How: Strategies for the Writer's Notebook* (2005, 113). The Buckner rubric assesses students on fluency and flexibility, thoughtfulness, and frequency. By year five in the classroom, I created a rubric *with* my students, which was a spin-off of a form Carl Anderson provides for teachers to use when assessing student writing (2005, 230). The rubric I created with my students (Appendix E) assessed their notebooks for meaning, genre, structure, detail, voice, conventions, and frequency. Regardless of the rubric I worked with in a given year, I always used the writing from students' writer's notebooks to factor in to their overall writing workshop report card grade.

Some teachers have challenged me with regard to grading students' notebooks. After all, the notebook is a place to practice craft, develop new ideas, and try out new concepts. However, if notebooks are a tool to help our students become better writers, then it is incumbent upon us to grade their notebooks to track their growth over time. In addition, grading notebooks allowed me to assess raw and in-process work, in addition to the polished writing that would come in at the end of a unit of study. This often gave me a better sense of what my students were capable of producing on their own.

Regular use of a writer's notebook not only helps students develop the identity of a writer, but it helps them become better writers. Grading a writer's notebook helps us get a fuller picture of students' capabilities as writers each day.

Challenge: Review photocopies of the completed rubrics you used to assess your students' writer's notebooks. When it comes to report card time, review each of the photocopies so you can remark on the progress each student has made in his or her writer's notebook throughout the grading period.

Reflective Practice:

- What are the most important things you want to assess in your students' notebooks? How will you use their notebooks to be meaningful to you when assigning a grade to their overall writing performance?
- How will you weight your students' writer's notebook grades among the other things you use to assess your students?

Switching Views of Student Writing

If you look at life one way, there is always cause for alarm.
—Elizabeth Bowen

Often when we look at student writing, we're alarmed. We notice everything the student is not doing, everything that is wrong, everything that could be better. The struggle ensues—they worked so hard—but the writing isn't perfect. Instead of being alarmed by students' writing, perhaps we should switch our view. By putting on a different set of lenses, we can assess student writers more accurately. There are many lenses to use, but three simple lenses are **process**, **craft**, and **conventions**.

An effective **writing process** is a key to successful writing and a practical means of assessment. When students use their writer's notebooks, embrace revision, or peer edit, they are developing writing processes. Workable processes should be recognized, as are solid conventions.

Craft, the way a writer uses language, is a second lens to use when assessing writing. When we look at writing through the craft lens, we can see how students attempt to use specific strategies or techniques to communicate meaning. Because they are less-experienced writers, they will not write with sophistication, but they will approximate craft. Recognize the craft moves students attempt in order to encourage and support them as they become more proficient writers.

Teachers are most comfortable using the lens of **conventions**. We take out our red pens and bleed all over student writing, fixing all of the mistakes. Although we have good intentions, remember the experience level of our students. We aren't looking for all of the conventional errors in their writing, rather we are looking for generalities in the kinds of errors students make. For instance, perhaps we noticed lowercased proper nouns, missing ending punctuation, or no paragraphs. If we can focus on one convention a student should master (and master soon), then we will be able to help the student to focus on learning one skill well before moving to the next.

We have less cause for alarm and more meaningful insight when we look at student writing through the lenses of **process**, **craft**, and **convention**. This allows us to give accurate feedback so students can grow as writers.

Challenge: Plan to spend time looking at student writing through these three lenses. Make notes as you approach the writing with the different perspectives.

Reflective Practice:

- Which lens was easiest for you to use to assess writing? Why?
- How will you give students feedback after assessing using these lenses?
- How will you translate your assessment into a grade?

Two Grades for Everything

When people don't agree on big things, the little things take on enormous significance.
—Shelley Harwayne

When I taught in the New York City public school system, I found report card time frustrating. The report cards didn't provide much space for elaborating on students' skills within a subject area. A "4" meant a student was exceeding the standards; a "3" meant a student was meeting the standards; a "2" meant a student was approaching the standards; and a "1" meant a student was falling below the standards. I inserted plus and minus signs after the numerical indicator to augment students' performance. In addition, I used the smallest handwriting possible to write comments in the space provided to explain the numerical indicator for the parent. Frankly, there wasn't enough space on the report card to show a parent how the student was really doing.

I taught fourth grade when I began working at the Learning Community, a public charter school in Rhode Island. We created our own report card because fourth grade was new to the school the year I started. The fourth-grade team, along with our instructional coach and an outside consultant, spent several hours determining what should be assessed in each subject area based on national standards. For writing, in particular, we decided to assess students in the following components of writing: writing genres (styles), writing process, conventions, word choice, spelling, and habits. Within each of those components, we had twenty-three subcategories that allowed us to assess students in specific ways.

With this unique grading system, a student received two grades on the report card for every area in which the student was assessed. Students received a *benchmark grade*, which was the level at which a student was performing at a given point in the year based on the national standards for that grade. The benchmark grades consisted of a ✓+, ✓, and ✓-. Students also received an individual progress grade, which described a student's progress over a period of time for every area in which the student was assessed. The *individual progress grades* were E, for excellent progress; S, for showing progress; and U, for unsatisfactory progress. Therefore, a student who worked diligently each day but was working below the benchmark for a given point in the school year could receive a ✓-/E, which would demonstrate the student's effort, despite his or her inability to meet or exceed the standard at a given point in the school year.

If we come to view more in-depth summative assessments as providing a meaningful way to understand our students, then perhaps it's time to think about assigning more than just one grade in writing. For instance, if we claim a child is meeting the benchmark, then we must quantify why the child is meeting the benchmark by explaining the skills he or she has attained to reach the benchmark goals. Instead of assigning an overall grade to a young writer, perhaps we should create subcategories that help us communicate a fuller picture of our students' progress and abilities.

Challenge: The next time you offer formal written feedback, acknowledge both the benchmark and the effort of a student. In addition, consider organic ways to communicate why a student has received a particular benchmark grade.

Reflective Practice:

- How do you think more specific forms of assessing writers on report cards will help drive your instruction?
- What was your colleagues' reaction to the idea of examining more components when assessing students in writing?

Publishing Graded Writing

All great achievements require time.
—Maya Angelou

"Can I publish this?" A student stood before me with her writing in one hand and the rubric in the other.

"Sure, why do you ask?"

"Well, my teacher graded it, and I guess it could be better, but I think my little sister will like it anyway. So can I publish it or do I need to do something else?"

I looked at her for a moment, weighing my options on how to respond. I wanted to hug her. I felt this partly because our system of grading seemed to get in the way of her meaningful reasons for writing, which is often the case. The other part of me wanted to hug her because she was confident enough to ignore the grade on the page and believe in her work. I smiled at her.

"Publish away," I said and patted her on the shoulder as she headed off to select a cover for her book.

Provide students opportunities to return to their graded pieces with the intent to publish. When students are writing for authentic reasons with a true purpose and real audiences, then the most important part of the process is publication, not the grade. This mind-set is harder to fight as students move through the grades.

One of the keys is to remember Maya Angelou's words, "All great achievements take time." Just because a student didn't perfect a final draft of writing, doesn't mean it isn't worthy of publication. Helping students to focus on their purpose and audience will lift the level of their writing and make it publication worthy.

Challenge: Adopt the belief that writing doesn't have to be perfect to be published. Make this attitude obvious to your students through your words and actions. Consider posting this message in your classroom for everyone to see.

Reflective Practice:

- How will you make your belief about publishing evident to your students?
- What will you have to set aside to embrace publishing imperfect works?

Remember to Celebrate

"And now," said Max, "Let the wild rumpus start!"
—Maurice Sendak

Education is serious business. Sometimes this serious business causes us to get caught up in all the work we have to do. This is especially true when it comes to summative assessment. We want our assessments to be accurate, which causes us to take this work extremely seriously. However, there is also a danger in being too serious.

After the toil of working alongside students as they draft, revise, and edit their writing, then spending time assessing this writing, be sure to take time to rejoice. Writing celebrations should be among the most joyful memories students have of the school year. Members of a writing community share a unique bond—they understand the work it takes to produce good writing.

We are able to honor one another, let our hair down, and smile proudly when we gather together for a formal writing celebration, with everyone sharing a piece of powerful writing. Let's be intentional about allowing the nature of writers who embrace the joy of completing a project take over. Allowing the writing of others to touch us, and then offering a response to the writer, will positively affect everyone involved. For this to happen, we, as teachers, must relax and respond as more than teachers. Our response should be as writer to writer, as fellow travelers in life. This celebration of writers will bind the writing community even closer, give students a revived energy for their next writing project, and help everyone to become stronger writers.

At first glance, a formal writing celebration—complete with smiles, laughter, and cupcakes—may seem like fluff. However, speak to any writer, and he or she will tell you the celebrations that come after completing a writing project are essential to the vitality of their writing life. In the words of Maurice Sendak, "Let the wild rumpus start!"

Challenge: If you haven't scheduled a formal celebration, put it on your calendar now. Prepare yourself by considering ways you can enjoy the celebration as a fellow writer.

Reflective Journal:

- What (or who) will keep you from relaxing during the celebration? How can you prevent this from hindering your participation as a fellow writer?
- How will you prepare to enjoy the celebration?

Cycle 3: Standardized Tests

Nourishing Student Confidence

The great thing in the world is not so much where we stand,
as in what direction we are moving.
—Oliver Wendell Holmes

Anxiety has risen in classrooms as the stakes have risen for students to perform well on standardized tests. Teachers and students are both concerned about writing well to a prompt. This added dimension makes it necessary to consider writing prompts not only through the lens of a genre but also through the lens of a writer.

The best time to consider writing prompts as a genre is the few days following the end of a unit of study. By giving students writing prompts throughout the school year, teachers are able to gain a sense of what students can do on demand, in a limited time frame across a variety of genres and topics. This system provides the opportunity to teach the writing prompt genre in small doses over many months, while leaving the weeks leading up to the standardized tests available to focus on a student's writing persona.

Let's devote these weeks to celebrating the writers we have become during the school year. Identifying our growth and strengths as writers will go far in preparing for a standardized test.

- **What do we already know as writers that we can do in a snap?** As we help students learn to write well in response to a prompt, it is important to help them focus on the writing techniques they have mastered. By generating a chart of techniques students already know how to implement with ease, we keep the focus on everything students know how to do, instead of what they don't know (Appendix E).
- **How do we write the best first draft?** When we teach students to write their best first draft as opposed to a "sloppy copy" or "rough draft," we help them change their mind-set about their initial attempt at writing. By taking the time to write according to a plan, to use craft techniques learned in class, and to correct spelling and conventional errors as they draft, students can take a standardized test confident that their best first draft is satisfactory.
- **What's happening in our heads?** When I first began writing this book, I spent much time at my computer, but I had few words to show for it because I deleted everything I wrote. After a week of misery and a good lecture from Stacey, I realized my problem—I was listening to all the negative thoughts in my head. Bit by bit I lost confidence in myself as a writer. This happens to our students too, especially when they are under the stress of a high-stakes test. When a trustworthy adult acknowledges self-doubt and the accompanying negative thoughts that creep into his or her head, it validates this for students. They can then be taught to turn off these thoughts. If I had not told the negative voices in my head to "be quiet," this book would not have been published. If we listen to negative thoughts, we begin to believe them. Our students are too precious to believe lies about themselves as writers.
- **What are our comfort strategies?** Every writer has a strategy he or she prefers. I love to use a conjunction in the last line of my work. I also depend on dialogue, emotion, and sensory images when I write narrative. These are my comfort techniques. By helping students identify and develop comfort techniques, we give them a way to remain confident and relaxed during a writing prompt.

As students consider the genre of writing prompts, help them to focus on themselves as writers. By nurturing their confidence in themselves as writers, we give them a gift that will sustain them not just in a standardized testing situation but in writing situations throughout their lives.

Challenge: Use this list to develop a mini-lesson around one of the ideas. Consider how you will boost your students' confidence as writers.

Reflective Practice:

- What do you notice about your students' energy level as you prepare for the writing prompt?
- How will you nourish your students' confidence as the standardized test approaches?
- What are some ways you will keep the focus on being a writer instead of taking a test?

Doing Your Best on the Test

Duty is the most sublime word in our language. Do your duty in all things.
You cannot do more. You should never wish to do less.
—Robert E. Lee

While I was watching the figure skating competitions during the 2010 Olympic Winter Games in Vancouver, I noticed the broadcasters repeatedly saying, "This score is a personal best for ______________." Often the skaters who scored their personal best didn't stand on the medals podium. However, they walked away from the competition with their heads held high knowing they'd given it their all.

Even in this day of tying teacher compensation to test scores, we cannot ask our students to do better than their personal best when they take standardized tests. It would be unfair to expect all students to exceed grade-level standards. It *is* fair to expect our students to use everything they know about writing well when they take any standardized test.

When students are engaged in writing workshop, we can expect them to transfer the following skills to standardized tests:

- Keep their writing focused on the given topic.
- Structure writing in a clear, easy-to-follow way.
- Elaborate, using relevant and specific details to support thinking.
- Write with precision, selecting words that are chosen purposefully.
- Write with correct punctuation and syntax.
- Read directions and fulfill whatever the writing prompt asks of them.

Essentially, what we teach our students each day about writing well should be applied during testing. Students who use everything they know about writing well whenever they have to craft written responses will always showcase their talents.

Challenge: Set aside time to talk about the qualities of good writing with your students. Keep track of what they say. Then, together, create a chart about the features of good test writing. Make sure they understand the parallels between what they already know about writing well and how that will transfer to standardized testing.

Reflective Practice:

- Did your students seem more confident about their ability to write well on a test after your class discussion?
- How will you show students what it means to write well in response to a prompt? Will you show them well-written writing samples, or will you go about it in another way?

Take Time for Authentic Writing Experiences

What was once educationally significant, but difficult to measure, has been replaced by what is insignificant and easy to measure. So now we test how well we have taught what we do not value.
—Arthur L. Costa

The goal of No Child Left Behind (NCLB) was "to ensure that all children have a fair, equal, and significant opportunity to obtain a high-quality education and reach, at a minimum, proficiency on challenging state academic achievement standards and state academic assessments." At the time of this writing, policy makers in Washington, D.C., were considering reauthorizing the bill because teaching the nation's students how to fill in bubbles on standardized tests did not prepare them for the demands of the twenty-first century.

It's my hope that change will come with regard to the way we test kids in the near future. But where does that leave teachers who are preparing their students for state tests?

We all have a job to do and cannot be insubordinate. Closing our door and doing our own thing is not an option because our students need to be prepared for standardized tests. However, all of us can try to find time in the day, even amid the test preparation, to provide students with authentic, educationally significant work. Once the norms and expectations of writing workshop have been established, it is time to infuse independent writing projects into your classroom.

M. Colleen Cruz (2004) talks about balancing independent writing workshops and standardized testing season in *Independent Writing: One Teacher—Thirty-Two Needs, Topics, and Plans*. She states:

> *I was pleasantly surprised after having taught during testing season for awhile. The students, and what they were capable of, did not change just because we had a big test to prepare for. I realized that as students lived their independent writing lives during this time, they did not feel creatively stifled when it got close to test crunch time and non-test writing lessons became a rare commodity.*
>
> *Interesting, too, was that students' independent writing was thriving more than it had during other units of study. Students found that because preparing for the test was so classroom specific they had more time to work on their independent writing at home and during free time. January had become one time, other than the summer months, when students were able to prove their independent mettle because I was less available to confer, offer seminars, or support them in any formal way with their projects. (Cruz 2004, 133)*

If independent writing projects seem too daunting, consider carving out fifteen minutes of the school day for your students to drop everything and write, on the topic of their choice, for ten minutes, leaving five minutes for partner shares. Donald Graves and Penny Kittle have named this time "quick writes," but you can call it whatever you wish!

Challenge: Decide what works better for your classroom: independent writing projects or a consistent ten to fifteen minutes each day for the children to write. Then read Cruz's book (2004) or Graves and Kittle's book (2005) to help you flesh out how you'll implement this in your classroom.

Reflective Practice:

- Did you decide to work with your students to undertake independent writing projects? If so, how will you carry these out? Will you provide your students with guidance outside of the regular school day?
- What kinds of pressures or stress do you feel with regard to the upcoming state tests? Record a list of emotions and then write, in detail, about each emotion you're feeling.

Understanding the Rubric

The secret to happiness is not in doing what one likes,
but in liking what one has to do.
—James M. Barrie

I've spent too many hours studying exemplar responses to my state's writing prompt. Although most of this was forced on me, I'm glad to understand the rationale behind the grading practices of my state's standardized test.

Writing prompts are a fact of life for our students. It is unfair for me to ignore it simply because I have a philosophical discord with standardized tests. However, I realize it's my responsibility, as an educator, to understand the rubric and practices used to assess students' responses to writing prompts. Over time, I've learned about my state's assessment practices. Following are some suggestions:

- **Peruse your state department of education's Web site:** Many states have scored student samples online to share with teachers. Look at the samples as well as read the scoring rationale.
- **Go to workshop sessions on standardized test scoring:** I have been to my fair share of sessions about the scoring practices of writing prompts in my state. These have been influential in helping me develop an accurate understanding of the way responses are scored.
- **Practice scoring with colleagues:** When one person at the table knows the score of a particular response and everyone else must read and "score" the writing, much can be learned. As we discuss our rationales for the score we deemed and then come to a consensus, we can compare our score to the state score. Another discussion ensues as we theorize about why our score is the same or different from the state.
- **Participate in Webinars about standardized test scoring:** Standardized testing is ever changing. Something that is true one year may not be true the following year. State-sponsored Webinars help teachers stay current with the assessment practices for writing prompts.

Until the pressure to perform on standardized tests is lifted from schools, teachers, and students, writing prompts will continue to be a part of the writing lives of our students. It is our duty to understand the assessment measures used to evaluate our students.

Challenge: Look at the exemplar responses for your state's writing prompt assessment. Notice the imperfect nature of many of the top scores. When students are assessed on their response to a writing prompt, perfection isn't expected. Develop an understanding of the expectations for your students on a standardized test.

Reflective Practice:

- How will you increase your understanding of your state's assessment practices for the writing prompt?
- What will you do to protect your students' confidence when they receive their scores from the state test?

How Do I Know What to Write?

I realize much will be asked of me, yet I am resolved to accept it as a great and splendid task.

—Beatrix, Queen of the Netherlands

To be successful on a writing prompt, students must understand the task set before them. Helping students identify the key parts of a writing prompt will aid them in developing an understanding of what the prompt is asking them to do as writers.

- **Genre:** When students identify the genre, they are able to plan more effectively. They know whether to structure their writing in scenes or according to reasons of support. Genre also helps students determine how they will elaborate on their writing.
- **Audience:** The audience helps students establish a tone and make decisions regarding word choice. As students develop a strong sense of audience, their writing becomes clearer.
- **Topic:** Writing prompts give students a specific topic. It is important for students to identify this topic early on in the test so they are able to access their background knowledge and make connections to the topic. As students connect to the topic, they will be able to write more about it.
- **Key parts:** Often writing prompts scaffold students in planning specific parts of their writing. By helping students identify key information expected in the response, we ease the tasks of planning and elaboration. When students respond to the key parts, they stay on topic and accomplish the writing task.

Students are more likely to develop a solid response to a writing prompt when they take time to develop their understanding of the writing task. Without explicit instruction in how to decipher these important areas, many students will lack the necessary test-taking skills to perform well on a writing prompt.

Challenge: Plan to help your students develop the skills necessary to understand the task in a writing prompt. Gather several prompts to give students practice with identifying the key parts of a prompt so they are comfortable making decisions as writers when faced with the actual test prompt.

Reflective Practice:

- What part of understanding the task is most difficult for your students when faced with a writing prompt?
- How will you help your students develop a full understanding of the task presented to them in a writing prompt?

Two Audiences

> Whenever I write, whether I'm writing a picture book, an entry in my journal, a course handbook for students, or notes for the milkman, there's always someone on the other side, if you like, who sits invisibly watching me write, waiting to read what I've written. The watcher is always important.
>
> ***—Mem Fox***

"Who reads your writing when you respond to a writing prompt?" I asked a group of third-grade students.

These rookies in taking standardized tests looked back at me. I could tell they were considering my question. A few shrugged, and the rest glanced around. It was clear none of them had considered their audience.

As a writer, I know my audience plays a large role in the choices I make. When I'm writing for my children, I make different choices than when I'm writing for teachers. When students don't take into account their audience, their writing suffers.

Standardized tests offer a peculiar audience situation. Students are writing for two audiences—one from the prompt scenario and the other is the assessor. Both of these audiences play a role in the choices they make as writers.

First is the imaginary audience from the scenario in the prompt. Students must write with an awareness of this audience. Helping students learn to identify the imaginary audience is a crucial first step. Often word choice and tone are highly influenced by the imaginary audience. Throughout the year in our writing workshops, we give students opportunities to see texts written for different audiences, as well as a chance to write for different audiences. This supports them as they learn to adjust their tone to suit their audience. In preparation for a writing prompt, it is important for students to identify and adjust their writing for a particular audience.

The other audience, who is just as important, if not more important than the imaginary audience, is the person who will be assessing the writing. On a blustery day in February, I was asking third graders to consider this real-life audience. As I talked about this audience, a boy with freckles sprinkled across his nose blurted out, "Whoa! You mean my teacher isn't going to grade my writing?" His green eyes were wide with the realization and his classmates began to interject their thoughts too.

Because audience plays a powerful role in writers' choices, it is important to understand the audiences involved in standardized testing. Our young writers need concrete images and understanding of abstract concepts. An audience they have never met, sitting in a room miles away from their classrooms, isn't likely to motivate our students to write well.

Therefore, following the advice of Barry Lane, we asked the third graders to draw a picture of the person who would be reading their test. They considered facial expressions, T-shirt sayings, and even included speech and thought bubbles. This gave students a concrete image of an audience, and it gave me insight into their confidence regarding the writing prompt.

Focusing on the basic needs of a writer when helping students prepare for a writing prompt is worth workshop time. Helping students define their audience before the test is useful. When we write with an audience in mind, we write well.

Challenge: Plan to help students visualize the person who will read their writing prompt. Ask them to conjure up an image, complete with speech or thought bubbles, and then to share the image with others.

Reflective Practice:

- How does audience influence your own writing?
- How will you help your students understand they are writing for two audiences during a standardized test?

Think, Organize, and Respond

Few of us express ourselves well in a first draft. When we revise that early confusion into something clearer, we understand our ideas better. And when we understand our ideas better, we express them more clearly, and when we express them more clearly, we understand them better . . . and so it goes until we run out of energy, interest, or time.
—Joseph M. Williams

On almost every standardized test elementary school students take, an extra page is provided for students to plan their writing prompt response. As someone who helped score standardized tests in the past, I can tell you it's uncanny how many students don't use that page or use it to doodle on! Although it's easy to tell students to organize their writing before they get started on a standardized writing task, we must show them how to organize their writing, because planned, written responses are often stronger.

Every state has different writing tasks for students in each grade to complete. No two look the same. However, we can provide our students with various devices to help organize their thinking before they respond to a writing prompt.

- **Outlining:** This traditional organizational method is one most of us learned in school. It doesn't matter whether students use roman numerals or boxes and bullets. What matters is that students identify the main and subordinate ideas they will prove in their writing by organizing them in a logical sequence, which will help them respond to the writing task in a thoughtful manner.
- **Graphic organizers:** It's useful for some students to organize their thinking using a graphic organizer. Students can learn how to use T-charts to help sort facts from opinions or Venn diagrams before comparing and contrasting. Two things are most important about using a graphic organizer: (1) that students understand which one to use based on the type of question they encounter and (2) that using a graphic organizer doesn't become too time consuming. Using something for the wrong purpose or spending too much time organizing one's thinking can be detrimental to a student, so it's important to make sure graphic organizers don't impede students' abilities to accomplish the writing task.
- **Time line and storyboard:** Some writing tasks ask students to write a narrative with a clear beginning, middle, and end. Therefore, teaching students how to quickly use time lines or sketch storyboards can be useful to helping them plan all parts of the story before they actually write it.

Providing students with more than one option for organizing their response honors multiple learning styles. When we provide students with a variety of ways to organize their thinking for a writing task, we honor them as writers by giving them the license to use the organizational tool that works best for them.

Challenge: Schedule time to teach your students a variety of ways to organize their thinking before they attempt a writing task. Be sure to talk with each student to ensure the student has an organizational process that works before test day arrives.

Reflective Practice:

- Which type of organizational device seemed to work best for the majority of your class?
- Which type of organizational device do you gravitate toward? Do your students have similar preferences?

Keep Writing!

I have been impressed with the urgency of doing. Knowing is not enough; we must apply. Being willing is not enough; we must do.
—Leonardo da Vinci

Often young writers run out of steam. They abruptly end their writing and decide there is nothing more to write. Under normal writing circumstances, this isn't a big deal, because students can revise at another time. During writing prompts, however, students do not have this option. Therefore, they ought to know some ways to keep writing even when they don't feel like it.

There isn't a simple solution to this issue, especially since students quit writing for a variety of reasons. By discussing the reasons people stop writing, as well as offering alternatives to quitting, we provide students with the necessary tools to keep writing even in the face of adversity.

Reasons Writers Don't Complete the Prompt	Ways to Keep Writing
Tired	• Stretch • Rub your eyes • Take a few deep breaths
Plan too much	• Watch the clock • Make a short plan, write the beginning, then come back to the plan • Know your best planning strategy
Don't know what else to write	• Reread the prompt question • Reread your draft • Determine the genre and add appropriate details
Not interested in the topic/bored	• Make a connection to the prompt • Reread your writing and focus on doing your best
Nervous	• Take a few deep breaths • Use positive self-talk
Confused by the question	• Reread the writing prompt • Make a connection to a similar situation you have experienced

As students work toward writing their best first draft in the daily work of writing workshop, they will gain confidence when writing for standardized tests. By addressing why young writers run out of steam, we validate these situations. This encourages students to use the necessary tools to continue writing, even when they run out of energy.

Challenge: Generate a list with your students of ways to keep writing during a writing prompt. Prod them to consider ways to elaborate when writing narrative as well as nonnarrative genres.

Reflective Practice:

- What is the primary reason your students seem to run out of steam when writing a practice prompt?
- How will you empower students to write their best first draft?

Proofreading

Grammar is my enemy.
—William Stafford

I've spent a lot of time analyzing writing test results with colleagues. After examining the scoring guidelines alongside the students' scores, it became evident students were often losing points on standardized tests because they weren't proofreading their writing.

Some states will tell you what types of Standard English are being assessed; others simply request that students "use proper conventions." Therefore, if you're unsure of what students are proofreading for, you can encourage them to make the following checks once they've responded to a writing prompt:

- Reread the response silently to make sure it makes sense.
- Fix spelling errors by using three of Ardith Davis Cole's strategies from *Better Answers: Written Performance That Looks Good and Sounds Smart* (2009, 135):
    - Write it five ways: Write the word in question five different ways in an attempt to figure out the correct spelling.
    - Use a synonym: Find another word, with the same meaning, to replace the word that can't be spelled.
    - Use what's right there: Use the prompt, the directions, and other information in the text to spell words correctly.
- Cross-reference the writing with the directions and the passage to make sure the proper pronouns were used. That is, if a writing prompt asks the student

to react to a character's actions, it's important that the student knows whether the character was male or female.

- Include transition words or phrases appropriately throughout the text to help the reader transition from one idea to the next.
- Make sure every sentence includes appropriate ending punctuation and is capitalized appropriately.

Finally, the most important thing we can do is to teach our students to try their best to draft with Standard English, so the need to proofread isn't as great. This is something students can practice every day as they write in writing workshop so that writing with conventions becomes second nature on state tests.

Challenge: Show your students a few pieces of writing, with various commands of Standard English, and have them discuss how they can be edited and improved so they're easier to read. Then teach your students how to proofread their own written responses.

Reflective Practice:

- Is it easier for your students to find their mistakes or someone else's? Why do you think this is?
- How will you help your students remember to proofread their writing before they close their test booklets?

Give Kids a Boost of Spirit

Stop worrying about the potholes in the road and celebrate the journey.
—Barbara Hoffman

My mother-in-law, Linda Schaefer, is a literacy specialist at Brookside Elementary School in Norwalk, Connecticut. When we usually talk shop, it's about great read-aloud books, effective mini-lessons, or ways to get through to students who struggle with reading. Therefore, I looked at her quizzically in February 2006 when she told me she was organizing a pep rally for the third, fourth, and fifth graders at Brookside. Noticing my puzzled look, she explained what was up.

Brookside Elementary School is a workshop school that throws celebrations such as poetry slams and publishing parties for its students. However, they're also a public school, which means their students have to take the Connecticut Mastery Tests, or CMTs, each March. Because the teachers spend time preparing their students for the CMTs, Schaefer thought it would be fun to let the kids know that they were all in this together. Therefore, on the last day of each year's test prep unit of study, the third-, fourth-, and fifth-grade classes, along with the school's administration, come together as a community in the school gymnasium for a pep rally.

The pep rally is a twenty-minute event with music, sheet cakes, positive messages, and cheering. Schaefer and her principal praise the students for working hard during their test prep unit of study and remind them they are well prepared. When each one speaks, they ask that students do their best on the test. Teachers are also recognized for their hard work. Each teacher is given a gift, such as a poetry book, for the classroom. The event ends with a school cheer:

> Brookside School is ready to take this test,
> Brookside kids always try their best,
> Brookside School is better than the rest,
> Brookside School is the BEST!

A class- or schoolwide pep rally helps students overcome pretest anxieties.

If each state test you take is several days long, then it helps to provide your class with a little downtime after each testing session. Providing in-class choice time, doing a special art project, or scheduling extra recess after each testing period always helps students unwind. After each testing period was over, I always threw a small party in my classroom. I brought in juice boxes, Munchkins, and baked goods. A good thirty minutes of unstructured time always followed so my students could just hang out before getting back to work. Finally, whenever possible, I tried to schedule a field trip for the day after the end of each testing period as a means to celebrate my students' hard work.

No matter how well your students may have performed on the test, it's important to celebrate their best efforts.

Challenge: Talk with your grade-level colleagues or your principal to determine how you will celebrate with your students before and after the testing window.

Reflective Practice:

- If you chose to throw a pep rally, take some time to write down what made it successful. Did students leave knowing they would be able to do well on the test? How did you get positive messages across to your students?
- How did the after-party in your classroom allow you to show your appreciation for your students' hard work on the test?

Closing Thoughts

Theoretically, we've traveled together for an entire school year, refining our writing workshops. Unlike other coworkers, though, it is unlikely we've ever met, have ever shared a laugh beside the copier, have ever poured over student writing together. Still, that doesn't keep us from wanting to celebrate with you at the end of this journey.

Completing 180 discussions and challenges doesn't mean you've arrived at the destination, any more than we have by writing them. This journey of becoming more proficient teachers, coaches, and administrators of writing workshop doesn't end after a year of study and reflective practice. It is a lifelong endeavor.

It won't always be an easy quest. To become more skilled at teaching writing takes dedication and tenacity. Know it is a worthwhile adventure and the joys will triumph over the hardships. So we wish we could be in the same room as you, take a deep breath together, look you in the eyes, and wish you Godspeed on this continuing journey. Because that is impossible, one final quote will have to suffice:

> I wanted a perfect ending. Now, I've learned, the hard way, that some poems don't rhyme, and some stories don't have a clear beginning, middle, and end.
> Life is about not knowing, having to change, taking the moment, and making the best of it, without knowing what's going to happen next. Delicious ambiguity.
>
> ***—Gilda Radner***

Appendix A: Routines

Sample Plan Boxes

Here are a few plan boxes created by Kiambra, a fifth-grade student, which illustrate the work she planned to do during the independent portion of writing workshop.

Plan Box (11-12-06)

I'm going to follow the prompts. I'm going to get my topics and choose at least 3 prompts. I'm also going to write however many non-narrative or narrative stories. And use my thinking to push myself.

I'm going to write about my braces and how ~~many~~ my room can look messy and clean. I am also going to write about my family.

Plan Box (11/29/06)

Today I'm working independently. I'm going to push my thinking into getting more stories. And then I'm going to write them on index cards. And tonight I'm going to interview my mom and dad.

Plan Box (12/4/06)

I'm going to write down statistics in every envelop because I feel that this strategy is much easier. I will also try to make some time to write mini-stories and lists.

Plan Box (3-5-07)

I think what's best for me is reasons. I can use other supporting claims also. I am going to infer on a lot of things from the text. And go through the text.

Collecting Ephemera Homework

Find Three Artifacts from YOUR LIFE!

Raid your junk drawers, your closet, or your room.

Look for items that bring back memories. Ticket stubs, pictures, postcards, or even candy wrappers. **Anything that represents YOU!**

** Remember, you are going to be taping/ gluing these things into your writer's notebook. Get permission before you bring items to school!

DUE: ___________

Find Three Artifacts from YOUR LIFE!

Raid your junk drawers, your closet, or your room.

Look for items that bring back memories. Ticket stubs, pictures, postcards, or even candy wrappers. **Anything that represents YOU!**

** Remember, you are going to be taping/ gluing these things into your writer's notebook. Get permission before you bring items to school!

DUE: ___________

Find Three Artifacts from YOUR LIFE!

Raid your junk drawers, your closet, or your room.

Look for items that bring back memories. Ticket stubs, pictures, postcards, or even candy wrappers. **Anything that represents YOU!**

** Remember, you are going to be taping/ gluing these things into your writer's notebook. Get permission before you bring items to school!

DUE: ___________

Find Three Artifacts from YOUR LIFE!

Raid your junk drawers, your closet, or your room.

Look for items that bring back memories. Ticket stubs, pictures, postcards, or even candy wrappers. **Anything that represents YOU!**

** Remember, you are going to be taping/ gluing these things into your writer's notebook. Get permission before you bring items to school!

DUE: ___________

Bilingual Publishing Party Invitation

Please join fourth-grade students as they celebrate the publishing of their personal narratives.

Date: Tuesday, 10/21/08

Time: 9:45–10:30 a.m.

Location: Room 310

Hosted By: Ms. Shubitz

Por favor únase a los estudiantes de cuarto grado mientras ellos celebran la publicación de sus narrativas personales.

Fecha: Martes, 10/21/08

Hora: 9:45–10:30 a.m.

Lugar: Salon 310

Ofrecido por: Sra. Shubitz

Publishing Celebration Feedback Form

Writer's Name: ______________________ Date: ______________

Title of Essay: ______________________________________

Reviewer's Name:	Comments:

Allergy Questionnaire

Dear Parents/Guardians of Class 5-310:

Periodically, I will be baking cookies, cupcakes, brownies, and other goodies for the class. To prevent any allergic reactions, I will only serve food to your child if you sign off on the checklist below. Kindly include any other pertinent information you feel I should know about your child. Thank you, in advance, for your assistance.

Kind regards,
Ms. Shubitz

(Please cut off and return the bottom portion.)

++

My child, ______________________________, does not have any allergies. Therefore, you may serve any kind of food/beverage.

OR

My child, ______________________________, does have allergies.

Please check all that apply.

☐ Chocolate
☐ Dairy
☐ Eggs
☐ Nuts
☐ Wheat
☐ Other (please describe) ______________________________

____

______________________________ ____________

Signature of Parent or Guardian Date

Appendix B: Choice

Idea Sheet

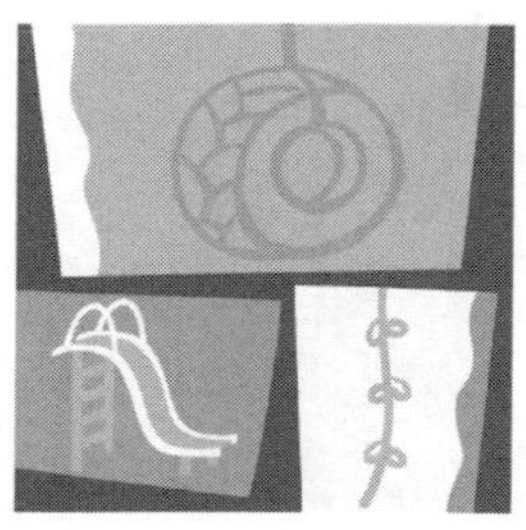

From Draft to Publication

- **Reread** your drafts and **select** one that is worthy of publication.
- **Imagine new possibilities** for the structure or craft/words.
- **Revise** by playing with the structure or craft.
- **Reread** for clarity.
- **Edit** for Standard English.
- **Reread with a partner** for Standard English.
- **Publish** your writing for your audience.

Writing Project Proposal

Name: ______________________________ Date: ____________

Congratulations on creating your own writing project! As a writer, there are several decisions you will make. Use this planning guide to help you with your thinking.

Questions to Ask	Writers Call This	My Thinking
What am I going to write?	Genre	
What am I going to write about?	Topic	
Who might be interested in reading my writing?	Audience	
Why is this important to write?	Purpose	
What kind of notebook entries should I write?	Collecting and Envisioning	

Teacher Feedback:

Writing Project Proposal

Writer: ______________________________ Date: _______________

What are your "BIG 3"?

AUDIENCE: ____

GENRE: ____

TOPIC: ____

What texts are you inspired by? ______________________________

In the space below, describe your project idea.

Teacher Feedback:

Appendix C: Mentors

Dear Parent or Guardian:

As part of my learning process, I will be looking carefully at the daily activities that make up the reading and writing curriculum in our classroom. I especially want to look at the thinking processes of students as they read and write. I'll be interviewing the students about their processes and about their reading and writing as part of my teaching as I always do. Occasionally this year, I will also be audio- and videotaping these interviews and conversations. When the whole class shares and discusses their reading and writing, these conversations may also be recorded on occasion. The purpose of these recordings will be to give me a chance to examine my teaching methods as well as the students' comments more closely and repeatedly to catch things I might miss if I only hear them once. This practice will help me continuously improve as a teacher. I will also be making copies of some of the writing composed by the students, with your permission. I know the class will benefit from the better understanding we will have of the students' reading and writing processes.

I would appreciate your signing the permission form below so I may share the information I learn from your child with my former professors and colleagues from Teachers College, Columbia University, and possibly wider audiences of teachers.

Sincerely,
Stacey Shubitz
4th Grade Teacher

(Please cut off and return the bottom portion.)

++

☐ **I DO** give permission to you to include my child's image on videotape as he or she participates in a class conducted by Stacey Shubitz and/or reproduce materials my child may produce as part of classroom activities.

☐ **I DO NOT** give permission to videotape my child or to reproduce materials my child may produce as part of classroom activities.

______________________________ Child's Name

______________________________ Signature of Parent or Guardian

______________________________ Date

Craft Table for *Those Shoes* by Maribeth Boelts

Craft Move	Page Number(s)	Why the Author Might Be Doing This . . . (Explaining the Craft Move)
Commas and Dashes	17, 22, 25, 26, 27	Writers use punctuation, such as dashes and commas, to get their readers to pause while they're reading a sentence. For instance, Boelts used dashes on several pages to emphasize a word or a phrase (pages 22, 25, and 27). She used a dash to set those words apart from the rest of the words in the sentence, which helps a reader take note of that section or word. Other types of conventions you can use to set words apart are commas (page 26). In this case, Boelts separated the setting details (first part of the sentences) from the character's internal thinking (second part of the sentences). You can emphasize words or phrases as Boelts did by using commas or dashes in your writing.
Movement of Time and Place	13	To keep a story focused, writers have to know how to move through time in a clear way using words that truly describe a change in the story's setting. For instance, Boelts creates a quick change of scenes on page 13. I think she knew she only needed one to two sentences to explain where they traveled (i.e., how they went from thrift shop to thrift shop). These places are nearly insignificant, which is why they were reduced to just a couple of sentences a piece. Therefore, when you're crafting a story that has setting changes, remember to select specific words that accurately describe the way the characters are moving from place to place.
Points of Ellipses	17	Writers use ellipses points, which are three dots that look like three periods in a row, when they want a character's voice to trail off or when they want to show that the character is thinking. On page 17, Grandma wants to say something to Jeremy, but she is searching for the right words. When you want to show a character's voice trailing off or want to show a character pondering something deeply, you can use these dots in your writing as Boelts did.

Purposeful Use of Dialogue/ Setting Details	11	Writers use dialogue that moves their stories forward. Boelts must have chosen the spoken words the characters in the text said very carefully. For instance, on page 11, she uses dialogue to help the reader understand that there's going to be a setting change or a transition from one place to another. She must have put these words there to signal the reader that the setting is going to change so that you don't miss it. You can try this in your own writing to make your writing more meaningful and to help your reader understand when your characters are moving from place to place.
Repetition	20, 21	Authors often repeat words or phrases to get their readers to pay closer attention or to make their pieces sound more rhythmic. "Too-big" and "too-small" on page 20 bring a great emphasis to the size of something. On page 21, there are two sets of twin sentences. Each pair of sentences starts with the same word ("I," then "I"; "One," then "One"). This second example helps the words on the page have a rhythm. You can try this in your own writing by purposely repeating a word or a phrase a couple of times in a paragraph or in your narrative.
Show, Not Tell	7, 10, 12	One way writers help their readers make a movie in their minds is by showing their readers what's happening, rather than just telling them what's happening. Boelts used precise language to show, not tell, her readers what things looked like and felt like in *Those Shoes*. For instance, on page 7, Boelts shoes us that the shoes in the box were dreadful for Jeremy. She used precise words to describe what the ones he got looked like. That helped me make a picture in my mind. Another time Boelts showed us what was happening was on page 10. I could tell Jeremy was mad because he gripped his pencil tightly and thought he might burst, which means explode. Finally, on page 12, Boelts shows Grandma "sitting down heavy," which made me think there was a problem. The word *heavy* showed me that Grandma was feeling upset or mentally exhausted. All three of these places show us what was happening, rather than just tell us what was going on. You can try this in your own writing by using precise words to show your reader what the character is thinking, feeling, doing, or saying.

Strong (Action) Verbs	16, 18	One way to show your reader what a character looks like or sounds like is by using strong verbs. Strong verbs, which show action, help readers create a picture in their minds about what is happening. Boelts did this really well on page 16 of her book. She used verbs like *pounding*, *hitch*, and *shove*, which are descriptive ways to show what's happening to the character. She used strong verbs, *squeeze* and *limp*, again just two pages later when she wanted to help you envision what was going on with Jeremy when he put on those tight shoes. Using strong verbs is something you can try in your writing too. It'll make your story stronger because strong verbs that precisely describe the characters you write about will help your readers create a movie in their minds as they read your story.
Text Features	4, 23, 24	When authors want to call attention to a particular word or phrase in a text, they *do* things to that word or to a phrase to make it stand out. For instance, on page 4 of *Those Shoes*, Boelts emphasizes words by putting them in single quotes or italics. On pages 23 and 24, you'll see that Boelts uses italics, boldface, and quotation marks to bring greater attention to a phrase that represents what the character is thinking. Using text features, like italics, boldface, underlining, bigger font size, and quotation marks, makes something stand out to a reader. It lets the reader know, "Hey, this is important!"
Varied Sentence Lengths	2, 15, 30	Writers vary the lengths of their sentences when they write so that their writing has rhythm. If an author wants you to slow down, she or he uses lots of short sentences. The punctuation at the end of each short sentence forces you to pause, stop, and think. However, when an author wants readers to quicken their pace while they're reading, she or he will use longer sentences. Therefore, you can vary the length of your sentences when you write so that you can get your reader to slow down, just as Boelts did on pages 2, 15, and 30 of her book *Those Shoes*. Writing short sentences, as Boelts did, will get your reader to focus more on the words contained in the short sentences, which can provide description or give more information to the reader in short, quick bursts.

Blank Data Wall Example

	Title #1	Title #2	Title #3	Title #4	Title #5	Title #6	Title #7	Title #8	Title #9	Title #10
Alliteration										
Descriptive Language										
Endings (e.g., circular, surprise)										
Figurative Language										
Lead (e.g., action, dialogue, setting)										
Punctuation That's Interesting										
Strong Verbs										
Varied Sentence Lengths										

Appendix D: Conferring

Conferring Record Form for ____

Dates	Compliments	Teaching Points

Adult Conference Form

Student Name ______________________________ Date ________________

Reviewer Name ____________________________ Relationship ___________

To the reviewer: Another perspective is always helpful to writers. Please listen to the writer describe what he or she is working on and then respond as a reader. There is no right or wrong answer. The writer just needs to know your opinion on a certain section or issue with his or her draft.

To the writer: Determine what section or issue with your draft you would like feedback on. Consider the items we've discussed in class. Briefly describe what you want a response to in the space provided. Mark the section with a highlighter on your draft.

I would like a response to:

IF POSSIBLE, PLEASE . . .

If possible, please have the writer read the draft aloud to you (you may follow along). This helps the writer hear his or her words, as well as refine the craft and conventions of the writing. Thank you for taking an active role in this writer's education.

For the REVIEWER:

What did the writer do well?

What is your response to the section/issue indicated above?

Appendix E: Assessment

Small Moment Story Writing

Name: ______________________________ Date: ____________

TASK: Write about a true, one-time story that has happened to you.

TIME: 40 minutes

CHECKLIST:

_______ My name and today's date are on the top of each page.
_______ I put a page number on the bottom of each sheet of paper.
_______ My story has a title.
_______ I wrote about a true moment from my life.
_______ My story has a beginning, middle, and end.

REQUESTS:

- Skip lines so it's easier for me to read your story.
- If you decide to plan out your story *before* you begin writing, then please attach the papers you used when you were planning.
- If you finish early, then go back and edit your story for spelling, punctuation, capitalization, etc.

When "time" is called, please take a few minutes to reflect on this assignment. Please respond in complete sentences.

- What about this task was simple for you? Please explain.

- What felt challenging to you about this task? Please be specific.

- This assignment made me feel like I was (circle one):

an accomplished writer a good writer

a fair writer a writer in need of improvement

Class Conferring Manifest for the Week of ________________

Name:	Name:	Name:	Name:	Name:
Date: Teaching Point: Check-in Needed? Y/N √ when complete: ____	Date: Teaching Point: Check-in Needed? Y/N √ when complete: ____	Date: Teaching Point: Check-in Needed? Y/N √ when complete: ___	Date: Teaching Point: Check-in Needed? Y/N √ when complete: ____	Date: Teaching Point: Check-in Needed? Y/N √ when complete: ____
Name:	Name:	Name:	Name:	Name:
Date: Teaching Point: Check-in Needed? Y/N √ when complete: ____	Date: Teaching Point: Check-in Needed? Y/N √ when complete: ____	Date: Teaching Point: Check-in Needed? Y/N √ when complete: ___	Date: Teaching Point: Check-in Needed? Y/N √ when complete: ____	Date: Teaching Point: Check-in Needed? Y/N √ when complete: ____
Name:	Name:	Name:	Name:	Name:
Date: Teaching Point: Check-in Needed? Y/N √ when complete: ____	Date: Teaching Point: Check-in Needed? Y/N √ when complete: ____	Date: Teaching Point: Check-in Needed? Y/N √ when complete: ___	Date: Teaching Point: Check-in Needed? Y/N √ when complete: ____	Date: Teaching Point: Check-in Needed? Y/N √ when complete: ____
Name:	Name:	Name:	Name:	Name:
Date: Teaching Point: Check-in Needed? Y/N √ when complete: ____	Date: Teaching Point: Check-in Needed? Y/N √ when complete: ____	Date: Teaching Point: Check-in Needed? Y/N √ when complete: ___	Date: Teaching Point: Check-in Needed? Y/N √ when complete: ____	Date: Teaching Point: Check-in Needed? Y/N √ when complete: ____

Quick Publish Assessment

Name: ______________________________ Date: __________

TASK: Write a literary essay about ______________________________

by ______________________________

TIME: 60 minutes

THINGS TO REMEMBER:

- Take time to plan your essay before you write.
- Your essay should be four paragraphs long.
- Be sure to create a thesis and advance it throughout your essay.
- Grow your thinking about the characters, plot, or theme of the story.
- Quote lines from the story that advance your thesis.
- Your body paragraphs should have a topic sentence, evidence from the story to prove your topic sentence, and a concluding sentence.
- Be sure to make a connection (i.e., personal connection, intertextual connection, or a connection to the world) in the final paragraph of your essay.

PLEASE:

- Skip lines.
- Put your name and date on anything you turn in.
- Number your pages.
- Revise/edit if you finish early.
- Attach anything you used when you planned your essay.

Third-Grade Writing Analysis

Title of Published Piece: ______________________________

Author: ______________________ Date: ______________

Rating System: Please make each star a different color to represent your feelings about your writing life. Then complete the following reflection.

☆	☆	☆	☆
I am thrilled with my work!	I'm pleased with my work but am still learning how to do this.	I could have done better work.	I didn't understand this.

I used my writer's notebook to collect bits of my life. ☆

I made a plan for my writing. ☆

I worked hard when writing my drafts. ☆

I revised my draft to make my writing stronger. ☆

One thing I learned about myself as a writer is:____________________________________

One thing that helped me write well was:____________________________________

One thing I would like to improve so I can be a better writer is: ____________________

My feelings about writing are: ____

Writing Analysis

Author: ______________________ **Title:** ______________ **Date:** _____

If you know, where did the idea for this piece originate? ______________________

____

____

What did you do to plan? ______________________________

Was drafting easy or difficult? __________ What makes you feel this way? __________

____

List the strategies you used to revise:

- ______________________________
- ______________________________

What can you (as the writer) do to ensure a successful peer conference? __________

____

Explain how you edited your piece. ______________________________

____

What is the best part of this piece? ______________________________

____

What was the hardest part of writing this piece? ______________________

____

Our Class's Weekly Writer's Notebook Assessment (2009)

[This rubric was inspired by the Teacher's Checklist in Carl Anderson's *Assessing Writers.*]

Student's Name: ______________________ Assessment Date: __________

Teacher's Name: ______________________ For the Week of: __________

Number of Entries Completed This Week: ______ out of 7 *(If fewer than 5, notebook will not be assessed.)*

Trait	Goals	√ or x
Meaning	1. You communicated meaning in your writing.	
Genre	2. Your writing has the typical features of the genres in which you wrote (e.g., poems have line breaks; nonnarrative entries use prompts to push your thinking)	
Structure	3. You put your writing in an order that makes sense for the genre(s) in which you wrote.	
	4. You used leads and endings that help a reader understand the meaning of your writing.	
	5. You used transitions effectively.	
	6. You developed the heart of your story or wrote more in places that help a reader understand the meaning behind your writing.	
Detail	7. You included relevant details in your writing.	
	8. You used specific words in your details.	
Voice	9. You used a variety of sentence structures so your writing has voice and therefore sounds like you.	
	10. You used a variety of punctuation marks to give voice to your writing so that it sounds like you.	
	11. You included details that show who you really are as a person.	
Conventions	12. You used punctuation marks correctly.	
	13. You used GUMS correctly when you wrote.	
	14. You wrote in paragraph or stanza form, which makes it easy for someone to follow your writing.	

Number of √ out of 14: ________

Comments from your teacher:

Things We Know About Writing Well

- Plan the parts.
- Hook the reader's attention at the very beginning.
- Make the characters move, talk, and think.
- Speed up time during the boring parts.
- Slow down time for the exciting moments.
- Use capitalization and ending punctuation.
- Make paragraphs.
- Reread your writing.

References

Books and Articles

Anderson, Carl. 2000. *How's It Going? A Practical Guide to Conferring with Student Writers*. Portsmouth, NH: Heinemann.

———. 2005. *Assessing Writers*. Portsmouth, NH: Heinemann.

Angelillo, Janet. 2002. *A Fresh Approach to Teaching Punctuation: Helping Young Writers Use Conventions with Precision and Purpose*. New York: Scholastic.

Atwell, Nancie. 1998. *In the Middle: New Understandings About Writing, Reading, and Learning*. 2nd ed. Portsmouth, NH: Heinemann.

Bernet, Brenda. 2009. *Technology in the Classroom: What's Good; What's Not? Selecting Tools of the Trade Requires Battery of Questions*. Available online at http://www.amarillo.com/stories/111009/new_news1.shtml.

Black, Paul, and Dylan Wiliam. 1998. "Inside the Black Box: Raising Standards Through Classroom Assessment." *Phi Delta Kappan* 80 (2): 139–148.

Buckner, Aimee. 2005. *Notebook Know-How: Strategies for the Writer's Notebook*. Portland, ME: Stenhouse.

Calkins, Lucy, and Mary Chiarella. 2006. *Memoir: The Art of Writing Well*. Portsmouth, NH: Heinemann.

Capital Area Writing Project. 2009. "Programs: Teachers as Writers." Capital Area Writing Project. http://citl.hbg.psu.edu/cawp/teacherWriters.htm.

Clark, Roy P. 2006. *Writing Tools: 50 Essential Strategies for Every Writer.* New York: Little, Brown.

Cole, Ardith Davis. 2009. *Better Answers: Written Performance That Looks Good and Sounds Smart*. 2nd ed. Portland, ME: Stenhouse.

Cruz, M. Colleen. 2004. *Independent Writing: One Teacher—Thirty-Two Needs, Topics, and Plans*. Portsmouth, NH: Heinemann.

Davis, Judy, and Sharon Hill. 2003. *The No-Nonsense Guide to Teaching Writing: Strategies, Structures, and Solutions.* Portsmouth, NH: Heinemann.

Denton, Paula, and Roxann Kriete. 2000. *The First Six Weeks of School.* Turners Falls, MA: Northeast Foundation for Children.

Dorfman, Lynne R., and Rose Cappelli. 2007. *Mentor Texts: Teaching Writing Through Children's Literature, K–6*. Portland, ME: Stenhouse.

Edwards, Ali. 2007. *Life Artist: Scrapbooking Life's Journey.* Golden, CO: Creating Keepsakes Media.

Ehmann, Susan, and Kellyann Gayer. 2009. *I Can Write Like That: A Guide to Mentor Texts and Craft Studies for Writers' Workshop, K–6*. Newark, DE: International Reading Association.

Extended Day Girls, Stacey Shubitz, and Christina L. Rodriguez. 2007. *Deal with It! Powerful Words from Smart, Young Women*. Philadelphia: Xlibris.

Feigelson, Dan. 2008. *Practical Punctuation: Lessons on Rule Making and Rule Breaking in Elementary Writing*. Portsmouth, NH: Heinemann.

Fletcher, Ralph. 1996. *A Writer's Notebook: Unlocking the Writer Within You*. New York: Avon Books.

Graham, Paula W. 1999. *Speaking of Journals: Children's Book Writers Talk About Their Diaries, Notebooks, and Sketchbooks*. Honesdale, PA: Boyds Mills.

Graves, Donald H., and Penny Kittle. 2005. *Inside Writing: How to Teach the Details of Craft*. Portsmouth, NH: Heinemann.

Heard, Georgia. 1999. *Awakening the Heart: Exploring Poetry in Elementary and Middle School*. Portsmouth, NH: Heinemann.

Johnston, Peter H. 2004. *Choice Words: How Our Language Affects Children's Learning*. Portland, ME: Stenhouse.

King, Stephen. 2000. *On Writing: A Memoir of the Craft.* New York: Simon and Schuster.

Kotch, Laura, and Leslie Zackman. 1995. *The Author Studies Handbook: Helping Students Build Powerful Connections to Literature*. New York: Scholastic.

Kumar, Lisa, ed. 2004. *Something About the Author: Facts and Pictures About Authors and Illustrators of Books for Young People, Vol. 147*. Farmington Hills, MI: Gale.

Lamott, Anne. 1995. *Bird by Bird: Some Instructions on Writing and Life*. New York: Random House.

MacLachlan, Patricia. 1994. *All the Places to Love*. New York: HarperCollins.

McGregor, Tanny. 2007. *Comprehension Connections: Bridges to Strategic Reading*. Portsmouth, NH: Heinemann.

Moss, Marissa. Amelia's Notebook series. New York: Simon and Schuster.

———. 2003. *Max's Logbook*. New York: Scholastic.

Murray, Donald M. 2004. *A Writer Teaches Writing*. 2nd ed. Boston: Heinle.

Overmeyer, Mark. 2009. *What Student Writing Teaches Us: Formative Assessment in the Writing Workshop*. Portland, ME: Stenhouse.

Palmer, Parker J. 1998. *The Courage to Teach: Exploring the Inner Landscape of a Teacher's Life*. San Francisco: Jossey-Bass.

Parsons, Stephanie. 2005. *First Grade Writers: Units of Study to Help Children Plan, Organize, and Structure Their Ideas.* Portsmouth, NH: Heinemann.

Ray, Katie Wood. 1999. *Wondrous Words: Writers and Writing in the Elementary Classroom*. Urbana, IL: National Council of Teachers of English.

Ray, Katie Wood, and Lester Laminack. 2001. *Writing Workshop: Working Through the Hard Parts (and They're All Hard Parts)*. Urbana, IL: National Council of Teachers of English.

Shubitz, Stacey. 2009. *Using Mentor Texts to Differentiate for Young Writers*. *Statement* 45: 24–26.

Silverstein, Shel. 1974. "Sarah Cynthia Sylvia Stout Would Not Take the Garbage Out." In *Where the Sidewalk Ends*. New York: HarperCollins.

Smith, Emily. 2009. "Authors Can Be Our Teaching Partners: Finding Mentor Texts and Tapping into Their Power." Teachers College Reading and Writing Institute, New York. August 10–14.

Spandel, Vicki. 2006. "Assessing with Heart: Commentary That Is Honest and Compassionate Helps Student Writers Develop." *Journal of Staff Development* 27:14–18.

Sprague, Jessica. 2008. "Stories in Hand." Online class materials (paid registration required). http://spraguelab.squarespace.com/blog/2008/10/10/new-class-stories-in-hand.html.

Steineke, Nancy. 2002. *Reading and Writing Together: Collaborative Literacy in Action*. Portsmouth, NH: Heinemann.

Vopat, Jim. 2007. *Micro Lessons in Writing: Big Ideas for Editing and Publishing*. Portsmouth, NH: Heinemann.

Weaver, Constance. 1996. *Teaching Grammar in Context*. Portsmouth, NH: Boynton/Cook.

Wong, Harry K., and Rosemary T. Wong. 2009. *The First Days of School*. 4th ed. Mountain View, CA: Harry K. Wong Publications.

Yolen, Jane. 2006. *Take Joy: A Writer's Guide to Loving the Craft*. Cincinnati, OH: Writer's Digest Books.

Web Sites

- Baby Hands Production's Dictionary of Signs: http://www.mybabycantalk.com
- BookHooks: http://www.bookhooks.com
- Carbonite: http://www.carbonite.com/
- Cricket Contests: http://www.cricketmagkids.com/
- DonorsChoose: http://www.donorschoose.org
- Kids As Authors: http://www.scholastic.com/bookfairs/contest/kaa_about.asp
- Merlyn's Pen: http://www.merlynspen.org/
- New Moon Girls: http://www.newmoon.com/magazine/
- PBWorks: http://pbworks.com/
- Stone Soup: http://www.stonesoup.com/
- The MY HERO Project: http://www.myhero.com
- This I Believe: http://thisibelieve.org/
- Wikispaces: http://www.wikispaces.com/
- Writers' Slate: http://www.writingconference.com/

Index

Page numbers followed by *f* indicate figures.